A Passionate Pen

A PASSIONATE PEN

The Life and Times of Faith Fenton

Jill Downie

With deepest regards
on behalf of all of the
women of the twentieth
century — Jill Downie
per Faith Fenton
(Alice Freeman)
May 15th, 1996.

A Phyllis Bruce Book
HarperCollins*PublishersLtd*

First Edition

Canadian Cataloguing in Publication Data

Downie, Jill
A passionate pen : the life and times of Faith Fenton

"A Phyllis Bruce book."
ISBN 0-00-255405-4

1. Fenton, Faith, b. 1857.   2. Journalists - Canada - Biography.
3. Feminists - Canada - Biography.   I. Title.

PN4913.F45D6 1996   070'.92   C95-932444-5

96 97 98 99 ❖ HC 10 9 8 7 6 5 4 3 2 1

Printed and bound in the United States

There are two ways of spreading light: to be
The candle, or the mirror that reflects it.

Edith Wharton, *Artemis to Actaeon*

There are chapters in every life which are seldom read,
and certainly not aloud.

Carol Shields, *The Stone Diaries*

For Phyllis Freeman MacKay
With love and gratitude

Contents

Acknowledgements

My thanks go to the staffs and scholars of many libraries and institutions who gave generously of both their time and their expertise. I received invaluable help from the Clarke Museum and Archives in Newcastle, Ontario, the Simcoe County Archives, the City of Toronto Archives, the Ontario Archives, the Toronto Board of Education Archives, Ann Cummings at the National Archives in Washington, D.C., the Mills Library of McMaster University, the Robarts Research Library of the University of Toronto, Burlington Central Public Library, and Margaret Houghton in the Special Collections department of Hamilton Public Library. I am also grateful to Mrs. Pickard of the Oshawa-Whitby Genealogical Society, to Colin MacFadyen for his work at the Dundee City Archives, Scotland, Alex Wilkinson, research assistant at the United Church Archives in Toronto, Jack Webster, Force Historian of the Metro Toronto Police, and Glen Suyama at the Halton Board of Education. Special thanks are due to Charles D. Taws, Curator of the Bowmanville Museum, who gave me hours of his time and shared his extensive knowledge of Bowmanville's history with me. In the National Archives in Ottawa I would like to thank Sandra Burrows, and Anne Goddard of the Social and Cultural Archives Program. Heartfelt thanks go to Colleen Dempsey of the National Archives Manuscript Division for her invaluable and generous help with the Aberdeen papers and the VON archives, and Katherine Tait of the National Council of Women of Canada. In the Yukon, my grateful thanks go to Shauna McLarnon, Susan McClure and Fay Tangermann at the Yukon Archives in Whitehorse, Michael Gates and Margot Anderson at the Dawson City Parks Department, and John Gould and Rohan Quinby at the Dawson City Museum and Historical Society Archives.

I am very grateful to Faith's great-great-nephew, Barry Kent MacKay, who shared with me his own knowledge and opinions of Faith Fenton. I was fortunate in my editor, Phyllis Bruce, whose advice made this a richer and fuller story. My sincere thanks to Margaret Allen, Elizabeth Parr and Karmel Taylor, who honoured this project with their professional endorsement in my fruitless quest for funding. I am also grateful to my son, Andrew, for helping me understand my computer.

This book could not have been written without the help of my agent and friend, Frances Hanna, who was at my side urging me on through the muskeg and mosquitoes of a difficult journey, and who first introduced me to the MacKay family. It would also have been a far more daunting task without my one and only researcher — my husband, Ian, who spent countless hours rephotographing and printing faded photographs, searching through newspapers, street directories, censuses, obscure tomes and long-winded government documents in search of an elusive quarry. Equally important was his support and belief that I could do this, even when I started to lose courage.

I owe a debt of gratitude to Ruth Freeman and the late Phyllis Clements, Faith's nieces, who collected many of Faith Fenton's possessions before they disappeared altogether, and who then handed them over to Faith's great-niece, Phyllis Freeman MacKay.

There is no doubt at all that much of Faith Fenton and Alice Freeman's hidden life would have disappeared completely without the devotion, determination and diplomacy with which Phyllis gathered up every scrap of oral and written information she could find from what was now a scattered and divided family. Then, one memorable day about two years ago, she handed over these precious possessions to me in an act of extraordinary trust and generosity. That is why this book is dedicated to her.

Introduction

THE NIGHT OF FEBRUARY 17, 1896, WAS CRISP and clear, and a star-studded sky shone down on Ottawa. Fur-laden sleighs pulled up in swift succession before the great doors of the Parliament Buildings and, within the Senate Chamber, the voices and laughter of the people thronging the galleries rose above the sound of the orchestra tuning up for the most spectacular social event of the decade in Ottawa: the great Historical Ball hosted by the governor general and his wife, Lord and Lady Aberdeen. Peruked and powdered courtiers, Acadian peasants, helmeted Vikings, Venetian ladies and Puritan gentlemen jostled for space on the floor as the national anthem announced the arrival of the viceregal court.

Preceded by buglers, heralds and pages in the full panoply of state, Lord and Lady Aberdeen moved slowly across the great Chamber floor to the crimson-canopied dais. Behind them paraded members of the judiciary, the Cabinet, the consulates, and their wives, the women's court dress ablaze with jewels, the ostrich feathers in their head-dresses fluttering in the warm air. When the viceregal party reached the dais, a pictorial history of Canada gathered around them: Sebastian Cabot; Jacques Cartier; Sieur de Roberval; Kiotsaton, the great Iroquois chief. Viking and United Empire Loyalist, Indian and Acadian, six hundred of Ottawa's élite in costume circled the great Crimson Chamber.

Among the Empire Loyalists stood a small, middle-aged woman in a Mennonite costume, its simplicity in stark contrast to the brilliance of the scene. Since the only pencil she carried on this occasion was attached to the beautifully decorated programme that hung from her wrist, she would have to rely on memory to record every detail: the standard-bearers with their ornate heraldic flags, the Boadicean robes of the Norsewomen, the gold cross around the neck of the violet-eyed Evangeline in dove-grey gown and buckled slippers. From where she stood she could see the magnificent diamond coronet and pendant earrings of diva Madame Emma Albani, who had joined the Aberdeens on the dais for the performance.

Quadrilles, minuets, gavottes, hornpipes, lancers, the dances followed in a whirl of costume and colour before the viceregal court beneath the crimson canopy. The Mennonite member of the United Empire Loyalist group made her modest contribution to the evening's entertainment and watched as the last dance, the Sir Roger de Coverley, wound its way through the great Senate Chamber.

As the viceregal party led off the State quadrille, the governor general's aides-de-camp moved among the performers, handing each woman a souvenir of the occasion, a gold clasp bearing the Aberdeen motto, *Fortuna sequator*: Let fortune follow. The performance was over, but the evening had only just begun.

Fortune had indeed followed this particular performer—followed on the heels of adversity, disappointment, perseverance and years of struggle. Out in the supper rooms, down the luxurious corridors, Ottawa society mingled and laughed and circulated, the woman in the Mennonite costume among them. The Aberdeen motto had a special meaning for her, not just because of the gift itself, but because of the giver, the formidable Ishbel Aberdeen, who was now leading the assembled company into supper on the arm of her husband, the governor general. From all over Canada and the United States, the leaders of society had come to the great Historical Ball, and she, Alice, was there—in disguise. Alice was her secret, only one of the secrets she hugged to herself that glorious evening in 1896, at the zenith of her career.

This is the story of a woman who has all but completely disappeared from the history of her country. It is the story of a woman who invented herself, because there was no pattern to copy, no route maps for the journey she chose to make. Other women pioneers of her era faced the same challenge, but she became two women to protect the identity of the one who followed the path laid out by society, and in doing so became the woman she created.

The fact that she hid behind a name other than hers is only part of the reason she has vanished. She concealed her true identity for years, but the persona she adopted was well known to thousands the length and breadth of Canada. It is not surprising that Alice Freeman has been forgotten; what is puzzling is that Faith Fenton, "the head of the lady journalists in Toronto," as the 1898 edition of *Men and Women of the Day* calls her, has virtually disappeared.

From time to time one catches a glimpse of her—a footnote here, a sentence there—and one recent book has used some of her columns from the end of her career. The strange thing is that no writers seem to have halted in their tracks and wondered about pursuing this interesting quarry a little further. Perhaps it is understandable that contemporary writers have not done so—although it is curious that most histories of Canadian journalism do not mention her—because her disappearance has been so complete that by now most of the documentation that proves her significance exists only in family archives.

However, even her male contemporaries mention her less frequently than they do the other handful of women in her profession. Perhaps she wasn't pretty enough, or deferential enough. Perhaps it was because she gave a forum to the supporters of women's rights as no other woman journalist did in Canada.

Or maybe she was just too successful. The woman Alice Freeman created was famous at a time when it was difficult for a woman to be so unless she was an aristocrat or an actress, or had done something spec- tacularly scandalous. In fact, there was something rather scandalous about a woman being famous at all.

The woman who was Alice Freeman and whose byline was "Faith Fenton" was equally at home with the rich, the titled and the celebrated, and used her column to advance careers, causes, public and personal con- cerns. Politicians on both sides of the House courted her, the actresses and singers who were the stars of their day wrote her letters, gave her hand- written notes to get her through the stage-door to their dressing-rooms. Prime ministers and literary lions gave her signed photographs. Alexander Muir, composer of "The Maple Leaf For Ever," gave her autographed copies of his new compositions; Catherine Parr Traill sent her first edi- tions of her books, with personal letters tucked inside.

"How sadly strange it seems," she wrote in one of her columns, "and what a commentary on human greatness, that these perishable bits of paper should survive the hand that wrote, the brain that willed, the heart that beat. . . ."

Not sad in Faith's case, because it is in these "perishable bits of paper" which have been cherished by her family—invitations to fancy-dress balls and at-homes, longhand first drafts, pages of typescript—that a remarkable original has been preserved. Where she is truly revealed, however, is in the hundreds of columns she wrote for the nineteenth-century Toronto daily newspaper, *The Empire*. Most of those "Woman's Empire" columns are not in the private domain. They can still be found in any archive that holds copies of *The Empire*—and there they have lain, virtually undisturbed, for over a century.

I cannot claim to have gone searching for Faith, or to have stumbled on her while combing the archives for signs of lost life. My agent, Frances Hanna, is also the agent of Faith Fenton's great-great-nephew, Barry Kent MacKay, the wildlife artist and writer. It was Frances who introduced me to Barry's mother, Phyllis MacKay, Faith's great-niece. Phyllis has made it her mission to gather together and to preserve those "perishable bits of paper" that were distributed to a previous generation and were in danger of disappearing altogether. By sheer good fortune and by the generosity and good offices of others, I happened to be in the right place at the right time.

Before I began the project, I thought I would be researching a turn-of-the-century journalist who went to the Klondike to cover the gold rush. When I saw Faith's remaining possessions laid out on her great-niece's dining-room table, I realized, with growing excitement, that there was more to Faith's story than a tough turn-of-the-century female taking the Klondike trail. It was a treasure-trove of Canadiana: there were signed photographs of Lady Ishbel Aberdeen and of politicians like Wilfrid Laurier, writers and activists like Harriet Beecher Stowe, countless actors and actresses; there was a proof copy of Robert Service's *Songs of a Sourdough*, a programme for the Historical Ball in Ottawa with its little pencil still attached, a silver chain belt for a very small waist, a necklace of golden Klondike nuggets. There were letters from a stellar line-up of nineteenth-century personalities, including an extraordinary correspondence from the wife of Canada's governor general, Lady Aberdeen. Then, and over the next few weeks and months, I listened to Phyllis MacKay talk about the great-aunt she remembered, who was the stuff of family legend.

When I first saw the boxes filled with Faith's columns—about a thousand pages of small print in all—I was daunted. It was not so much the quantity that was challenging, it was the thought of wading through reams of material that would prove to be dated and have nothing much to say to a twentieth-century reader. How wrong I was! A century later, and her voice is still fresh, ringing with sincerity, passion, anger, humour, hope. That voice still reverberates because so many of the issues she dealt with in "Woman's Empire"—sexual discrimination, sexual harassment, child abuse, wage disparity—have not gone away.

Bur first I began to dig for Alice. There was very little about Alice Freeman in the family records, and as I searched through censuses, street directories, baptismal records, educational archives, I discovered that the two personae had existed side by side far longer than Faith had disclosed. Even her own family, and possibly her husband, did not have a true picture of Faith Fenton's *alter ego*.

Putting together Faith Fenton's life began with her columns, with the handwritten reminiscences of her husband and her nieces and with the correspondence that had survived over the years. There were books she had been given, and photographs, but there were no letters she had written, apart from one that I found in public archives. Fortunately, the archival collections of *The Empire* are reasonably complete, because, although hundreds of Faith's columns had been preserved by her family, they were not in chronological order. Few had dates and, of those supplied, many were incorrect.

Gradually, Faith and Alice's world became mine. When I walked the streets of Toronto, I saw the Grand Opera House and the crumbling mansions of the old eighteenth-century aristocracy on King Street, the whisky dives of Victoria Lane. I followed in Faith's footsteps to Dawson City and the Klondike, where the ghosts are never far away from the river and the crumbling shacks that still cling to the cliffs above Bonanza and Eldorado. Putting together the double life of this woman was a quest that immersed me, a first-time biographer, more profoundly than I would ever have imagined, in that turn of the century, Victorian Canada.

Why did she disappear? Part of the answer to the mystery lies in something that occurred just after her death, an event that caused a rift in what had been a close-knit family. So scandalous did it seem to her brothers and sisters, her nephews and nieces, they felt they could not speak about her or write about her, because it meant revealing what they believed was a betrayal of Faith Fenton. And, in protecting their beloved Faith, they drew a veil of silence over her achievements.

In the opening chapter of *Writing a Woman's Life*, author Carolyn G. Heilbrun observes that "it is a hard thing to make up stories to live by. We can only retell and live by the stories we have read and heard. We live our lives through texts. . . . Whatever their form or medium, these stories have framed us all; they are what we must use to make new fictions, new narratives."

Faith Fenton's story more than deserves to be read and heard and shared, for it helped frame a generation of women. Her writing made connection after connection between women isolated one from another in their homes from the Prairies to the Atlantic coastline, as she shared the stories of her fellow-Canadians one with another. Faith's story is an adventure, a romance and a mystery. It is the story of Alice, who was Stella, who was Faith—and who disappeared, almost certainly by the actions of others, but also by her own sleight of hand.

PART ONE

At the Foot of the Hill

I

Undercover

Toronto is, as a residence, worse and better than other small communities—worse in so much as it is remote from all the best advantages of a high state of civilization, while it is infected by all its evils, all its follies; and better, because, besides being a small place, it is a young place . . .

Anna Brownell Jameson,
Winter Studies and Summer
Rambles in Canada. *1838.*

THE SNOW HAD FALLEN HEAVILY that January day of 1894. By evening it lay thick on the dark streets and glistened beneath the glow of the streetlamps. So deeply had it fallen that at six o'clock the streetcars had ceased running and now, three hours later, the only sounds that broke the stillness of the white-folded city were the jingle of sleighbells and, somewhere in the distance, the sound of cheerful voices.

Alice Freeman pulled her threadbare ulster around her and struggled east along College Street, tugging an old cloth cap down over her forehead. The snow seeped in through the holes in the worn leather boots her sister-in-law had found for her in the kitchen—"Gaps and rents are the insignia of the class," said Elizabeth. "Remember, you are the type of woman who never wears anything but cast-off clothing."

Alice passed the imposing Romanesque façade of the Athletic Club, with its brilliantly lit windows.[1] Beneath the lamps at the entrance, a woman emerged from a cab, and Alice caught a glimpse of a delicate white gown, white arms beneath soft furs. From an upper window drifted the sweet sounds of an orchestra playing a waltz. With a shiver as much of apprehension as of cold, she laboured past the Hospital for Sick Children, on to Elizabeth Street, which lay almost buried in snow. Here, behind a high fence, was her own destination, the reason for her subterfuge: the House of Industry, which offered women in need bed and board in return for work. Steeling herself, Alice walked up to the entrance and knocked quietly but firmly until the shabby front door opened.

"I'm Mary Smith from Hamilton," she whispered. "I must find a place to stay for the night."

The disgruntled-looking individual behind the door greeted her with scant courtesy. "Shut the door, woman. Have you never been here before? A nice time to be taking people out of their beds. From Hamilton, did you say? Hamilton should take care of its own poor. Well, you can stay one night and no more."

He picked up a lantern, and Alice followed him along a passage and through a deserted courtyard to another building, where she was handed over to an elderly woman of frail appearance who added her complaints to the doorkeeper's. "What a time to be rousing people from their beds! Well, I suppose you didn't know any better, it bein' yer first time. Come along. Get yer things off and take yer bath—you don't need one, you say? It's the rules. We could have all sorts of women a-comin' in here and a-dirtyin' our beds."

There was nothing else for it but to undress and bathe under the watchful eye of the querulous caretaker. Then, putting on the nightdress provided and taking the clean blanket handed to her, Alice followed her guide into a large dormitory of sleeping women, where her escort pointed out an empty cot and departed.

The room was filled with the sound of mutterings and stertorous breathing, the air stifling, overheated by great coils of steam pipes that added their bubbling and hissing to the groans and whimpers around Alice in her truckle-bed. Somewhere in the room someone was crying, and Alice heard the clink of glass as a strong smell of whisky wafted into the fetid atmosphere. Perhaps if she opened the door to the passage the air would be fresher and the temperature would drop. Alice got out of bed and crept to the door.

"What are you doin'?" called a coarse voice from the darkness. "D'you want to let the rats in? It's real bold they are."

Alice scurried back to her cot. As she pulled back the serge blankets she saw something moving against the pillow. It was a column of plump, sluggish bedbugs—twelve, she counted them—moving steadily down into the bed. Horrified, she turned to the door, only to remember the rats.

"Is the bugs a-worrin' yer?" said a voice nearby. "You'll get used to them after a bit. They don't trouble me."

It was sound advice. She could not allow herself to be troubled if she was to remember every detail—the humiliation of the strip-bath, the oppressive atmosphere of the great dormitory, the ravings and profanities of the sleeping women around her for whom this world was an everyday reality. Alice pulled the clean blanket she had been given over the bug-infested pillow and lay down to wait out the night.

Who was this woman who trudged the snowy streets of Toronto a hundred years ago, alone and in disguise, when any other respectable unaccompanied female was behind closed doors? She was one of a rare new breed: a lady journalist in search of a story.

The city through which the lady journalist walked that snowy evening had changed a great deal since the first lieutenant-governor of Upper Canada, John Graves Simcoe, had designated it the new capital in 1793 because of its distance "from a foreign shore"—that foreign shore being, of course, the recently created United States of America.[2] Yet it was not so long since the forest to the north of the city was broken only by the slash of Yonge Street cutting through the trees, bringing the farmers with their produce to town. Proceeding by wagon down Gallows Hill to pay their dues at the Bloor Street toll-gate, they made their way to the St. Lawrence Market above the quagmires of Lower Yonge Street with grain and vegetables and pigs raised among the stumps yet to be cleared from the land.

Now the railway cut the city off from its beautiful curve of bay, and near the water the elegant brick houses of Toronto's early aristocracy, with their spacious courtyards and splendid gabled roofs, were falling into decay. The smart set had moved farther inland, away from the factories and businesses springing up around this new means of transportation.

The Toronto through which Alice Freeman made her way to the House of Industry was no longer a frontier town but a many-layered city of rich and poor. High above the bay, in his beautiful residence, The Grange, sat Professor Goldwin Smith, who had married into the Family Compact—Ontario's *crème de la crème*—by taking as his wife Harriet Boulton, whose house it actually was.[3] A fine example of the newly emerging upper class, British by birth, Oxford-educated, he had arrived in Toronto by way of Cornell University at Ithaca, New York, and won the heart and income of the recently widowed Harriet, whose first husband, William Boulton, former mayor of Toronto, had been deeply embroiled in the political scene of both city and province.[4] As he worked in his study, waited on by his butler, the impeccable Chinn, Goldwin Smith might well have been putting finishing touches to an article condoning Russian pogroms, or deploring the possibility of women's emotions muddying the clear waters of government.

Farther north lay Euclid Hall, on Jarvis Street, with a fountain at the foot of the grand staircase and a conservatory filled with orchids.[5] It was the home of Hart Massey, whose farm-equipment business had made his family wealthy, and whose philanthropy would enrich the cultured class of Toronto with Massey Music Hall—the city's first concert hall—in 1894, and the underclass of the city with the Fred Victor Mission in the same year. Tramps' Paradise, some would call the latter. But Hart Massey knew that tragedy and destitution could touch anybody. He planned to raise both edifices in memory of his son, Frederick Victor, who had died three years earlier from tuberculosis.

Around Euclid Hall on Jarvis Street were other houses built by industry: the rambling, comfortable home of Alexander Nairn, coal merchant and timber-supplier to the railways; the elegant, three-storey cut-stone mansion of John Fitch, whose interests in the milling industry had bought him spacious lawns, gabled roofs, stables and coach-houses.

The middle class lived in homes and lodgings on Spadina, Richmond, Adelaide and the streets around them, and on this cold winter's night they were probably gathered around the fireplace, a sand-filled bolster firmly against the bottom of the parlour door, planning the next day's expedition to Timothy Eaton's store on Yonge Street, perhaps to purchase a mahogany sideboard in the English style, or a modish chapeau in plum-coloured velvet trimmed with tightly curled ostrich feathers.[6]

And on King Street and Palace Street, where an early British aristocracy had once lived and promenaded and entertained, were the underclass of the city, living rough on the streets and in row housing and shacks to the east and west of the city centre, or huddled in the derelict remnants of stately mansions. They spoke with a bewildering array of accents—Irish, Scots, cockney, French—but they had two things in common: a complete familiarity with hard times and hard living, and a membership for life in that underclass. Knowing your place was an essential of Victorian society, and being in the Dominion of Canada made little difference.

After the rigours of a night spent with bedbugs and rats, Alice Freeman may well have taken a streetcar home on Saturday to bathe and to change before going to write and file her report on the House of Industry for her newspaper, *The Empire*, on Adelaide Street. Walking would have been difficult, because the ploughs on the horse-drawn trams threw up great piles of snow, much to the annoyance of the shopkeepers on their route, who promptly shovelled it back onto the tracks. As the tram descended Yonge Street, Alice would have been able to catch a glimpse of the bay and the Toronto Islands beyond—created by the fierce storms of the 1850s that smashed their way through the narrow sliver of sandbar near the mouth of the Don River. At this time, the bay would freeze solidly, and undoubtedly some of the passengers on the streetcar would have been carrying skates, which they buckled to their boots to skim across the surface of the lake among ice-boats and horse-drawn sleighs.

Perhaps they drew back from the woman in the scuffed boots and the tattered ulster as she boarded the tram. Perhaps they ignored her. Alice Freeman would have been no more surprised by such treatment than Faith Fenton. "Not belonging" was a condition she was more than used to in her life, even when not in disguise. Being different had been a habitual state for her as far back as she could remember. But knowing her place in that burgeoning, changing society was something she had always refused to do.

Once, years before, in a St. Catharines hotel, a clairvoyant called Madame Carreno, seventh daughter of a seventh daughter, had asked to cast the young girl's horoscope, to "lift the veil of the future and forecast the fortunes of those whom the planets favor." Ignoring Faith's reluctance, she had begun: "You were born in January, under a favorable augury. There is but one evil influence that crossed the constellation that was in the ascendant at your birth, and—"

At that point Faith had stopped her. There were events in her past she would share with only a very few people, and some she did not care to remember.

II

A Certain Charm

Bowmanville abounds in inconsistencies: perhaps that is
what gives it a certain charm.

> *Hamlyn, Lunney, and Morrison,*
> Bowmanville: A Retrospect.

Do you know that I lived in your town once, when I was
a little girl? Such strange memories I have of my three
child years there.

> *Faith Fenton to "Elfin" of Bowmanville,*
> *"Woman's Empire," 1893.*

THE COMMUNITY OF BOWMANVILLE lies about forty miles east of Toronto on
the shores of Lake Ontario. In the 1850s it was a patchwork-quilt of a village, named for Charles Bowman, who had bought the land from one of
the founding families, the Burks, and given a plot to the oldest girl in every
family. Why he did so in a patriarchal society is unknown, but it adds
intrigue to an otherwise ordinary Ontario town.

The roads grew in disorderly fashion around King Street, the main thor-
oughfare, and the Danforth road, which later became the Kingston road,
bent and curved its way around Liberty Street, then across Barber's Creek,
where it went on to circle the great bulk of Simpson's Mill.[1] The early settlers in what was once called "Darlington Mills" ignored such niceties as
road allowances if it meant they could avoid swamps and ravines.

To the hundreds of immigrants who arrived in Bowmanville from the British Isles in the early years of the nineteenth century, it was a more familiar pattern than the grid system of most new towns in Canada West, but nothing in the old country could have prepared them for the isolation of their little community. Asa Danforth's great highway joined them to other similar settlements along the wide shoreline of Lake Ontario and to the north of them, but until the middle of the century the Mississauga still came to fish for sturgeon and salmon in the fall, and grandfathers told tales of encounters with packs of baying wolves in the beech woods around the tiny hamlet.

In 1857 the little one-storey brick house of William Henry Freeman and his wife, Mary Ann, at 10 King Street was in the centre of a thriving community. The streets fanning out from King Street boasted some fine homes set in pretty gardens, and the smokestacks of the industries that had financed those homes rose at a discreet distance. Not only did Bowmanville have a cabinet factory on Elgin Street, it also was home to the second-largest piano factory in the country. Steamers and barges tied up where the Mississauga had fished for salmon, and left loaded with coal and apples. Alsay and Thomas Fox's brickyard was doing good business, and the Grand Trunk Railway from Toronto to Montreal gave the little town a feeling of connection to the outside world.[2]

William Henry and Mary Ann were far happier in the village of Bowmanville than they had been in Brooklyn, New York, which was where they had lived for a year after leaving England in 1854. After enduring a seven-week journey in a four-masted schooner to start a new life in America, the Freemans were shocked to discover that their new neighbours in the promised land were staunchly republican, and they bitterly regretted their decision to choose America over Australia. At the urging of a new friend, Edson Andrus, of Syracuse, New York, they had made their way north in 1856 with their two children, five-year-old Mary and two-year-old Henry, to Canada West, the western portion of the united province of Canada, which had been created in the 1840 Act of Union.

With one child born in London and one child born in Brooklyn, twenty-seven-year-old Mary Ann must have seen the brick house on its eighth of an acre as a haven on that cold January day in 1857 as she awaited the birth of her third child. Edson Andrus had not steered them wrong: William Henry's skills made him an ideal citizen of the townships of Darlington and Clarke. The little workshop attached to their home was already taking in orders for beds, tables, coffins, chairs, and William Henry was busy making them—busy, and happy, since the reason Edson Andrus had persuaded him to come to Canada West had nothing to do with furniture and everything to do with music.

Making furniture was William Henry's profession; making music was his passion. He could play the cornet and the violin, and he had a fine trained singing voice. Since his arrival in Bowmanville the previous year, he had become bandmaster of the Orono Band, of which Edson Andrus was a founding member. When his working day was over, William Henry was off to Edson's house for band practice—Edson also had "crossed the line" and come to live in Canada West—or to St. John's Anglican Church for choir practice. Soon he was leader of the choir. Music was everywhere: bands, glee clubs, church choirs, choral groups of every shape and size. And if William Henry was happy, so, for the time being, was Mary Ann.

Over a span of twenty-two years, Mary Ann would bear twelve babies, all of whom would survive well into adulthood. And on January 14, 1857, she gave birth to her second daughter, whom she named Alice Matilda. But whatever dreams Mary Ann may have had for this third child, her first-born Canadian, Alice would play a role in her country that her mother could not possibly have imagined.

Four-year-old Alice held tight to her sister Mary's hand as they walked through St. John's churchyard, past the graves of Bowmanville's pioneers and of those early settlers' children who had not survived. "This lively bird us awhile was given, transplanted now, brightly blooms in heaven" read one headstone, dedicated to five-month-old Mary Jane, who had died in 1843. By January 1861, Mary Ann had five children and she had managed to find time to bring the last three to be christened together by the Reverend Alexander Macnab. It was one of Alice's earliest memories, the wonder and delight of "the pretty windows" and the touch of the baptismal water on her forehead.

Alice's family was, in fact, anything but ordinary. The portrait of her paternal grandmother hung on the wall of the family parlour for everyone to see: pretty, with soft brown hair in a fluffy crown above her dancing eyes, white shoulders framed by her rich gown. Beside her was Grandfather Freeman in his eighteenth-century finery, an amused and very un-Victorian half-smile on his lips.

Grandfather and Grandmother Freeman were theatre people. The Freeman children all knew the story of how young William Henry Fenton of the ancient city of Colchester, destined by the family for the legal or medical profession, had run away to London with a Miss Lardner, an actress and opera singer, where he changed his name in a symbolic flourish to "Freeman" and became a writer and lyricist. "Here's a Health, Bonnie Scotland, to Thee" was one of his compositions, and his book of poetry, *Fancy or the Effusions of the Heart*, had enjoyed a modest success in the early years of the nineteenth century. Their father had been the only child of the union, and although he had trained as a cabinet-maker, those early days filled with music, when writers like Thomas Hood and Thomas Peacock were his parents' friends, had given him a love for musical performance.[3]

Mary Ann, too, had a story about ancestry, and the plot was pure Victorian melodrama. The walls held no pictures of Alice's Grandmother and Grandfather Lillie, but in-between endless chores and childbirth, Mary Ann related the tragic tale of her mother, filling Alice's imagination as she played around her own mother with her Dutch dolls and the pieces of broken china with which she gave them tea-parties.

A certain Private Lillie, a man "of philandering propensities," according to the recollections of family members, wooed and won the heart of a girl of good family, Mary Kesner, while he was stationed in Ireland. He was, say his descendants, "a knockout of a soldier with dash and feminine appeal," and Mary Kesner ran away with him to England. Her family disowned her.

In England the hapless Mary found herself living in the soldiers' residences of the Tower of London, where her husband had been posted. Her daughter Mary Ann was born a stone's throw away from Traitors' Gate, through which so many had come to certain death. She had only to look up to see the room where Sir Walter Ralegh had been imprisoned for loving the wrong woman.

A brilliant but difficult man, Mary's husband began to rise swiftly through the ranks, and took little responsibility for his family. The early death of her mother left young Mary Ann with no one to care for her. On her death-bed her mother told her she must go to a certain large house in Chelsea which stood behind great iron gates in its own grounds; there she would find relatives who would take her in.

Perhaps she was on her way there, weeping bitterly, when—so Mary Ann told her children—a wealthy woman stopped her and asked her why she was crying. When she heard the child's story, she took her into her own home, educated her and cared for her. The happy ending seems almost too good to be true, but it is the ending Mary Ann related to her children and she never changed her story.

Somewhere around the end of the 1840s, William Henry Freeman, the son of the runaway marriage of a songwriter and an actress, met Mary Ann Lillie, the daughter of the runaway marriage of a handsome soldier and an Irish heiress. They were married in Chelsea in 1851, both aged twenty-one.[4]

Six years later, in his new country, William Henry rediscovered his artistic roots with a passion. What with the band, the choir, the choral group—a quartet, consisting of the Misses Kyle and McMurtry and the Messrs. Meynard and Freeman—he was making as much music as he was furniture.

Mary Ann, meanwhile, was making babies. With the birth of Rosa in 1865 she had seven children younger than thirteen, and the Freemans moved to the corner of King and Scugog streets, where they had a little more space. William Henry was busier than ever, because he had joined the local militia, which was training in case the Fenians tried to invade from across the border.[5]

"Don't you remember sweet Alice, Ben Bolt—
Sweet Alice, whose hair was so brown,
Who wept with delight when you gave her a smile,
And trembled with fear at your frown?"

Alice Freeman with her curly brown hair and her emotional response to the world around her loved it when her mother sang that song specially for her. Such moments were becoming rarer as the children grew, filling Mary Ann's time and wearing out her patience. Years later those who remembered her would call her "the brigadier-general type." But someone had to take charge in a household of nine people, particularly when the master of the house was never there. And everyone had to share the responsibilities.

Most of the burden fell on Mary Ann's shoulders—as her journalist daughter later expressed it: "the housekeeper and mother, whose work is never done; who from early morning until late night hours moves back and forth with ceaseless steps and tireless fingers, planning, arranging, devising, guiding; the centre of the household and the final court of appeal." But the burden also fell on the shoulders of the oldest child, Mary.

When Rosa was born in 1865, Mary was thirteen years old and was attending the Bowmanville Union School—at least, from time to time.[6] A list of pupils from the Union School for the spring of 1865 records the performance of Mary and her brother Henry. Henry was sixth of sixteen in the Second Class and late nine times. Mary was fourteenth in a class of twenty-one and late twenty-three times (only one child had more latenesses: twenty-four). And this did not include her absences, which were not counted as a misdemeanour. At the age of thirteen Mary did not by law have to attend school at all, but obviously she was still trying to, in between helping her mother after the birth of another baby. Alice never forgot what happened to her big sister:

> It is a cruel thing that is being done every day, especially with daughters, whom parents educate in a desultory way, keeping them at home for household duties until they are of marriageable age, then refusing to supply them with anything beyond mere necessities. . . . It is a cruel thing to wait until a girl's training days are past, until perhaps the early youth has gone. . . .

Most of the happy memories of Alice's childhood that Faith Fenton later shared with her readers had to do with books. There was already a bookstore in Bowmanville, The Gift Book Store, run by Robert O'Hara, and the Freemans seem to have given their children access to much of their considerable library. Faith Fenton would always urge her readers to expose their children to a wide range of literature as early as possible, specifically recommending Scott, Thackeray, Hawthorne and Dickens: "I do not think it does a child any harm to be turned into a full library of such writers and permitted to browse at will."

Walter Scott and Charles Dickens are the writers whose style and themes would most profoundly affect Faith Fenton, but William Makepeace Thackeray's tolerance of human frailty, for which some of his contemporaries criticized him, would not have escaped the lively intelligence of Alice. Journalist Faith Fenton would later have little problem agreeing with Thackeray's credo: "if they [people] are good and kindly, to love and shake them by the hand; if they are silly, to laugh at them . . . if they are wicked and heartless, to abuse them."

Nathaniel Hawthorne is the only American writer Faith specifically mentions from this period, and undoubtedly she would have read *The Scarlet Letter* and taken note of Hawthorne's attitudes towards cant and hypocrisy, his sympathy for those who rebel against orthodoxy.

Not only were there plenty of books in the home, but the children were given them as gifts. One of Alice's most precious books was a copy of *The Arabian Nights,* whose tales of faraway places, with its exotic illustrations, filled her imagination: "How I pored over it, dreamed over it, carried it about with me." She would later speak fondly of "dear old *Pilgrim's Progress*," and remember ruefully a Christmas gift entitled *The Christian Woman, Her Place and Character,* when she had been hoping for the poems of Elizabeth Barrett Browning—"the shock," said Faith Fenton, "was tremendous."

Elizabeth Barrett Browning was not the only woman writer in Alice's collection. She also read Jane Austen, Maria Edgeworth, Mrs. Gaskell, Charlotte Brontë—women who in some cases concealed both their writing and their sex, and whose writings often questioned the status quo, however gentle that criticism may seem to a later generation. Elizabeth Barrett Browning, for instance, is mostly remembered now for her romance with the poet Robert Browning and for her love poems, but in her own era one of her best-known poems, "The Cry of the Children," was a plea for the children working in the mines and the factories of the Industrial Revolution. Alice adored Mrs. Gaskell's cosy cathedral-town novel, *Cranford*, but Mrs. Gaskell's other work is far less charming and comfortable to read.

Reading brought an inner joy that Alice would always carry with her: "My most treasured literature lies in memory nooks, where song and story, high thoughts and brave deeds are stored away, safe from the dust that gathers and the moth that corrupts."

Poetry would have been very much part of that secret store, as it was for many of Alice's contemporaries, and, from the few references there are to her early writing, her earliest ambition was to be a poet. Reading, learning, and even writing poetry was not considered as exotic an undertaking as it is today, and Faith's favourites from that nineteenth-century flowering of English poetry were Alfred, Lord Tennyson, Queen Victoria's poet laureate, and Robert Browning. Again, like most of her contemporaries, she also enjoyed poetry that sounds bathetic and banal to modern ears. Given the nineteenth-century practice of concealing authorship, it is difficult to identify Faith Fenton's poetic works, but from the ones that can be identified it would seem that her own compositions tended towards Victorian sentimentality and symbolism.

Books were not just a solitary pleasure. One of the family rituals was to gather together after the evening meal, the hour when the tea and the candles were traditionally brought out together, to listen to William Henry reading aloud from one of his store of books, and the memory would remain with his daughter for ever:

> I made my first acquaintance with [Dickens] when, as a ten-year-old child, I listened to my father's daily after-dinner reading, and the scenes that excited my mother's laughter are the ones most vividly impressed upon my memory today.

Another memory that stayed with Alice, and was later recalled by Faith Fenton, was of not doing what she was told. Years later the adult could recall the pain of the child:

> One of my earliest memories is of a great, unfinished kitchen, where I stood—such a little child—beside a low table helping to stone raisins for the Christmas pudding. And somehow the raisins found their way to my mouth so frequently that I was finally sent away in disgrace—away from the warmth and cheer into a big, cold, bedroom, where everyone forgot me, and I cried myself to sleep.

Alice's mother, however, had a more serious problem than a strong-willed child—namely, William Henry. Even if he had stayed up all night, it would have been impossible for him to bring in enough money from the business, because he was always singing, or conducting, or violin- or cornet-playing. There was fierce competition in Bowmanville in the furniture business, so no prospective customers had to wait around for their tables and chairs until William Henry came home from band practice. To make matters worse, he had left the Bowmanville-based Orono Band and was now forming a new band farther afield, in Newcastle, which required even more time and attention.

Some of the band members would have seemed less than ideal to Mary Ann's middle-class eyes. There was Billy Wyman, who went around the country with a travelling show; Thomas Thornton, whose father ran a liquor store; and George Druery, who worked in Asa Collins' hotel. While William Henry was indulging himself, Mary Ann was worrying herself sick over so many mouths to feed—and perhaps anxious lest her husband return to the bohemian half-world that had lured his father away from his middle-class Fenton roots in Colchester.

There is no evidence that the solution to her problem arrived at Mary Ann's urging, but there can be little doubt it was for her a blessing. Somewhere around 1868—possibly in late 1867—the Freeman family moved all the way to Barrie, a fast-growing community about a hundred miles north of Toronto. The railway had reached Barrie in 1865, and they had been told by family friends that opportunities there were good for a cabinet-maker.

For a musician, they were regrettably mediocre. The Barrie Glee Club had reached its zenith in 1865 and was now a shadow of its former self, and reviews for the Barrie Temperance Band in the local newspaper,

The Northern Advance, give an idea of performance standards by the use of such withering adjectives as "inept" and "discordant." There is no evidence of William Henry ever playing music again after his ten Bowmanville years.

Though life changed for the musician and his family, it changed most of all for ten-year-old Alice. Without a word of explanation she was shipped back to Bowmanville to live with the Reverend Thomas Reikie of the local Congregationalist church and his wife, Margaret, who were childless, and she was never told why she was the only one to be cast out "in disgrace."

Her parents saw her off on what Faith Fenton later described as a "long out-reaching" pier in Toronto, putting her aboard a Royal Mail Line steamer to travel on her own the forty miles to Bowmanville. It required "much child-courage," she said, to walk up the gangway with her small valise, but she said nothing to them of her terror at "the great labouring monster" that was taking her away from them, and they still offered her no word of explanation. She remembered putting her head down on a stack of life-preservers, her pulse-beats calming a little, and finally falling asleep.

To Alice Freeman, aged ten and sobbing herself to sleep on a pile of life-preservers, it must indeed have seemed that an evil influence had crossed the constellation of her birth. In fact, the heartbreak of being cast out of the family was the best thing that could have happened to her.

III

Liberty of Conduct

It is a cruel thing that is being done every day, and
especially with daughters, whom parents educate in a
desultory way . . . then if [the daughter] asks for
greater freedom of action to tell her that if she is not
content she is at liberty to make her home elsewhere. . . .
there are hundreds of women . . . who are thus living a
life of irksome subjection, with no more liberty of conduct than a five-year-old child.

> Faith Fenton, *"Woman's Empire," 1890.*

A LESS LIKELY PASSPORT TO LIBERTY OF CONDUCT and self-expression than the
Reverend Reikie, Alice's new guardian, it would be difficult to imagine.

Born in Glasgow, Scotland, Thomas Miller Reikie had been
appointed minister of the Bowmanville Congregationalist Church in
1855.[1] A dour, dignified man, he followed on the heels of the more flamboyant Reverend Climie, who had unashamedly mixed politics and religion, and had founded Bowmanville's local newspaper, *The Canadian
Statesman*, as a Liberal organ.

Not that the Reverend Reikie lacked missionary zeal. During the first
year that Alice was his house-guest, he was the driving force behind the
formation of the Society for Total Abstinence in the town, and in
December 1868 he was appointed its president. Although he was often
away from Bowmanville on missionary work, his trips took him, not to
exotic outposts of Empire, but to neighbouring communities, where he
preached to young men at the local YMCAs on the virtues of Total
Abstinence. He was for some time editor of *The Canadian Independent*,

the official publication of his church, and he spent many hours on a committee formed to erect a monument to his predecessor, the Reverend Climie, for his efforts "to advance the high interests of temperance, education, philanthropy and religion." He appeared the very model of propriety.

With her husband away so frequently, Margaret Reikie was often very lonely. Born into a family of missionaries in Caithness, in the northern Highlands of Scotland, she had for a while wanted to be a missionary herself, but what she liked above all was teaching. In fact, it was while she was running classes for the young wives of fishermen in Thurso, the most northerly town on the Scottish mainland, that she had met her husband. Thomas Reikie was still a student at the time, and his marriage to the daughter of a distinguished evangelistic family helped not a little in his advancement. Now here she was in Canada, miles away from her loved ones. There were occasional family visits—her young sister, Harriet, had been over to stay with her—but her health was fragile, and she had been denied what she had been brought up to believe was the purpose of a married woman's existence and the greatest of all gifts: children.

Margaret Reikie loved children; her husband's twelve-year-old sister, Christine, had also been a visitor in their home, and the Sunday school Margaret ran was a vital part of her life. She must have wondered at the fickleness of fate that gave young Mary Ann Freeman more babies than she could manage, and herself not one child to cherish. It is unlikely that the Anglican Freemans would ever have taken part in any of the town's Congregational activities, but in a small community like Bowmanville the two wives could have met on other occasions.

Perhaps Margaret Reikie needed a new table and, being careful of her pennies—good Scottish housewife that she was—came to William Henry, who was slower but cheaper than the bigger businesses.

Maybe she had to wait for the order to be completed, and was asked in for a cup of tea by Mary Ann, who practised, as Faith Fenton would recall, "not so much a giving as a sharing, and [whose] tea-table is rarely without the presence of some Feeble-Mind or Ready-to-Halt, whom she warms and feeds and comforts a little on his weary journey." Perhaps it was at her mother's tea-table that Alice Freeman first met the woman who was to be her mentor and surrogate mother for four of the most crucial years of her young life. Margaret Reikie would have understood a mother's need for money with so many mouths to feed. She must have marvelled at the children's energy and vitality, for none of them was weak or sickly. Whether Mary Ann displayed her offspring like a litter of puppies and allowed Margaret Reikie to choose one for company, or whether the precocious Alice engaged her mother's visitor in conversation and won her heart, can only be guessed. Margaret Reikie chose the child who was the odd one out.

The solitary little girl whom lonely Margaret Reikie met off the Royal Mail Line steamer in late 1867 or 1868 thought of herself as a "stolid child," a "homely little maiden . . . with few bodily graces, the last person you would notice in any gathering."[2] She had inherited her father's strong nose, and she had a habit of looking straight at people with her big brown eyes that was not quite proper. Her generous, mobile mouth was far from the Victorian rosebud ideal; it would take a hundred years for such a mouth to be considered beautiful. Her sisters were more delicately featured, like their mother. In appearance, Alice was different.

She was different in other ways, too. From what Faith Fenton later told her readers, she was taught to play the piano like all the other children in this musical family, but it was never one of her strengths, as it would be for her younger sisters, and she counselled her readers to give a child piano lessons only if the child wanted them. From her outburst about the fate of daughters, it seems likely that Alice would not allow family priorities to deflect her from attending school regularly. And, according to the recollections handed down by family members, Alice started to write at an early age—taking herself off to any quiet corner she could find in that busy, overcrowded household. When she was handed over to Margaret Reikie, she saw it as abandonment—being cast out from the family circle—and Faith Fenton would never be able to travel on a steamer without remembering the pain ten-year-old Alice had felt.

That the Freemans offered no explanation of their actions was only to be expected of authoritarian Victorian parents. It may, of course, have been an act of love. As Mary Ann watched this clever, difficult, little girl of hers struggling to use her intelligence and her creativity against great odds, she may have seized the chance to free her from the conventional obligations of a Victorian family. From the records of the Bowmanville Union School, it looks as if pupils had to pay a small fee to attend, and any amount of money would have stretched the Freemans' limited budget. The Reikies had more disposable income and—as good Scots—believed in the value of education, even for girls. They could have been trusted to fulfil that part of the bargain.

By the time Alice was ten, it would have been clear to Mary Ann that her daughter would not catch a husband with her looks and, worse still, that her cleverness might well put off any prospects. Alice would have to find her security another way.

Though none of her doubts about her parents' reasons for sending her away were ever resolved, in the first days with Margaret Reikie all her fears vanished. Alice became the cherished child when Mrs. Reikie took her under her roof.

And what an exotic roof it was! Four years before Alice Freeman's arrival, the Reikies had moved into the new octagonal parsonage that had been built for them by the Congregational church trustees.[3] Set amid spacious lawns with trees and shrubs, its eight stuccoed walls surrounded two storeys, with a "lantern" or cupola on the roof, flanked by two chimneys. The proponent of such architecture, an unconventional American with no formal training named Orson Squire Fowler, touted its properties for making families "constitutionally amiable and good." It was supposed to put an end to "fretfulness and ill temper, as well as exhaustion and sickness." Perhaps the elders of the church had the frail health of the childless Mrs. Reikie in mind when they chose the octagonal shape.

Valise in hand, Alice stepped into her splendid new home on Division Street and into a new life. No longer did she have to share not only a bedroom, but a bed, with her sisters. She now had her own room where she could read and work, a private place for herself.

Looking out from between the louvred shutters of those strangely shaped rooms with their angled corners, she could see the homes of some of Bowmanville's upper crust. Across the road was Waltham Cottage, built by a former mayor of Bowmanville, with a verandah on three sides and a pretty transom over the front door. Dr. George Low's nieces, Catherine and Julia Welch, ran their private girls' school there, and Alice would have seen the young ladies arriving to be instructed in the three Rs and the equally important art of being gentlewomen.

The middle class of Bowmanville were now prosperous enough to ensure their daughters acquired the accomplishments considered essential by society. Their mothers could teach them how to scald cream for butter, to pickle a ham or stuff a pillow with goose-feathers, but the Misses Welch could show them how to work at an embroidery frame, paint a pretty watercolour, sing sweetly to their own piano accompaniment, or pluck charmingly at the strings of a harp, with their cumbersome skirts arranged becomingly around them. What had ensured the success of their mothers in early pioneer society was now not enough for their daughters' survival.

Kitty-corner to the parsonage was John McClung's red-brick home, with French doors leading on to the verandah, an edifice built on the success of his dry-goods business. Shortly after Alice's arrival, Mr. McClung added a second floor, making his home more impressive than ever.

With Margaret Reikie, a punctilious observer of the social niceties, as her guide, Alice did not need to attend the dame-school across the way. Had the proper Mrs. Reikie changed the original spelling of the old Scottish name *Reekie*, with its somewhat odoriferous connections? It was always pronounced in the old way, but in the local newspaper it was spelled *Reikie*, or even *Reike*.

Margaret Reikie soon had her small companion trained in the finer points of etiquette, and Alice was a willing pupil. There had been no time for such niceties in her old life, but her parents would undoubtedly have reminisced about past glories and social graces as they looked up at the portraits of the actress and the writer on the parlour wall.

Alice enjoyed carrying carefully composed invitations and notes to Mrs. Reikie's various acquaintances in the town, and above all she loved to deliver a spoken message. Here, her theatrical blood rose to the occasion. Carefully coached by Mrs. Reikie, Alice, with her long, curly brown hair neatly brushed and tied back with a pretty ribbon, would walk primly along Division Street to Silver or Temperance Street, or wherever the social errand was taking her, and make her little speech: "Mrs. Reikie presents her compliments to Mrs. Fisher, and requests the honour of her company to tea on Thursday next." The admiring comments of the ladies who received her were a balm to the little girl who had always felt in the wrong somehow, left out for some reason.

Tea was a social event of consequence in small-town Ontario life, a ritual with established rules, and it is likely that Margaret Reikie's tea-parties followed the accepted pattern. She and Alice would set up one or two tables covered with heavy linen tablecloths, with the teapot and the tea-service, a coffee pot, cups, saucers and teaspoons. When the guests arrived they would greet each other, walk about and socialize, sipping their tea and exchanging pleasantries. Gloves would, of course, be worn, and hats retained, the hostess keeping her head covered with a small lace cap.

It is unlikely that the crinoline was much worn in Bowmanville—after all, it was still considered by many a rather decadent French fashion, introduced to a shocked world by the Empress Eugénie—but it was now on its way out, as the ladies of Bowmanville would have seen from the Paris fashion sheets and *The Illustrated London News*. Like sailing-ships on Lake Ontario, their voluminous skirts would have billowed about them in Mrs. Reikie's drawing-room in shades of mauve and grey, and the ever-present black of mourning. The more daring among them may have exchanged the soft colours of the 1860s for the vivid yellows, emeralds and magentas made possible by the new aniline dyes. Glancing at themselves in the gilt-framed mirror over the mantelpiece, with their small hats perched in the newly fashionable angle over their foreheads, they would have smiled graciously at the little girl who freshened the tea in their cups of fine Derby china.

They would then have settled themselves in Margaret Reikie's damask-upholstered armchairs or on her mahogany-framed sofa to partake of a selection of small cakes handed around by their hostess and her helper. In the summer, home-made lemonade would be served, and maybe a cooling jelly or blancmange, while an observant ten-year-old absorbed the elements of polite conversation and social chatter from her perch on the cross-stitch–covered footstool near the parlour chiffonier.

Being a minister's wife meant endless social occasions. In between the tea-parties at the parsonage, there were numerous events in aid of the Congregational church, such as the conversaziones held at the Town Hall in aid of the organ fund, with music provided by local instrumental and vocal groups and by the choir—musical life in Bowmanville continued to flourish after the departure of William Henry—and refreshments arranged by ladies of the church. Mrs. Reikie's name does not figure largely in newspaper accounts of the events, so obviously she kept a low profile in church affairs and concentrated on her Sabbath school. And on Sundays, Alice would accompany Margaret Reikie to church, sitting beside her while her husband preached with "the even tenor of his way in a calm, moderate fashion."

Alice probably never crossed the road to the McClung home. John McClung was rabidly Conservative and actively involved in local and provincial politics. The Reverend Reikie held the Tory party in low esteem because of the deplorable lifestyle of its leader, John A. Macdonald, who clearly was no supporter of the Temperance Movement. On the rare occasions he was at home, Thomas Miller Reikie would have read *The Canadian Statesman*, nodding approvingly at the editorial attacks on the Tory leader for displays of public drunkenness: "If those in high positions would only discountenance the liquor traffic as they should do and work with those who are endeavouring to obtain mastery over 'the curse of Canada' we might hope for better things."

The outspoken Alice would have known well enough to hold her tongue on the subject of temperance. She came from a staunch Tory family, and their views would always colour her own. The theatrical side of Alice responded to Macdonald, the colourful, charismatic figure who had led Canada into nationhood in 1867.

This dashing, debonair figure, with his black curly hair and humorous expression not unlike that of Alice's bohemian grandfather, had undoubtedly already graced the town of Bowmanville with his presence. One of Macdonald's oldest friends was the Reverend Alexander Macnab, who had christened Alice and her brother and sister. He had sold his home, Dundurn, on Concession Street, in 1867 to John Milne, a fellow-Scot, who had tried and failed to beat the Grit stranglehold on Bowmanville in the first national election that never-to-be-forgotten summer, when Alice's father's band marched through cheering crowds to celebrate the new Dominion. Sir John attended more than one party in the town and it is likely he came during the 1867 campaign to John Milne's home.

Perhaps young Alice Freeman slipped away from home to peek at the crowds in their best finery, to try to catch a glimpse of the famous man with his second wife, Agnes, standing in the shade of Dundurn's columned porch to accept his local supporters' best wishes for his success against his arch-rival, George Brown, editor of *The Globe* newspaper in Toronto, whose editorials played no small part in publicizing Macdonald's drinking bouts.[4] It would have been Alice's first glimpse of the larger world, her first taste of its glamour and excitement.

If Alice knew to hold her tongue over politics, she did not feel the need to keep quiet over religion. During the time she was with the Reikies, she regularly interrogated the Reverend Reikie on the differences between the religion of her parents and the Congregationalist interpretation of the Bible. It was probably Thomas Reikie that journalist Faith Fenton was thinking of years later when, covering a General Assembly of the Presbyterian Church for "Woman's Empire," she told her readers: "a Scotsman is in his element when he has some metaphysical hair to split, especially if the said hair be pulled from some theological sheep or goat."

Quite often the answers she received did not satisfy her, and it is to the Reverend Reikie's eternal credit that he allowed himself to be quizzed by the small sceptic under his roof. He would have been surprised to know that his lasting gift to the woman Alice Freeman became was a dislike of cant and a wide tolerance for the religious beliefs of others. "We travel pretty much the same spiritual paths that our forefathers trod," she was to say later. In her case, it was the Reikies whose beliefs she followed, for she stayed in the non-conformist faith as an adult and did not return to the Anglican fold, which she later characterized as "the finest and most frigid body of people on the face of the earth." For Alice, warmth was in the religion she shared with Margaret Reikie.

Margaret Reikie had something private she shared with Alice. She was a poet. In between the endless parish chores and the observances of her religion, she lived a secret creative life that nourished her lonely heart. For about fourteen years she set aside a period of time in the middle of the day that her husband thought was spent in prayer for the parish. She was indeed praying, for she was a deeply religious woman. But it is also likely that this was when she wrote her poetry.

Loyalty to her husband would never have allowed Alice's mother to tell her daughter why she had given her into the keeping of Margaret Reikie, but in doing so she brought kindred spirits together.

It was only a brief walk along Wellington Street from the octagonal parsonage to the Bowmanville Union School, which Alice attended regularly for the next four years, a pleasant walk past Temperance Street, beneath the maples and the chestnut trees to the head of Silver Street, where the school occupied what was originally the old Town Hall. In the summer the well-kept grounds of Waverley Place, home of the general manager of the Ontario Bank in Bowmanville, perfumed the air with the scent of roses and the peppery tang of geraniums.[5] David Fisher's elegant home across the road from the school was one of the finest in the town.[6]

Union School by now was overcrowded, with more than seven hundred pupils in attendance, and some of the younger children were moved to the Sons of Temperance Hall for their lessons. Classes of sixty or sixty-five were not unusual in any school at the time, but in 1868 poor Miss

Pollock's Division had eighty-five children in what should have been accommodation for sixty-five. Boys and girls were, of course, segregated, but in the Union School they were brought together "in the first class only and for the purpose of recitation." Authorized books were used exclusively: the *Canadian Reader*, the *Royal Reader*, the *Ontario Reader*.[7]

In this structured, overcrowded environment, Alice Freeman thrived. Her presence there day after day represented freedom, a triumph after the deprivations of her sister Mary and her own struggles, and she grasped the opportunity. Year after year Miss A. Freeman appeared on the prize lists, winning awards for French, Classics, English Literature, Etymology, Botany, Grammar, Geography, History and, probably by dint of much application, Arithmetic and Algebra. Numbers affected her, she later said, "like sledge-hammer blows." Interestingly, she never seems to have won a prize for Composition. In creative work which allowed her spirit to roam free, her original mind and unconventional opinions possibly came as a shock to instructors who went by the book.

She could still be one of the girls, piercing her own ears fearlessly. She even survived being made to write with her right hand, although she was sure she should have been left-handed. There were teachers she adored—teachers like Miss Jane Kyle, who taught the top Division in the Union School for fifteen years. Alice was lucky that Jane Kyle did not leave until just after she graduated. Miss Kyle accepted a position in Port Hope, where they offered her better conditions and more money, and *The Canadian Statesman* opined in an unusually radical outburst against the local school board: "We cannot blame her in the least for giving some attention to her own interests. . . . We can only hope that the School Board of this town will not find that in allowing Miss Kyle to depart they have been 'penny wise and pound foolish.'" The girls' gift to their beloved Miss Kyle was decorative and not in the least practical: a pair of gold bracelets which they said were given, so *The Canadian Statesman* recorded, as "a memento of our love, not on account of [their] intrinsic value."

In her letter of farewell, Jane Kyle asked her "dear girls" to cultivate three things: "a firm will to do right, a tender conscience and a loving heart." With role models like Jane Kyle and Margaret Reikie, Alice moved with growing confidence into her teenage years.

Then, early in 1871, something unforeseen happened. Margaret Reikie became ill—probably not an unusual occurrence, but on this occasion

things took a turn for the worse, and all the magical powers of the octagonal house could not save her. After three weeks of painful struggle she gave
up the fight and died on March 1. Dr. W. Allison, who signed the death
certificate, put down "bilious fever" as the cause of death.

Before the advent of antibiotics and sulpha drugs, there were many
infections that could kill a frail woman like Margaret Reikie. It is
unlikely to have been typhoid fever, because that would have been stated
on the death certificate. However, it could have been a recurring infection connected with repeated miscarriages that had weakened her over
the years, and finally ended her life.

The death notice in *The Canadian Statesman* was brief: "On 1st
March, at the Congregational Parsonage, MARGARET W.S. REIKIE.
The funeral will take place on Saturday afternoon, first, at 2 o'clock."

Sitting between the flowing mourning veils of Margaret Reikie's
twenty-year-old niece who had come from the United States to nurse her
aunt in those last days, and the good ladies of the church who had
brought provisions and prayers to the octagonal house, a heart-broken
fourteen-year-old Alice fought back feelings of panic and claustrophobia
as the women knelt to pray and the veils fell over her, enclosing her completely. In later years she would recall the feeling, never directly identifying the occasion. She would avoid wearing veils over her face—with only
two notable exceptions, one on an extraordinary journey.

As the Reverend F.H. Marling from Toronto intoned the closing
words of his sermon—"Margaret had a stormy passage across the river,
but that is over now, and she has entered the everlasting rest. She is
spending today her first Sabbath in heaven"—Alice must have wondered
what the future held in store for her.

Years afterward, Faith Fenton would tell the person she loved about
her stay in the large octagonal house with the Reverend and Mrs. Reikie;
she would remember word for word the little speech she had been taught
for her oral invitations; she would remember how she would cross-
examine the Reverend Reikie. She never mentioned that Margaret Reikie
died while she was there.

There was, of course, no question of her remaining in the parsonage
without Mrs. Reikie. She returned to her parents in Barrie. The name
Alice Freeman does not appear in the midsummer prize-giving list of
1871 for the Union School, and she is listed in the Barrie census for that
year. But before she left, a poem appeared in *The Canadian Statesman*

under the following heading: "LINES composed by the late Mrs. Reikie, when her husband was absent from home on a missionary tour, and found in her portfolio." It could have been the niece who found them, but it is much more likely to have been Alice who took what was then the unusual step of naming the author.

Most poems and articles in journals and newspapers at the time were published under a pseudonym or, at most, the initials of the author, and certainly most women writers would never have dreamed of identifying themselves, particularly in their home town. In naming Margaret Reikie, Alice gave her benefactress one brief moment of posthumous recognition and glory:

> Memory presents a page so bright,
> Of olden days gone by,
> That sitting here, and gazing there,
> My thoughts o'er power me nigh.
>
> E'en now I hear a father's voice,
> A mother's loving tone,
> And straight I'm locked in fond embrace—
> Oh Mother! "Home, sweet, Home."
> . . .
> But why stoops down this weary head,
> Why flows this gushing tear?
> My aching heart, oh why this throb
> Of anguish sad and drear?
> . . .
> List, list, they speak, they cry to thee,
> Press on, press on, my child,
> Earth's not thy home, a pilgrim thou
> To heaven, serene and mild.
>
> Prize precious time. His glory seek
> With heart, and mind, and soul.
> Faint not, e'en should the way be steep.
> On Him thy sorrows roll.

The poem, which is untitled and has fourteen verses in all, is typical of other offerings on similar themes, but it cries out with Margaret Reikie's loneliness and her attempts to comfort herself with her faith.

From that moment on, Alice deliberately cultivated the positive frame of mind she took with her into the future. If that meant closing her mind to some great writers, such as Tolstoy, and some great works of art, then so be it. She would write: "At least grant that Truth is prismatic and that I have as much right to choose the brighter reflections as you the darker shades." Paintings that depicted human suffering gave her written criticisms a touch of outrage, even a note of hysteria: "What right has an artist to thrust the horrible before us?" she would ask her readers.

Alice Freeman had seen Margaret Reikie's life come to an end at forty-two, a life full of good works, charitable deeds and personal creative endeavours, yet with an emptiness at its centre. When she wrote, as Faith Fenton, "Like the Lady of Shalott, the women of today have become half-sick of shadows, and, turning from the tower, the spinning-wheel and the mirrored reflections of life, have floated down the broad stream that bears them into the real, busy, burdened, world," she might well have been thinking of what had been Margaret Reikie's life.[8]

Even in Barrie there would be consolations; there were Alice's brothers and sisters, with whom she was still close, and there would be all her father's books: works by Scott, Hawthorne, Thackeray and, above all, Dickens. *David Copperfield* was her favourite and always would be, just as it always was Dickens's own "favourite child." The parallels between the lives of David and Alice are obvious; both are cast away at ten years old by their parents without explanation.[9] It would have been easier to explain to her parents that it was Dickens who made her weep, rather than their abandonment of her and the loss of Margaret Reikie.

Alice returned to Bowmanville after the summer. Again she travelled on her own by steamer from Toronto, "a solitary but intrepid young traveller . . . watching the fair girls of happy family parties, who lean caressingly over grey-haired fathers or flit in and out of state-rooms with books or caramels, who chatter of 'Montreal" or 'Quebec.'" She may have been alone, but this time she did not cry. Instead, she made herself a promise to explore the far-off places down the river: "I will go down the big river and find out what is there." It was a promise she was to keep a thousandfold.

Alice again appears on the prize lists for the Union School closing exercises for 1872, and this time she is part of the entertainment, reciting a poem titled "Somebody's Darling," which she "rendered with feeling, with clear and distinct pronunciation, and [which was] highly appreciated," said *The Canadian Statesman*. She would always feel unsure about her looks, and from time to time she would wonder about her talent, but in the end the conviction Margaret Reikie had given her that she was a worthwhile individual—that she had indeed been "somebody's darling"—would transcend all her doubts and drive her onward.

She probably stayed with the family of one of her girlfriends for that final year. Perhaps that was the girl who took one of the poems her clever friend Alice had written and sent it to *The Canadian Statesman*.

Many years later Faith Fenton recalled the shocking circumstances surrounding its publication, referring to herself in the third person:

> She wrote some verses on the death of a minister's wife; very pathetic verses they were to her thinking, and she was very proud of them. Many months afterward she showed them to a school girl friend, who, thinking that her chum was a second Mrs. Browning, sent them to the editor of a local paper. And those (unattributed) verses on the death of that minister's wife came out in the paper a week or two later, on the day that he surprised his congregation by bringing home wife number two.

The Reverend Reikie, of course, is not mentioned by name, and there were other ministers' wives in Bowmanville, but none appeared in the death notices of *The Canadian Statesman* in 1871 and 1872. Moreover, starting with Mary Reikie's death certificate and following up with the census of 1871, something very strange happens to the Reverend Reikie's mathematics. He told Dr. Allison that his wife was forty-two, when in fact she was forty-six, and he told the census-taker that he himself was forty-five in April 1871, when in reality he was born on January 30, 1819, and was therefore fifty-two years old. Moreover, in the nominal return of deaths on the census, Margaret Reikie has dropped two more years to become forty, one month after she was declared dead at forty-two.

Why would an upstanding man of the church who would unquestionably have believed that lying was one of the cardinal sins have made both his dead wife and himself younger? Was he simply temporarily out of his mind with grief?

Well, out of his mind perhaps, but not with grief. In 1873 this notice appears in *The Canadian Statesman*: "PERSONAL—Rev. T.M. Reikie, who for the past eighteen years has been Pastor of the Congregational Church in this place, has resigned his charge, and left town on Tuesday last, to proceed to Scotland, where he contemplates residing for a time. Mr. Reikie is a devoted and faithful minister, and was universally esteemed as a worthy citizen—a good man. May the place he has vacated be filled with one equally worthy."

The notice appeared after Thomas Reikie had left, so the departure seems to have been speedy, leaving the congregation without a minister, and a Reverend J. Allworth filled in for a year before a permanent minister was found.

The cause of all the upheaval? In 1872 Thomas Reikie, aged fifty-three going on forty-five, married Marion Charlotte Thomson, who was twenty or twenty-two years old, depending on which census is correct. There appears to be no record of the marriage in Ontario, so they were probably married in Montreal, where Marion's wealthy father ran a dry-goods business. They could have met on the Reverend Reikie's missionary travels, as a branch of the Thomson family lived in Ontario.

What a shock it must have been to the small community when the upright Thomas Reikie, President of the Society for Total Abstinence, demonstrated that he had not had all his appetites under control! The Reverend Reikie soon discovered that his former reputation as a devoted and faithful minister was not enough to make his marriage to a woman more than thirty years his junior, hot on the heels of his first wife's death, acceptable to his appalled congregation and to the town of Bowmanville.

At the time many men remarried younger women, because many first wives died in childbirth, but Thomas Reikie stretched the goodwill of the Congregational church by his imprudence. Whatever he may have told the census-takers—or even the second Mrs. Reikie—the church fathers were in no doubt about how old he was. It was in their records.

From then on his career in the church lost its sheen. The sinner was not rejected, but he never again held the position he had had and, on his return to Canada in 1876, was shunted from parish to parish in Toronto, even returning at one point to the Presbyterian Church, in which he had originally been ordained in Scotland. His last parish was in the country area of Wiarton, where he died on December 12, 1900.

What a tangled web Thomas Reikie wove when he lied about his age! He continued to misrepresent his years on the census of 1891, where he declared he was sixty to his wife's forty—in fact, he was seventy-one, and had taken the bold step of dropping three more years from the truth. By now he was also the father of three children—two boys and a girl—and short of money in consequence. The family moved about Toronto a good deal, usually living with relatives of Marion Reikie, where she was listed as a housekeeper—this in spite of the fact that her father had retired to Toronto and that his estate was worth a quarter of a million dollars when he died in 1889, having apparently disinherited his daughter.

The passion of Thomas Miller Reikie for his young wife has to be read between the lines of censuses, street directories, notices in newspapers, and the records of the Congregational church. Nowhere does anyone display outrage, disapproval or the vaguest hint about their ages; appearances are maintained. One commemorative biographical record manages to avoid the issue by simply mentioning the second marriage and, more revealingly, the year. Thomas Reikie's obituary in *The Canadian Congregationalist* states the correct date of his birth—but presumably by this time it had dawned on Marion Reikie that things were other than they had seemed thirty years earlier, when a middle-aged minister on a missionary tour had converted her to his cause.[10]

On the edge of the Reverend Thomas Reikie's dangerous liaison stands a fourteen-year-old girl, watching and drawing conclusions. Even before she had any idea of her guardian's plans, Alice showed that something about Margaret Reikie's life with Thomas Reikie disturbed her.

Her unusual introduction to the publication of Margaret's poem— "LINES composed by the late Margaret Reikie while her husband was absent from home on a missionary tour"—suggests that the minister's wife may have written her poems in secret while her husband was not there to censure her, or that she wrote because she was often left alone. They hint that Alice was developing an eye for hypocrisy. Did the reference to the missionary tours imply that Reikie had less than lofty motives? After all, Thomas Reikie had started lying about his age a month after his first wife's death, even adjusting her age to fit his own new-found forties.

And although Alice says the timing of her own poem was unintentional, she probably knew full well that Thomas Reikie was coming back to town with a girl only four years older than herself to fill her beloved Margaret's shoes. The editor of *The Canadian Statesman*, after all, just happened to be the son of the Reverend Climie, the Congregational minister who had served prior to Thomas Reikie. Twenty years later, Faith Fenton wrote: "How softly we walked during the following days, for fear we would be associated with the contretemps. But the editor took pity on us and kept the secret." Maybe the editor was only too happy to be part of the conspiracy.

The contretemps touched Alice when she was moving from childhood into womanhood and beginning to think about love and marriage. In her own home and in the Reikie household, she saw two very different women in two very different marriages: her mother, ground under by children and domestic chores; Margaret Reikie, childless and weighed down by the barren nature of her existence. Were you then, as a woman, damned if you did, and damned if you didn't? What other alternative was there?

Faith Fenton the journalist was often sceptical about love and about marriage—even when she heard about a good one: "It means very much to us women, who, because of the knowledge that comes to us every day, are compelled to grow somewhat cynical concerning the existence of any such thing as unselfish love in men. We are glad to know that it does exist in the world—somewhere."

Life was moving Alice swiftly on towards a point where she would have her own experiences with love and loss. On January 4, 1872, she performed at the closing exercises of the Union School and received her last prizes. By the end of the year she was in Toronto, where she was about to commence her training as a teacher at the Toronto Normal and Model Schools: an apt profession for a woman whose looks might not guarantee her a husband.

PART TWO

On the Delectable Mountains

IV

Through the Looking-Glass

And moving thro' a mirror clear
That hangs before her all the year,
Shadows of the world appear.
There she sees the highway near
Winding down to Camelot.
Alfred, Lord Tennyson, "The Lady of Shalott."

THE IMPOSING EDIFICE THAT HOUSED the Toronto Normal and Model Schools reflected the buoyant optimism of mid-Victorian society and its growing awareness of the importance of education. Built in 1852 in the centre of the fashionable seven-and-a-half-acre park known as St. James Square, its architecture was more reminiscent of an English stately home than of an institution. Amid manicured lawns and shade trees, a curving carriageway led to an elegant sweep of façade and a porticoed entrance with Roman Doric columns and decorative details in the Renaissance Revival style, topped by a tall, open cupola surmounted by a cross.

St. James Square is long gone, and all that remains now of F.W. Cumberland and Thomas Ridout's edifice is a fragment of the front façade in the quadrangle of what was called the Ryerson Institute of Technology when it was built on the site in 1963. Much the same fragmented fate has befallen the records of the young men and women who studied in that "educational pork-packing factory," as one of its ex-students, writer Robert Barr, described it.[1] Sometimes single sheets of information have survived, sometimes whole ledgers; sometimes there are gaps of months, years, decades. There is no record left of Alice Freeman's six-month session in Model School in 1872, or of her Third-Class Certificate, except that she appears on the prize list and as part of the entertainment in *The Globe*'s coverage of the closing exercises of her session, and her attendance there is noted in the Entrance Register for the Normal School in 1874.

When Alice Freeman first passed through the doors of the school in 1872 to begin her six months of study, she would have been one of a growing number of her sex crossing that lofty threshold. In 1871 Egerton Ryerson, Chief Superintendent of Education and prime creator of the educational system in Ontario, had guided through Parliament one final, major piece of legislation before he retired.[2] It brought the old grammar schools under the full authority of the provincial Department of Education and legislated attendance in school between the ages of seven and eleven, the growing need for teachers thus opening the Model School doors on Gould Street to many more women.

These were not the only doors that Alice could have chosen. There was a Model School in Barrie, and she could have lived at home while she studied for her certificate. Indeed, her Certificate of Moral Character—necessary for every Model School applicant—was not provided by the Reverend Reikie, whose own moral character was now suspect, but by the Reverend Edward Morgan of Barrie.

The move to Barrie had brought financial security to William Henry and Mary Ann Freeman. Their establishment, Crystal Palace Stores, with its pretty white gingerbread frontage and its name evoking memories of courtship days in London in the 1850s, was already a landmark. Wordy advertisements in the local newspaper, *The Northern Advance*, bore witness to the quality and quantity of the stock carried:

To Persons
ABOUT TO MARRY
(and no doubt the number is large, considering the late
bountiful harvest)
W.H. FREEMAN
Begs to announce that he has on hand a LARGE &
WELL-SELECTED
STOCK OF FURNITURE
consisting of

Tables of all kinds,	Bureaus of all kinds,
Bedsteads of all kinds,	Cupboards of all kinds,
Chairs of all kinds,	Washstands of all kinds,

Sofas and Lounges of all kinds

To those who are ALREADY MARRIED, and blessed with the sound of little feet pattering around the house in joyous expectation of the coming
CHRISTMAS PRESENTS!
we would say that we have the largest and best stock of TOYS AND FANCY GOODS in the County of Simcoe—in fact the very storehouse of SANTA CLAUS himself; to which is added an excellent assortment of PURE CANDIES and CONFECTIONS from the best makers in Ontario. STOP A MINUTE, we have not done yet!

This advertisement of December 1868 covers an eight- by five-inch space in *The Northern Advance* and goes on to list an impressive assortment of wools, silks and other household items, before ending with personal thanks from the Freemans "to their numerous friends and the inhabitants of Barrie generally for the liberal support they have met with. . . ."

William Henry Freeman had clearly diversified his business and found prosperity within the first year of his arrival in Barrie. The store was initially rented from one of the area's leading property-owners, Robert Ross, but by the time of his retirement William Henry would own Crystal Palace Stores. At the age of thirty-eight, all musical passion spent, he had settled down to become a true member of the bourgeoisie, a storekeeper. He left any artistic activities to his offspring, particularly his tenth and twelfth children, Florence and Grace. They appear in newspaper accounts of receptions for various events such as the arrival of the new minister for the Reformed Episcopal church, and Florence played the organ in the Anglican church from her early teens.

By 1872 there were nine Freeman children in Barrie, with two more yet to come: Arthur in 1873, and Grace in 1875. At a time when little was known about the importance of prenatal nutrition and the dangers of infection—puerperal or childbed fever, caused by streptococci bacteria, killed women by the score—giving birth and surviving was difficult enough. Then, if she survived childbirth, a woman might face a lifetime of gynaecological complications: recurring infections, a prolapsed uterus or untreated pelvic tearing. Childbirth would not end for Mary Ann Freeman until the age of forty-four, and the onset of menopause, which came earlier to nineteenth-century women—a not-uncommon reproductive pattern for married women of the era, if they survived childbirth itself.

Alice Freeman did not choose to return to the bosom of her family. It is possible that returning was not an option and she was simply expected to fend for herself. There was no charge for attending Model and Normal School, but her lodging would have cost her $2.50 or $3.50 a week, and although textbooks were subsidized, she would have had to pay half the cost. Given her scholastic achievements, she may have received some sort of scholarship, but Bowmanville Union School was short of funds—as the loss of Jane Kyle and the size of the classes illustrate—and probably the Freemans helped their daughter financially at this point. William Henry was by now better able to do so.

Besides, Alice was about to embark on training that would ensure her financial independence from the family "before marriage or a move to another career provided an escape from teaching," as a government study bluntly put it. Most of the young women with her were doing just that: finding a respectable way to keep themselves before they found a man to keep them instead. It was what they had been told all through school was the supreme purpose of life for their sex, that "high and holy estate," as Faith Fenton put it in one of her columns: marriage and the bearing of children.

But at least one of the girls sitting before Mr. James L. Hughes, the Model School principal, and Mrs. Martha Cullen, Head Mistress of the Girls' Model School, that first day in the great auditorium of architects Cumberland and Ridout's palace of learning had other plans. The enquiring mind and natural scepticism developed during Alice's religious debates with Thomas Reikie had been further sharpened by the events of 1871, and every time she went home she saw her mother, now approaching middle age, nursing another baby. Alice Freeman did not see marriage as an escape—from teaching, or from anything else. She had looked into that mirror and she had not liked what she had seen. It was not an escape she was seeking, but a route to freedom, and she already knew the road she wanted to travel in that "move to another career." First, however, she had to survive Model School, James L. Hughes and Martha Cullen.

James Hughes would later deplore the training that taught him his "supreme duty was to criticize destructively," but, when Alice Freeman was a student in Model School, positive reinforcement was a distant glimmer on the twentieth-century educational horizon. Hughes's punitive approach undoubtedly played a part in the heavy drop-out rate—a third to a half of the girls did not finish the course or qualify for a certificate— but it was behaviour they would already have been used to in a class-room situation, where corporal punishment and the complete authority of the teacher were the order of the day.

The women were usually young girls straight out of school, unlike many of the men, who had already been teaching before they came to qualify and were often in their twenties. Combined with the stress of a rigorous course would be the anxiety of separation from their families. Such very young Victorian females would have led confined lives within the walls of home, school and church, with little experience of the outside world.

The fifteen-year-old who had weathered a five-year separation from her family would have found boarding-out in Toronto less of a challenge than would most of the other young women. The strict controls placed on behaviour by the Model School system extended to the students' private lives and to the approved boarding-houses in which they stayed while they studied. There was a curfew at night, attendance at church on Sundays was compulsory, and the fate of any student caught talking to a member of the opposite sex was immediate expulsion. Indeed, females were expressly forbidden "to form any new male acquaintances." Given the extreme innocence and lack of experience of the girls under the care of authorities who had to board them out in private homes—albeit "approved"— around a big city, this was not so much unenlightened as sensible.

Since Alice Freeman was not looking for a mate at this time in her life and had spent every Sabbath for the last five years in church with Margaret Reikie, none of these restrictions presented a problem. In fact, from the fragments of the picture that remain of student life in Model School, fifteen-year-old Alice enjoyed herself very much. She was in Toronto, which was part of her dream, and she was embarking on a career that would lead her—however winding the highway—to the most important part of that dream: being a writer. She had already told her brothers and sisters and girlfriends that she had set her heart upon it.

First of all, however, there was History, Geography, Chemistry, Arithmetic and Mensuration, Algebra, Geometry, Drawing and Linear Drawing, Euclid, Natural Philosphy, Book-keeping—not to mention reading, writing, calisthenics, religious instruction, practice in the use of school apparatus and, of course, instruction in the general principles of the science of education and the art of teaching. Specialization, like positive reinforcement, was on the distant twentieth-century horizon; the nineteenth-century teacher had to be able to do it all.

Classes commenced at nine o'clock and finished at four o'clock, with an hour's break between twelve-thirty and one-thirty for lunch back at the boarding-house. Curfew was a surprisingly generous nine-thirty and, given the weighty timetable, it is likely many students spent their evenings studying—particularly if they had been chosen at the end of the day to teach class in the Model School and had a lesson to prepare before facing whichever division they had been assigned.

Division One was particularly dreaded. It was no easy task to face a class of children close to your own age who knew you were a student teacher, and who also knew they were in the only educational establishment in the province where corporal punishment was not permitted. Of course, you *could* send a child out of the room if push came to shove, but it was your shove that would be judged as failure, not the behaviour of the child who had provoked you into it.

The Model School had the cachet of a private school and was always inundated with applicants, although it was not free. At the turn of the century it was "fiercely imperial," one of its ex-students recalled, and the day started with a hymn, a prayer and the younger ones marching around the classroom with Union Jacks over their shoulders, proclaiming that they were "soldiers of the queen, my lads"—even if they were lasses. There is little doubt that it would have been the same in Alice's time. From kindergarten on, of course, they were as strictly segregated as their student teachers.

Saturday was free for the students and teachers, except that the men were required to attend an hour's drill under the direction of an ancient drill-sergeant who was a veteran of the War of 1812—they soon found that the best way to ensure an easy morning was to get him going on his war stories.

It was probably on Saturdays that Alice Freeman got to know the city she would grow to love—however harshly she might come to judge some of its institutions and public figures, its hidebound mores or its religious bigotries. Wherever else in the world she travelled, she always came back to Toronto, where she had first tasted independence.

By the end of her training Alice Freeman knew Toronto better than did most women who had lived there all their lives, because she had walked miles along its streets, clambered up the sides of its ravines, saved her pennies for the ferry ride over to the Island, where she learned to row in the lagoons and sheltered waters. Working her mind was not enough; she had to burn up her considerable physical energy. When she was older, and of necessity more aware of the proprieties, she would take her younger brother Fred along with her on her outings, but it was always she who knew the way and suggested the route. And she had probably found the way as a young girl with a girlfriend or two from the approved boarding-house.

It was no doubt Alice and her friends who first made the explorations that Faith Fenton would describe to her "Woman's Empire" readers years later, when she wrote about the joys of running along the desolate winter shore amid the deserted boat-houses below High Park, with the grey waves splashing beneath a grey sky and the trains roaring past behind them to Mimico and points west. As long as they were back by curfew, their landlady was probably quite happy to have her young lady lodgers out of her way, racing each other in the cold yellow light of a late winter day up the long alley from the lakeshore to Colborne Lodge. There they would stop at the grave of its owner, John Howard, high on a hill overlooking the trees of the Humber Valley. It was John Howard's architecture that had shaped much of the city's fashionable face, and High Park itself was his gift to the city.[3] Then they would make their way back, slipping and sliding over the frosty ground, across the ravines of the valley to the Dundas Street bridge and the streetcar home before darkness fell, filling the shops with light, the sidewalks with cheerful, effervescent Saturday-night crowds, and the roads with horses and sleighs and the silver sound of sleigh-bells.

It may well have been as a student that Alice Freeman first became acquainted with that "Other Half" of Toronto society that reminded her of characters in *The Old Curiosity Shop*, *Great Expectations* and *Oliver Twist*, the lost souls of which Faith Fenton was to write with such eloquence and passion, the echoes of her beloved Charles Dickens never far from her character-studies and her prose. She and her friends would have walked past the once-splendid mansions on King Street, with their boarded-up courtyards and rag-filled windows, torn shutters and refuse-covered lawns, and seen through the broken panes the "miserable, hunted" faces of the street-people who now frequented them.

Since the students of the approved boarding-houses seemed to have helped with some of the day-to-day chores such as grocery-shopping, Alice probably discovered the delights of the St. Lawrence Market on that first six-month stay at Model School. It would always be one of her favourite places, with its jostle and bustle of storekeepers and housewives and those members of a "Lower Bohemia," the Gypsy fortune-tellers and jugglers who wheedled small change out of you, all the while keeping a wary eye out for the policeman on his regular beat around the market.

Alice would have had little time for her own creative writing, but she undoubtedly recorded some of her adventures, honing her skills for choosing the telling detail, painting the original vignette: the little girl selling newspapers with her eyes on her feet beneath her ragged frock, one in an old boot much the worse for wear, the other in a frayed blue satin dance-slipper she had picked up from somewhere, "its steel beading aglitter beneath the light"; the old man with the long white beard "that swept his shabby coat to the third or fourth button," passing her on the winter street on a sled pulled by a large black dog "for all the world like a bankrupt Santa Claus."

As the weather improved, she and her fellow-students would be off to Yonge Street and the ferry to "that little sandy bar that we term in local parlance 'the Island,'" where they would walk between cottages called "Seabird" and "Rosebud," "Idle Wyld" and "Far Niente," and listen to the whistle of the ferry-boats at Hanlan's Point and the monotonous music of the steam-organ on the carousel. They would stand a while to watch the entertainers with fancy names, like the juggler "Dr.

Marigold," in "the glossiest of beavers and the whitest of cuffs, with his curly hair resting lightly upon his coat collar" and wonder at his marvellous gift of the gab.

Then, back to the boarding-house—perhaps on or near Church Street, because the "approved" locations would be close to the school and also close to churches of many denominations. There they could choose the sitting-room provided for them by the landlady under the Model and Normal School boarding-house rules, with its tea and toast and laughter, or the bedroom that two girls shared, where ambitions and dreams were confided. Alice would always treasure her female friends, refusing to see other women merely as rival fillies in the marriage stakes. "Women," she would say later as Faith Fenton, "are kind and tender to each other, no matter what men may say to the contrary."

Outside in the street they might hear the lilting sounds of the Italian organ-grinder's barrel-organ playing "The Money-Musk" or "Il Trovatore" in the late twilight, giving fifteen-year-old Alice dreams of "other skies full of sunshine and glitter, rich colour and passionate life."

Silence filled the streets on Sunday. Not a child playing, and certainly no organ-grinders, the clatter and rattle of the streetcars stilled. Church bells broke the Sabbath hush as Alice and her friends walked to the church of their choice. Then it was back to the boarding-house to prepare for the following day, so that you could tell Mrs. Cullen or one of the other instructors how degrees of longitude are reduced to statute miles, or sketch briefly the *third* invasion of Greece by the Persians, or write an essay on *Should a parent be compelled to educate his children?*, or explain the formation of dew. Or you might have to stand in front of a class of girls about your own age and explain how to divide 71.417 by 0.98762 *duodenary* scale, and to carefully mark the position of the separating point in the quotient.

Mrs. Cullen was probably a widow who had returned to work in teacher-training. She marked so harshly that Model School principal James Hughes occasionally took it upon himself to regrade the results of some of the female students to a higher "rate," as the levels were called. Alice's reports have not survived, but many have, and Mrs. Cullen's opinion of poor Miss Cameron has come down to posterity: "slow and lifeless, kept her eyes constantly on the book. In Arithmetic did all the work herself and that very slowly. A wretched teacher." She was graded as fifth-rate. Likewise the report on Miss Hall, who said to her class,

"You wasn't reading that well. Read again." Then there was Miss Davidson, who pronounced "barrel" as "barl"—"to the amusement of the class"—and was judged "a miserable teacher"; Miss Hill, who got "confused and excited"; and Miss McLaughlin, who "said a few words and then gave up the class"—hardly surprisingly after her dramatic exit, she was judged "too nervous and excited to teach well."

Then there were the good ones, like Miss Carter, who was "not accurate in speech [but] teaches well, has energy, is enjoying teaching, succeeds with practice. Excellent." She was judged second-rate. Miss Connor, who did not read well, but prepared and taught with energy, apparently talked too much and "did not pay attention to the position of the class," but was judged as capable of being successful "with practice" and given an "almost" second-rate grading.

It was to this latter group that Alice Freeman belonged, so she was no doubt judged as second- , perhaps third-rate. A first-rate girl does not seem to have existed—and there were only one or two males judged first-rate in a session. In later years Faith Fenton's family recorded that she had done "brilliantly." There is no reason to doubt the truth of the memory, and some evidence to support it.

The Model School closed in the summer of 1873 with its usual exhibition and distribution of prizes on Friday, June 21—an event given full coverage by *The Globe*. What a flutter of excitement there must have been among the girls who had made it through the reefs of destructive criticism to reach this moment! Dressed in white, with sashes and hair ribbons in different colours for the different divisions, they sat in the great hall, turning around to see if they could catch a glimpse of their parents among the audience of local dignitaries, including the great Egerton Ryerson himself.

The first part of the entertainment was a cantata presented by the girls: *Crowning of the Rose*. Among the thirteen roles featuring various flowers were Rose, played by Katie Alley; Dandelion, portrayed by Mary Yale, who would eventually be weeded out from Normal School after two attempts to obtain her permanent licence; and Japonica, acted by Alice Freeman. In a garden of sunflowers, mignonettes, tulips and hollyhocks, the exotic Japanese quince stood out, with her strong features and her beautiful voice. The musicality of that voice would be remarked upon again and again by ex-students and teaching colleagues when they spoke of the woman they had known as Miss Freeman and later rediscovered as Faith Fenton.

Among the memorabilia that has survived the years is a studio portrait of Alice in a white dress, her curly hair tied back with a ribbon. It is most probably of Alice in her Model School Graduation dress; it is also testimony to the presence of her parents in the audience on that June day. William Henry and Mary Ann Freeman watched their maverick daughter's moment of glory when she walked up to the stage to receive her prizes in the Girls' First Division, Senior Section: a First Prize in English, and a Second Prize in Natural Science. Alice, the castaway, had not merely survived; she had triumphed.

The journey, however, had only just begun. The Third-Class Certificate Alice was awarded was not permanent, and she would need to do some practical teaching in the classroom before she could sit the entrance examinations for Normal School to work for her Second-Class Certificate. So at some point in 1873 Alice packed her bags again and was off by steamer to a country school on the Niagara Peninsula, near Fort Erie, to stay with a Mennonite family while she worked as a student teacher for about six months.

Alice's life among the "peculiar people"—a description she said they delighted in—and the details of her days as a student teacher in Niagara can only be pieced together from fragments, some of which she herself provided as Faith Fenton. If her descendants had not kept that knowledge alive, her "Woman's Empire" column in 1888 on the Mennonites, and her article on a visit to the Niagara Peninsula, would seem to be simply the work of a journalist who felt something on the history and customs of those people and that part of the world would make good copy.

It is clear from her article, written fifteen years later, that she accompanied her new foster-family to church, just as she used to accompany Margaret Reikie, standing at the back of the church with "the carnally minded," as outsiders like herself were called. With her Mennonite family she shared the ceremonies of their religion—ceremonies like the washing of the feet, a significant occasion they called "a big ceremony," that served as a general rendezvous for the Mennonite community throughout the Niagara Peninsula in the spring and autumn of every year.

The Mennonite church Alice attended was a simple structure of white-washed walls and plain wooden benches that would, she said, "appall some of our luxurious city pew-holders," and the pulpit was an enclosed platform with hat pegs on the walls at the back and cuspidors on the floor in front of it. The men, with their clean-shaven faces and "round shocked hair," sat on the right, the women in their caps and kerchiefs on the left, many holding their babies in their arms.

Faith Fenton describes in her article a conversation with "a professional man"—possibly a doctor or another teacher working in the community—about the dress of "the peculiar people" and its significance to their sense of who they are and what they believe: "Take it away and the people lose their individuality at once. They have come to regard it as an essential of their religion rather than an accessory." The perceptive professional man saw that it was the similarity of the Mennonites' dress that preserved their individuality; it was their uniform, their "strong barrier" against the encroachment of "the carnally inclined" world.

Equally, the literal interpretation of the Scripture that is an essential part of the Mennonites' beliefs would have fascinated the girl who had quizzed Thomas Reikie on his interpretation of the Bible. In the feet-washing ceremony she observed the community literally fulfilling Christ's admonition, "If I your Lord and Master wash your feet, ye also ought to wash one another's feet," and was able to overcome her first reaction of amused scepticism to see beneath the outward form the heart and purpose of the exercise: ". . . the effect to a thoughtful mind is impressive . . . giving a deeper realization of the self-abasement of the One who 'took upon him the form of a servant.'"

The first Mennonites in the Niagara area arrived with the Empire Loyalists at the end of the eighteenth century, principally from Pennsylvania, looking for religious freedom and, above all, good farming land. They gradually spread from their original settlements along a creek near the Niagara River to Lincoln County, and then to Welland County.[4] Alice Freeman taught in a school near Fort Erie, so it was probably in Welland County that she stayed with her Mennonite family.

There is also a possibility that she taught in a school largely attended by Mennonite children—hence her stay in a Mennonite household, which seems strange unless she had some part to play in the community. By the 1870s there was real tension in the Niagara region between conservative and progressive factions, and the differences had first appeared in attitudes to education and the involvement of the state in the school-ing of their children. Some were all for more secular involvement, and started to send their children to local schools outside Mennonite control. Alice may have been part of such a community. Faith Fenton later observed: "A church quarrel is the bitterest thing on earth, so it seems to me," and Alice Freeman would have seen something of those tensions in her time with the Mennonites.

For about six months, sixteen-year-old Alice made her way from that old log house to the village school. The Education Act of 1873 had brought some welcome changes to country schools, and a report for the Welland area notes the improvement in basic school supplies, the plant-ing of shade-trees, the digging of new wells and privies. As she walked along the path, Alice could hear the shrill whistle of the mother-turkey calling to her brood in the orchard and see the swarms of bees over the white, perfumed blossoms of the buckwheat. She was light-years and cultural miles away from the classrooms of the Model School in which she had written out for Mrs. Cullen an explanation of the formation of dew. Now she was teaching children whose parents did not know the sci-entific explanation of that atmospheric vapour, but believed absolutely in its magic and its Creator.

Two other "Woman's Empire" columns were also inspired by her stay as a sixteen-year-old on the Niagara Peninsula. In one, Faith Fenton describes in detail an old log house in the country, where she once lived, although she does not say when. The description of the interior matches that of the typical Ontario Mennonite home, from the low ceilings with heavy rafters, to her own bedroom three steps up from the entrance to the cellar, "with its cemented floor and rows of milkpans." Many Mennonite homes of the time started with a bedroom or two on the ground floor, and then were added to as the family grew—which is how Faith Fenton describes the house in her column. The focus of the article is the kitchen garden that functions as a source of supply for the house-wife's "cure-closet."

This garden is described in not just minute, but loving, detail. She knows where the sweet herbs grow—marjoram, lavender, rosemary—and where to find the medicinal herbs—pennyroyal, tansy, catnip, anise and bitter horehound. She makes her way along the bark paths, past beds of snapdragons, pinks and sweet william, noting the vines climbing over the old picket fence and around the gnarled bark of an old plum

tree. She points out the rose of Sharon and dark-spotted tiger lilies, pop-
pies and the tall stems of the gladiolus. Then she takes the reader back
indoors to "the house-mother's cure-closet" with "its rows of bottles,
bunches of dried herbs carefully labelled, and jars filled with rare jellies
. . . 'to take the taste out of the mouth.'" Here she tells her "Woman's
Empire" readers of the woman's complete faith in "mysterious conditions . . . attached to the preparation of her drug," which should be
gathered when the first snow falls, or on the day in spring when you see
the first toad, or before the dew dries. These were Mennonite beliefs,
and at the time Alice was with them they probably still held their
"Braucherei," a form of charming done with prayer incantations.

In the second of her columns on the area, Faith Fenton recalled a
visit to St. Mark's Church in Niagara, where she talked at some length
with its rector, the Venerable Archdeacon McMurray, who could remember as a small, three-year-old boy watching the American fleet coming
around Toronto Island to attack the then city of York.[5]

It is "the chain of living memory" that touches her most: the old
man remembering the Americans "drinking and rioting" about the
streets, and one of them "in a kindly way" giving him a toy bugle. She is
moved by the old, yellowed church register that records the marriages
and deaths of those early Canadians—among them the marriage of
Moses and Phoebe, "negro slaves of Mr. Secretary Jarvis,"[6] the burial of
"Cutnose Johnson, an Indian chief," and the birth of Allan Napier
MacNab, Tory leader and first prime minister of Upper and Lower
Canada.[7] Outside the church the old rifle pits thrown up by the
Canadian soldiers still wind their way among the graves like a dry
riverbed, and she can see on some of the large, flat gravestones the
hatchet marks of the American soldiers who had used them as tables for
meat-cutting when they held the town.

From the banks of the Niagara River, with its glimpses of Brock's
Monument high above the trees, from the peninsula that held the old
capital of Upper Canada, Alice brought back with her to Toronto "vivid
records of Canada's early struggles" and a sense of her country's history
that she would take into the classroom with her.[8] An older and more
reflective woman would view those years differently. There is a sense
throughout the piece that thirty-three-year-old Faith is nostalgic not only
for the lost time of an earlier age, but for her own young womanhood,
slipping "from the warm sentient present into that silent, pregnant past."

So, in 1874 it was back to Toronto, to St. James Square and boarding-house life, to be reunited with some of her friends from the Model School: Rose Katie Alley from the cantata, and Dandelion Mary Yale, soon to be uprooted and sent away, certificate-less, after her two sessions. Attending two sessions was not in itself uncommon, particularly among the girls. Most of them were very young and had limited experience in the classroom, and even clever Alice Freeman completed two courses before she received her permanent Second-Class Certificate.

Alice's sessions in Normal School were marked by two scandals that made headlines in *The Globe*. The first involved the no-new-male-acquaintances rule. The valiant efforts of the Normal School authorities to separate the sexes were, not surprisingly, unsuccessful, and in fact were routinely ignored by many of the students, with the knowledge of the staff, who seem to have thrown up their collective hands and retired from a losing battle. The principal of the Normal School, Dr. Davies, finally had to take action when the matter was brought to his attention.

The headmaster's immediate response was to order the girls involved into his office, demanding they confess and grilling them until they broke—at which point, apparently, they were "rebuked . . . for confessing, otherwise he would have known nothing. . . ." Damned if they did, and damned if they didn't, the young women were learning what they should already have known in Victorian society: that, when it came to the sins of the flesh, it was woman who was the temptress, and man her helpless victim. Four women and three men were suspended for one week, and one man was permanently expelled.

The most harshly punished, smarting at the injustice, wrote a lengthy letter to *The Globe* that gave his own version of the affair, suggesting he had been singled out because he came from Michigan, and accusing Dr. Davies of harassment—even his clothing and squeaky boots were criticized, although "Dr. Davies wore a pair fully as bad in that respect." He described the head of the Normal School as "the most successful failure I ever saw." The letter incidentally throws some light on why Alice Freeman received a prize in Natural Sciences, an unusual area of excellence for her. Virtually the only teacher praised in the letter is the Science Master, Thomas Kirkland, who was both popular and extremely competent. Obviously Alice had striven to do her very best for an able teacher who used constructive, rather than destructive, criticism.

But the most interesting aspect of his letter is the picture that "Justice" (the writer's pseudonym) draws of the harassment of the women students by the principal, largely by ridiculing them in front of the class. Dr. Davies used language as an instrument of punishment quite as effectively as the strap: "Now, Miss, if you open your mouth much wider I can see what you had for breakfast," or, "Now, Miss, you are like an old cow that gives a pailful of milk and then kicks it over," or the picturesque and pithy "There you go again, hagglety-bang chuckle-cock as usual." "Justice" adds: "Some fathers might hesitate to send their daughters to such a school were they acquainted with the treatment they might expect from the Principal."[9]

Some fathers maybe, but Alice's father now had little say in his daughter's destiny. When William Henry Freeman handed his daughter over to others, he handed her over to herself. It is highly unlikely Alice was ever moved to break the rule of sexual separation, since she had other roles in mind than that of temptress, or wife. But the verbal cruelty and sexual discrimination Alice undoubtedly encountered in her training was the perfect preparation for the intolerance and ridicule she would meet on the road to her chosen career. There would be a lot of name-calling in Faith Fenton's future; the names would hurt her, but never break her.

The second scandal would undoubtedly have brought back memories of Margaret and Thomas Reikie. Dr. Davies's predecessor, Dr. John Herbert Sangster, had divorced his wife of eighteen years and the mother of his seven children, and then married a much younger woman. The woman had been a student at the Normal School when he was the principal, and then a teacher in the Model School during his tenure, which lasted until 1871.

Aspersions were cast, accusations hurled, but no action was taken until Dr. Sangster attempted to run for a seat on the Council of Public Instruction.[10] Discretion was finally thrown to the winds by some who had kept silent about the affair, and the matter was the subject of much letter-writing and extended editorials in *The Globe* under such headings as "The Sangster Scandal," "Sangster Again," and "Sangster Once More." At the time, scandal and rumour were grist for even the most respectable newspapers' mill. *The Globe* even went so far as to print the text of one of the headmaster's letters to his pupil, calling it "disgusting." In the sexual sense it is not in the least disgusting, but the selfishness of the writer and the psychological pressure put on a very young girl are disturbing. According to

The Globe, the forty-year-old doctor not only had paid "devoted attentions" to a sixteen-year-old girl who was his student, but had forged his wife's signature to a document in which she purportedly confessed to adultery, driving her "in poverty to the States."

Dr. Sangster had friends in high places, men who swore they had seen his wife sign the document, who accused her of drunkenness and adultery, of having a child with another man. In fact, "the amatory headmaster," as *The Globe* dubbed him, probably committed bigamy when he married his "lady love" in Detroit, since no one ever saw his divorce papers. He maintained they had been destroyed in the fire that devastated Chicago in 1871.

Egerton Ryerson does not come out of the story well. *The Globe* claimed that the situation had been brought to his attention in 1870 by the understandably distressed parents of the girl and, although Dr. Ryerson ordered that the affair should cease, he took no further action when his order was ignored, and proceeded to sweep everything under the Establishment rug, even holding on to documents and letters that implicated Dr. Sangster—a man "who took advantage of his position, age and experience to attract a comparative child by his attentions"— while, according to *The Stratford Beacon*, delivering "homilies" against male and female students even speaking to each other.

Passion. Hypocrisy. The power of the male Establishment. While Alice Freeman pondered such matters and discussed them with her friends, she may also have given some thought to the power of the fourth estate. In the Sangster scandal it was newspapers such as *The Globe*, and even smaller regional papers like *The Stratford Beacon, The Guelph Mercury* and *The Owen Sound Advertiser*, that gave a voice to the wronged parties, and exposed what those in power would have preferred hidden from the public eye. It would probably also not have escaped Alice's notice that the Liberal *Globe* had not taken a stand along party lines, but had attacked the former Reformer Ryerson and his Liberal school-board friends.[11] The newspaper threw its support behind Professor Goldwin Smith, who hastened back from a visit to England to run successfully against Dr. Sangster, thus proving that the majority of teachers "have no sympathy with Free Love and Chicago divorces," as *The Globe* put it.

The newspaper reports would have done nothing to soften Alice's sceptical outlook on the "high and holy estate" called marriage. When the wronged wife faced her husband with his behaviour, he and his supporters held this against her as proof of unreasonable jealousy. When she refused to go away quietly for $300 a year and leave her children behind, he concocted the scheme for the divorce and spread scandalous stories about her. In the end she was forced to leave the country without support, rather than lose her children. So much for the protection that marriage afforded!

In the minutes of the Toronto Board of Education for 1875 there is the following entry: "That Miss Alice Freeman, holding a Second-class Provincial Certificate, Grade B, be appointed 5th Division Teacher, Palace Street School, in the place of Miss Sefton, resigned." It is signed by W.W. Ogden, Chairman of the Standing Committee on School Management.

In October 1875, Alice Freeman entered the service of the Toronto school board. Her salary was less than $300 per annum, under half what any of the males from her Normal School course would receive. In an 1875 editorial *The Globe* suggested "it would be far better for young ladies to turn housemaids than school teachers," but by 1882 the same paper is saying that, after all, "the lady teacher's connection with her profession is but temporary." Alice, however, would remain in the Toronto school system for nearly nineteen years.

V

The Lady Vanishes

I should think it well nigh impossible to read a writer
thus [weekly] and not know something of him. . . .
Women writers betray themselves in their writings more
readily than men. It is natural that they should, being by
nature more emotional, less secretive and repressive.

Faith Fenton, "Woman's Empire," 1893.

IN 1873, WHEN ALICE FREEMAN was attending Model School, Prince
Edward Island entered Confederation and the Dominion of Canada finally
stretched *a mari usque ad mare*. The year also marked the beginning of a
recession and the resignation of John A. Macdonald from power. In the
General Election that followed in 1874, the Reform Party—as the Liberal
party was also called then—took office under Alexander Mackenzie.[1]

The fall of 1875 in Toronto was marked by religious violence. Hard
times exacerbated the tensions always simmering between Protestants and
Roman Catholics, and they finally. erupted in October during a Sunday
march of Roman Catholics celebrating the Jubilee of St. Paul's Parish.

The parade started peacefully enough, making its way from St.
Paul's on Power Street to St. Michael's Cathedral, and then along Bond
and Queen streets to St. Patrick's Church. At St. Mary's, on Bathurst
Street, the crowds began to gather and, rather than force the issue, the
marchers chose another route. However, at the junction of Queen and
Spadina, a large crowd awaited them, throwing debris gathered from a
nearby brickyard on men, women and children, and the police inter-
vened. The parade pressed on in spite of violence every step of the way,
with gunshots adding to the terror.

In the aftermath of the riot the newspapers fulfilled their obligation to reflect public opinion, covering both the ensuing court cases against the young thugs, with their unlicensed firearms and their unreasoning hatred, and the pronouncements by the leaders of various groups. Ogle R. Gowan, head of the Orange Organization, maintained the responsibility for what happened lay with the Catholics for insisting on "walking the streets in procession."[2]

The Globe dealt with that statement in no uncertain terms: ". . . delusive nonsense is frequently aired to the effect that Ontario is a Protestant country, and Toronto a Protestant city. Anything more transparently false could not well be uttered. . . . Ontario is a *free* country in the broadest sense of the term, and Toronto is a *free* city, which implies all that is best in 'Protestant', and a great deal more." It kept the full force of its sarcasm for the self-righteous statements made by the British press about riots in the colonies: "If the occurrence of riots is a reliable indication of governmental imbecility, England is one of the most incapable countries in the world."

Alice would undoubtedly have been moved by *The Globe*'s final, eloquent appeal: "If we cannot permit every citizen the free exercise of his religion . . . then all our boastings about freedom are a delusion, and all our claims to superiority over the benighted and bigoted population in Europe and elsewhere are baseless as the mere dream of the shadow of smoke."

In that troubled Toronto of 1875, struggling to free itself from the recession of the early 1870s, the violence was not always on a large scale. In August, when Alice was probably being interviewed for her first teaching position, the headlines in the papers were about the violence inflicted on one human being: a young woman called Jeannie Gilmour.

July 31. A hot Saturday night in the city. Nicholas Rooney, warehouse watchman, is on his way at a few minutes before eleven o'clock to check his company's premises on Jordan Street. As he makes his way along Melinda Street, he sees a wagon stopped on the side of the road, with someone in the driver's seat, and a man and woman standing on the sidewalk beside it. Peering through the summer darkness, the watchman

sees a box in the back of the wagon. Suspecting he has interrupted a robbery, he starts to run towards the group, whereupon the woman jumps into the wagon, alongside the driver, who whips up his horse and drives off. Acting on the spur of the moment, Rooney throws himself in front of the man, preventing him from leaping onto the wagon.

"What are you doing with a wagon out here at this time of the night?" he demands.

"I know nothing about it," says the stranger. There is a white handkerchief tied over the lower part of his face, partially concealing his features.

At this point another night-watchman, called Bluett, arrives on the scene. "Follow that wagon! Stop it if you can!" Rooney shouts at him. As Bluett takes off in pursuit, the stranger with the kerchief over his face starts to walk towards Wellington Street with watchman Rooney at his heels.

"What were you doing? I said," Rooney repeats.

"I was telling them the way to Yonge Street," says the stranger.

"Then they're headed in the wrong direction," Rooney observes. In the distance he sees Bluett hastening back towards them, shouting.

"All's well. I caught up to it—there's only a coffin inside—likely sent from Phillip's coffin-store on Jordan Street."

Although not satisfied, Nicholas Rooney has no option but to let the stranger go. He continues on his way, still uneasy about the box and its contents.

At half-past one in the small hours of Sunday morning another watchman, Watts by name, observes a woman alight from a buggy and enter the home of a Dr. Davis on Scott Street, just east of King, off Eastern Avenue.[3]

Sunday morning. At the Mansion Saloon on King Street, the innkeeper's daughter, little Mary Whyte, is up early. Her parents are probably sleeping in after a busy Saturday night behind the bar. Wandering into the backyard she peers curiously into one of the barrels, where something has caught her attention. In it she finds a black and white straw hat, a lavender grenadine waist and skirt, a black cape trimmed with black fur, white knitted stockings, elastic garters, and a nightgown. A piece of fabric has been cut out of the neck of the nightgown where a name or initials might have been embroidered.

Later that morning, some distance beyond Bloor Street and the city limits, a section foreman on the York Roads, Charles Lovell, sees a white wooden box lying in one of the ditches east of the Northern railway track. It is partly covered, but he can see blood on the box, and the marks of wagon-wheels near it. He alerts a local farmer, who arrives with his son-in-law and an axe to open the box. The son-in-law recoils at the smell coming from the box, so Charles Lovell takes the axe from him and opens it.

Inside they find the body of a young woman. She has blue eyes and dark brown hair. She is naked. Her chemise lies beside her on her bed of straw.

Murder most foul? That is how it was viewed by *The Globe* in its coverage of the case, and that is what Dr. Davis, the abortionist, and his wife were charged with. One heart-warming aspect of the newspaper accounts and the letters printed in connection with the case of "one more unfortunate" is the condemnation of "the wretches [who] have robbed this poor young woman of her life . . . for a few dollars," rather than of "the poor forsaken corpse."

Jeannie Gilmour's story is only too familiar. In the courtroom, her Glasgow-born father told the story of his arrival in Canada from Scotland in 1872 with his son and daughter, to take up farming and preaching in the Presbyterian Church. He seems to have done little, if any, farming in Scotland, and, like the Reverend Reikie, to have spent most of his time on missionary work away from his family, although he was not ordained until after his arrival in Canada. Mrs. Gilmour and two other daughters were to follow when the family were settled.

Young Jeannie was an independent girl. She had already been making a good living since her mid-teens as a successful saleswoman in a linen shop in Edinburgh, where the family had moved, and as soon as they arrived in Toronto she found work sewing for a Mrs. Calloway on Temperance Street. In fact, her father's first job offer came about only because the Lowrie family of Woodbridge were anxious to acquire the services of capable, likeable Jeannie rather than those of trainee farmer John Gilmour and his fragile son, who had "never had a tool in his hand—nothing but a pen."

From John Gilmour's statement emerges a picture of a battle of wills between daughter and father: one resolved to make her own way in a new country that was giving her plenty of opportunity to do just that, the other determined to hold on to a valuable asset. When John Gilmour was ready to move on from the Lowries, he found to his surprise that his Jeannie dug in her heels and refused to go. So John Gilmour left with his sickly son to rough it in the bush, periodically returning to the area, where he did some of his preaching—"all without any remuneration, of course."

After about two years Jeannie Gilmour suddenly went off to work with relatives of the Lowries, the Nattrasses. She only told her own family afterwards, and when John Gilmour went to make enquiries he was not made welcome by the Nattrass family, because they too did not want to lose the services of such a strong, capable young woman. Once they came to fetch her back when she was taking a few days off with her father "because they were going to have a logging bee and could not do without her."[4]

The reason for the sudden move almost certainly was one of the six Nattrass boys—"all single, all at home." She was seen from time to time driving out with one of them, "the teacher," although she denied being engaged to him. Perhaps that was not the way Jeannie Gilmour wanted things to be. Her father told the court she had previously refused the hand of a young farmer while with the Lowries, and it was "not the only one she rejected, also respectable." It would seem that capable, likeable Jeannie Gilmour had fallen hopelessly in love with young Nattrass the teacher.

Although John Gilmour skates over the real reason he wanted to get Jeannie away from the Nattrasses, it certainly wasn't to get her back in the bosom of the family, because he placed her first with friends in the country, and then with people he knew in Toronto, the Clements, "as a friend." When their servant left they found work for Jeannie, but even in Toronto she was under pressure from the Nattrasses, because members of the family—among them, presumably, her sweetheart—visited her there.

Reading John Gilmour's statement one has the uncomfortable feeling it suited the Nattrass family well that the indispensable Jeannie was in love with one of their boys. Jeannie may have tried to break free, because while she was in Toronto she attended her father's ordination and was received into the church herself—at her own suggestion, according to her father.

Or it could be that Jeannie was by now pregnant and terrified, and, having lost her virtue, was trying to save her soul.

At the end of June, Jeannie sent little gifts to her mother, sisters and brother. At the beginning of July she left the Clements. Her father received a letter from her telling him she "didn't seem to agree with the city." Two weeks later, on July 24, she was seen by a friend of the Clements at Union Station with two of the brothers, who said they had come in "on business." By the first day of August, Jeannie was dead in a ditch. John Gilmour ends his statement thus: "We know no more of our poor child till her body was found. I may add that to my certain knowledge she had no money saved of her own, and must therefore have been furnished with means by someone to put herself into the hands of her murderers. Truly the moral aspect of this case is most mysterious and perplexing."

What perplexed John Gilmour is how a girl from a God-fearing family could end up in a ditch. For him, his daughter Jeannie's seduction by Nattrass the teacher remained a mystery. Whatever most women readers may have thought about poor little Jeannie Gilmour and her fate, many of them would have understood better than John Gilmour the attraction that led an independent, strong-minded young woman to her death at the hands of an abortionist.

Astonishingly, too, any woman reader who followed the case would have been given surprisingly graphic details of the brutality of that botched abortion. Even now, when we have been numbed into insensitivity by the daily depiction of violence, those details still horrify; in an age that hid "the facts of life" from the tender sensibilities of females, the gruesome evidence given by the coroner and the physicians who examined the body must have been beyond belief.

For Alice, who always read every newspaper she could because she was hoping to get published in one of them, some of the extensive coverage must surely have broken through the protective wall she had put up around herself. However hard she may have tried to skip over the unpleasantnesses, some of the particulars of the case would have caught her attention as a woman and a budding writer.

For it is the small details that chill and touch the heart over a century later: John Gilmour telling the court what a credit and a comfort his Jeannie was to him; a "citizen" writing to complain of the treatment of "the poor unfortunate" at the city dead-house, where she lay naked, "dirty and bloody with the marks of the surgeon's knife about her person"; "surely," he adds, "the proper officials could at least have covered the body over, and with a little ice and disinfectant made the corpse look Christian-like"; a nightdress found in the backyard of a tavern with the embroidered monogram cut out of it—the hand-sewn nightgown of Jeannie Gilmour, whose manner and skill in an Edinburgh linen shop was good for business and made her "a general favourite."

Life, Alice was discovering, had a way of continually confronting you with the ugly and the tragic, particularly if you chose to join its broad stream. And even if you only watched it in reflection, the "shadows of the world" were often frightening. She was continuing to evolve a personal philosophy that would give her the courage to face up to grim realities, while remaining optimistic. The tragedy of Jeannie Gilmour was just the sort of event that fuelled her writer's imagination and aroused her sense of social justice.

Palace Street School was far from palatial; it was tough. It was so far east on Palace Street—later called Front Street at this point—on the corner of Cherry Street, that it was almost outside the city limits. Even today, when Toronto has spread far beyond the boundaries that Faith Fenton knew, when Yorkville is no longer a village but a central area in the city, Cherry Street lies beyond the prosperous heart of Toronto. The large red-brick building that housed Palace Street School still stands, spared the wrecker's ball by its remoteness from the city's core.

Palace Street School was housed in the southern section of the building that was also at one time the Eastern Star Hotel, and later a warehouse. Today, part of the structure is The Canary Restaurant, with its large yellow plaster canary perched over the door, as it has been for the past thirty years. The school's pupils came from some of the rougher areas of the city, the layer at the bottom of the social cake. On the other side of what at that time was a dirt road still stand some of the narrow brick row houses from which those children came, crushed one against the other, barely the width of one cramped room.

In 1874, an inspector's report revealed that about half of the ten thousand pupils in the Toronto school system were absent for half the school year, and Palace Street School was no exception. Its students made a poor showing on the annual prize lists, and at Christmas there is no mention of the decorations adorning many of the other schools, so presumably Palace Street School didn't have any. There are reports in the press about vandalism by boys from the school—windows were often smashed during the weekends.

When eighteen-year-old Alice Freeman faced her first class, she would have needed every scrap of that positive outlook of hers. She must have been nervous, but she was probably not terrified. Terror was the "great labouring monster" of a steamer that had separated her from her parents at the age of ten. Terror was seeing Margaret Reikie die, all creative ambition frustrated. Terror was feeling the mourning veils falling around her fourteen-year-old face. She was to stay until 1877 at Palace Street, when she transferred to Niagara Street School in the west end of Toronto, at about the same layer of the social stratum, but nearer the centre of the city.

Even in an age that believed in corporal punishment, Niagara Street School used the strap somewhat more liberally then was common. This practice led to a charge of assault being brought against the headmaster, Mr. Spence, while Alice was a teacher there—not for the whipping itself, but for its severity. The victim was Letitia Wright, a disobedient child who stole other children's mittens and used "profane language." On this occasion she was punished for skipping school and having the gall to claim she had Mr. Spence's permission. Letitia claimed she was tied up with a "red cord" to a corridor wall and beaten on her legs and back for at least ten minutes, until the skin was broken. From eyewitness reports the red cord seems to have been Letitia's invention, but the whipping was undoubtedly severe and was not carried out with the strap, but with an umbrella rib.

The ensuing investigation by the school board, however, suggests that Mr. Spence may have been made something of a scapegoat because he had expelled the son of a school trustee and, as a follower of the Temperance Movement, had been involved in the passing of an act allowing municipalities to ban the sale of alcohol—an unpopular move among many bibulous trustees. Harsh as it was, the punishment inflicted on Letitia Wright may not have been out of the ordinary for the times, although the chairman of the school board was of the opinion that there was no point in whipping girls because "their nature was so peculiar and so very different from boys that whipping did them no good; and neither could one reason with them as with boys." To the school-board chairman, not only were girls a different sex, they were not of the same species.

None of this seemed relevant to Mr. Spence, who said he never whipped children with the hope of doing them any good; he did it as an example. That kind of control through fear lasted another hundred years in the school system, but twenty years later the Toronto school board regulated the length and size of the instruments of control to rubber straps, "fifteen inches long and one and a half inches wide."[5]

In the midst of whippings, vandalism, absenteeism and discrimination, Alice Freeman established a style remembered by her contemporaries as remarkably different from that of most other teachers. In a young country having only recently attained nationhood, in which history meant what happened in Europe and America, and whose classrooms were as "fiercely imperial" as those of the Model School, Alice Freeman's students walked each day into a schoolroom dominated by the message placed at the top of the front blackboard: "Canada our home."

Pupils in other classes envied those under Miss Freeman's "mild sway," for her control was not through fear. She used her low, musical voice and "the gentleness of her looks" to win over the most recalcitrant of pupils, and that mild sway of hers worked even in the halls and playgrounds of the school. Perhaps the most effective tool she had was her love of learning and her own desire to excel. She fostered a spirit of comradeship in her classroom, and other teachers marvelled at how she could inspire even the most difficult of students to behave well.

Alice made good use of the dramatic talent inherited from her grandparents, and she may well have drawn on it when she faced her first Palace Street class. Many years later a colleague recalled how she was helped at the beginning of her career by words of wisdom from the experienced Miss Freeman, who "saved my heart from breaking." In the classroom Alice found a legitimate outlet for her acting ability, reciting poetry, reading Dickens and Scott and Thackeray in her musical voice, encouraging her charges to create their own dramatic scenes from favourite stories and poems.

When they grew up, many of those children remembered Miss Freeman the teacher—even those who could only observe "the gentleness of her looks" as she walked through the schoolyard while they suffered under tougher regimes. In fact, Miss Alice Freeman, who moved again to John Street School in 1881, and from there to Ryerson School in 1883, was successful enough to read papers on the teaching of literature before the Toronto Teachers' Association and to be published in their official journal, *The Canadian Teacher*.

Ryerson was Alice's school for the next eleven years. It was a large school, with around a thousand pupils, and was the site of the provincial examinations. It had a high attendance record, class sizes slightly smaller than average, and low incidence of lateness and corporal punishment. Miss Freeman was regarded as a high-profile, extremely successful teacher, with a particular talent for handling very young children. A fellow-teacher later said that, as soon as salaries were scaled according to length of service rather than seniority of grades, Alice chose to teach the Junior Book Classes, "because she loved the little children."

True. But there may well have been other reasons—in fact, the school board changed its policy in 1886, and the records show that Alice transferred to the Junior Book Classes in the fall of 1881, when she joined the staff at John Street School. Perhaps it was just her love of the little ones, but it may also have been that Alice sought out a lighter workload when something reawakened the slumbering ambition of the young teacher who wanted to be a writer.

The pen-names and pseudonyms affected by nineteenth-century journalists—both men and women—protected them from recognition in a career not considered entirely respectable. Journalism was not quite as suspect as the theatre but, for a woman especially, mixing with ink-stained hacks in offices where dubious views that questioned the status quo might be expressed, and in improper language, was unthinkable—and, even worse, was the possibility that she might begin to express radical, or simply original, thoughts herself. Copperplated on their copybooks and in their minds was the admonition: Be Good Sweet Maid And Let Who Will Be Clever. By the 1880s a handful of women were using the convenient protection of assumed names, a convention already adopted by many male journalists, challenging the assumption that goodness and cleverness were incompatible.

In late 1884, a twenty-two-year-old teacher who wrote for *The Courier* in her home town of Brantford was hired by *The Globe* to write a series of articles on the New Orleans World's Fair that celebrated the hundredth anniversary of the cotton industry. By May 1885 she was writing a weekly column for *The Globe* under the name "Garth Grafton." Her real name was Sara Jeannette Duncan.[6]

Did the two schoolteachers who wanted to be writers ever meet? If they did, it would not have been during their training, because Sara Jeannette Duncan attended Model School in Brantford, took her Toronto Normal School training in 1882, and never taught in the Toronto school-board system. But it is more than likely that they knew of each other's existence, because it may well have been Sara Jeannette Duncan's success that spurred Alice on.

Week after week "Garth Grafton" wrote about her visits to exhibitions and institutions, not only in *The Globe*, but also in *The Montreal Star*. She visited the Montreal Winter Carnival and described for her readers the wonders of the procession and the great fancy-dress ball attended by the governor general, Lord Lansdowne, and his wife. She expressed her views on the modern woman and on marriage. She answered letters from her readers on every subject under the sun.

Alice's connections were not in Toronto, but in Barrie. Her father had strong links with the Conservative party—Tory senator James Gowan, High Court Justice for the district of Simcoe, was a lifelong family friend—and the local Barrie newspaper, *The Northern Advance*, which was the first daily newspaper to be established north of Toronto, had a circulation of around 1,300 copies and was staunchly Tory.

William Henry Freeman had become a man of property. He had started acquiring houses in Toronto at the end of the 1870s, and for a time Alice lodged in her father's properties on John and Richmond streets, usually with her brother Fred. However, as soon as William Henry retired to Toronto, Alice stopped living under his roofs, and as soon as her brothers acquired houses, she started living with them—a move that was to prove invaluable in her career as Faith Fenton.

Unlike Sara Jeannette Duncan, however, Alice could not rely on her father for the financial support that would take her out of teaching; William Henry seems to have been reluctant to help his children further their careers if their choices were not strictly practical. If an 1894 "Woman's Empire" column is about him, as it seems to be, William Henry the property-owner seems to have done everything to stop his children following in the steps of William Henry the musician:

The young girl, you know, is of artistic temperament, and longs for a chance to study at Art School; her sister is a book-lover, with a passion for pretty stories and verse. But father keeps every cent invested in real estate, and mother has to go without a servant; so the young artist takes to office work, which she dislikes, the reader contents herself with ten-cent paper editions, or trashy novels from the library, and the years develop them into two restless, mentally dwarfed young women, instead of the bright, clever, happy creatures they might be, were their parents conscious of the Sin of Saving.

The reader of trashy novels is undoubtedly Mary, the unpaid servant trapped at home without an education; the artistic sister is probably Florence, who was a stenographer in Toronto at the time, and had obviously given up any dreams of being a concert pianist—Faith Fenton has merely changed the artistic discipline. Unlike "Garth Grafton," Alice Freeman would have to stay in teaching for the time being. It is probably as well she did not know how long that "time being" was to last.

Alice Freeman's first published articles for *The Northern Advance* were probably submitted with a covering letter from one of her father's influential Tory contacts. Maybe the contact had been a personal one, made at some fund-raising dinner or social event. She opened with a two-part series on a trip she made on the lighthouse supply boat—a forerunner of a longer and more ambitious series of articles on a similar trip for *The Empire*. The newspaper introduced her as "a Barrie lady," and she signed off the second article with her initials: A.F. They are our first introduction to the intrepid traveller who never let the fact she was a woman stop her doing anything she wanted. She seems to have travelled with two equally venturesome and unnamed women friends, and their journey took them "along the islands of the Canadian coast," from Detroit into Lake St. Clair, through Lake Huron, up to Sault Ste. Marie.

The two columns show Alice the writer at an early stage of development: she uses such phrases as "I hardly know where to begin," and "The scenery along the river is beautiful, but more skilful pens than mine have already described it." Faith Fenton usually knew where to begin, and if she passed over a chance to describe scenery, she would never have denigrated her own ability to do so. A.F. already uses some of the little word "snapshots" that became one of Faith Fenton's trademarks, such as the episode when the second mate fell overboard:

> I sprang to the side of the vessel in time to see his upturned face as he drifted past, dangerously near the screw. Fortunately one of the boats used for the supplies was ready alongside . . . and in less then ten minutes he was on board again. He is a French-Canadian of somewhat economical habits, and his first words as they approached him were, "Boys, save dat good hat first, nevare mind me." The poor fellow has been unmercifully chaffed ever since.

There is also a glimpse of the active Alice, always keen to use her muscles as well as her mind whenever she got the chance: "In the evening of the same day we reached Killarney, a little village, beautifully situated on the extreme north shore of Georgian Bay. . . . As we had to remain here for some hours, after tea we obtained the loan of an old wooden punt, and pulled down the shore, passing here and there sail boats, manned by Indians and laden with berries, bark and babies."

Such a classically romantic picture she draws for the reader: the three young women in the old punt rowing along the river in the setting sun, with the shadows of the trees lengthening across the water, the cry of the whippoorwill echoing through the dusk, the gleam of the camp-fires along the shore where the canoes were now drawn up at rest. "We returned to our 'water home' in a very dreamy and contented state of mind, being filled with the beauty of our Canadian Killarney."

Alice Freeman used her 1886 summer vacation to satisfy her wanderlust and to provide material for her *Northern Advance* columns. It was a pattern she would continue for the next eight years.

Killarney wasn't St. Louis, but it was a start. For the response to the articles was such that the editor offered her a regular spot on the paper—or Alice suggested she should have one. Her articles seem to have been more or less weekly, although the gaps were sometimes longer.

Perhaps the arrangement was not fixed, which would have suited Alice Freeman the teacher very well.

The name Alice chose for herself was "Stella"—a romantic *nom-de-plume* meaning "star." The first column was entitled "A Toronto Letter" (there is an interesting echo here of Garth Grafton's "A Woman's Letter," which was a regular feature of her column) and signed "STELLA" in darker type no larger than that used for the rest of the article. It was about two hundred words long, and covered the weather, the visit of a well-known preacher to Toronto,[7] and an epidemic of diphtheria, finishing with some fashion notes. The next column a month later is about three hundred words long and is called "Stella's Toronto Letter." By the end of 1886 the column has doubled in length and the title is in a large typeface; "Stella" had obviously acquired a following.

To a modern reader it might not seem essential for Stella to be separate from Alice; after all, she wrote in an out-of-town paper, and there was little likelihood that the connection would be made. However, such was the level of paranoia about the morality of female schoolteachers in general—let alone those who wrote in the newspapers—that Alice was unlikely to have let it be known she had another persona.

The Toronto school board was still uneasy about the growing numbers of women in the teaching profession, and discouraged the hiring of women over thirty, because they had no business by that age not being wives and mothers. If they married and acquired husbands to support them, they had to resign. The dress code was so strict that a teacher who rather foolhardily wore bloomers shocked one trustee so profoundly he didn't know whether to call her a lady or a prostitute. At one meeting of the school board, the chairman tabled a motion that women with corns on their feet, tight shoes or coloured stockings not be hired. Coloured stockings and corns aside, one thing is clear: the surveillance of every aspect of women teacher's lives was absolute. The identity of "Garth Grafton" could be an open secret—many of the letters to the column began: "Dear Madam"—but Alice and Stella would have to keep silent about each other.

If indeed it was her father's influence she used, then William Henry was one of the first threads in a web that A.F. started to weave, a network Stella would continue to fashion and that Faith Fenton would strengthen, building up a complex pattern of contacts in the worlds of stage, politics and the aristocracy over the next sixteen years.

"Stella's Toronto Letter" gave Alice a chance to develop the skills she needed to be a successful journalist. Writing a column for a newspaper, as she discovered, was a very different matter from writing poetry. There were the constraints of time and space, and the growing realization that it was not enough merely to report on the events of the day. Something more was needed: originality, immediacy, style. Stella was learning what Faith Fenton would tell those who besieged her with samples of their work for her approval and advice: ". . . that they must not only have something to say, but also that it must be said in an attractive way to catch the eye and please the mental palate of the jaded reader. . . . the product of a writer's brain must be carried to market like any other supply."

In "Stella's Toronto Letter," Alice started to explore the themes she would write about for the next sixteen years: fashion, politics, literature, religion, travel, social events and social evils. Sometimes her columns jump from the latest society wedding to coverage of a political meeting, to the budget allocated for Toronto's new city hall and courthouse—a practice used by other columnists and one that she was to continue in *The Empire*.

At the age of twenty-nine Alice Freeman finally had a published space she could call her own, somewhere she could air her views on anything under the sun she cared about—and there were many such things. The joy and elation of the young woman who had finally made a significant breakthrough sings through her prose; it is girlish, sometimes melodramatic, sometimes humorous, bubbling with vitality:

> Of course we are all grateful that our Queen has been permitted "to reign over us, happy and glorious," for so many years . . . [but] many absurd modes of commemoration are being proposed, for instance: "Jubilee" or "Jubilee Victoria" is the appellation now received at the font by multitudes of little innocents the world over. In the name of all infancy "thrown upon the lap of time" during the present year I protest against such a sacrifice of sound and sense. "Jubilee"—think of it, picture your wee baby girl ten or fifteen years hence . . . answering to such a cognomen—"Jube" or "Bilee"—for the name is sure to be curtailed.

Stella had to provide her own fashion notes—not for her the syndicated American article she could insert into her column, as was the common practice. They give her observations a spark of originality, because they come from her own life experience, and Faith Fenton would often use the same approach:

> "Why does not Stella give us some spring fashion notes?" I hear some of my pretty young country friends saying. Because Stella is not a fashionable individual, my dears . . . gray, pink and heliotrope take present precedence, as a walk down King or Yonge Street on any bright shopping day will show. . . . In "'trimmings' feathers are entirely out," as my milliner severely assured me, when I ventured to suggest them.

Stella's stories are cloyingly sentimental for today's tastes, but her readers would have sighed and delighted over them—such columns as "A Sketch of Life among the Lowly," in which Stella recounts visiting a night lodging for men on "a quiet street that was once the favourite resort of fashion and wealth." She uses her December visit to create a Christmas story of the birth of a child in the midst of poverty and suffering. It reads like Dickens at his most mawkish and requires a hefty suspension of disbelief:

> But presently the roughest man among them touched with tip of his horny finger the tiny hand that lay like a drifted flower petal upon the flannel covering, and said in a husky voice: "Well, chums, we can't pass round the hat for him, seeing we're nigh cleaned out ourselves, so let's hope God A'mighty will keep the little chap from ever bein' the likes of us" . . . the cathedral chimes rang out a joyous peal of welcome . . . to the new-born babe, dropped in all its purity from the angel world. . . .

Since Faith Fenton occasionally indulged in similar passages, the writing cannot be put down to immaturity. Like so many of her Victorian contemporaries, male and female, Alice Freeman enjoyed a good cry—what she herself called "the luxury of tears." A *good* cry had little to do with true suffering and much more to do with escape from it, and a flight from reality. The tough-minded, sceptical side of Alice had no problem switching from the sublime to the bathetic. Besides, understanding the tastes of her women readers would always be one of her great strengths. Her inability for so many years to remove herself from the daily grind to full-time journalism had one great advantage: it kept her in touch with her public and that public responded well to blatant sentimentality.

The greatest charm of those early columns is watching Stella grow into Faith Fenton, the columnist who would mix sentiment with satire, fashion notes with social commentary, travelogues with personal, political and patriotic observations, never afraid to reveal her convictions, her loves, her anger, while all the time concealing her true identity. Reading "Stella" one watches Alice take the first steps through the mirror towards a new woman. The hard-edged journalism that would take her to the top is already there in among the bonnets and the feathers and the frou-frou.

Frou-Frou, in fact, is the name of a play she reviews for her readers, and Stella does what Faith Fenton would later do: she assures her readers that it is "all right" to like the theatre, and that Miss Fortescue, the actress, is "the most perfect embodiment of the word 'lady' I have ever seen upon the stage." In another article she moves from discussion of a fashionable preacher to a play by Robert Louis Stevenson at the Grand Opera House with the words: "Do not look aghast at the change of topic, my good friends. Divinity and the Drama are not so widely separated as at first appears. Worthy exponents of each occupy the same high platform as preachers and teachers, while *unworthy* exponents of either are an evil to be equally deplored"—a daring concept, for Stella is suggesting that excellence itself is a virtue, quite apart from considerations of conventional morality.

In those early columns Stella covered some of the educational interests of Alice Freeman the schoolteacher. She reports on a Normal School reunion she attended, and on the political ambitions—and character flaws—of School Inspector Hughes, quoting a schoolteacher who told her that "while the Inspector is taking a flitting through the country, he cannot pop into my classroom in that unexpected way he has, that's one comfort."[8]

She also confides in her readers that "Dame Rumour hath it that two lady candidates are to be brought forward to contest seats at the Public School board now occupied by male representatives," and ventures the opinion that their election wouldn't do much harm, because the seats "are too often regarded as mere stepping stones to civic honours, resting places in the ascent(!) to aldermanic dignities," a state of affairs only too familiar a century later.

Alice's professional involvement is never revealed, for obvious reasons, but it is still a daring move, given the school board's attitudes. As the years go by, Stella's successor, Faith Fenton, will grow even bolder.

There is a refreshingly self-deprecatory quality about Stella's society notes: "Everybody who is anybody went to hear Mrs. Scott-Siddons last week. It was quite the thing to do, so we all did it, and therefore, despite the downpouring rain, she had a large audience."[9] In all the forty-odd columns she wrote for *The Northern Advance*, never is there the slightest hint of condescension from the city woman to her country sister, never the suggestion that her city sophistication made her superior to those who lacked her advantages.

Stella brought preachers, politicians, actors and teachers to the women of Barrie in her Toronto letter. When she told them about the death of Her Majesty's Inspector of Customs, the Honourable James Patton, Stella could say that she had been sitting with him in his Customs Office only two weeks earlier and that "he referred frequently to your own pretty town, in the welfare of which he appeared much interested, and with whose early history he was so intimately connected." And when William Holmes Howland ran for mayor of Toronto as the Temperance candidate—"the citizens' candidate"—against David Blain, Stella was there to cover the campaign and the events of election day from the point of view of the hundreds of women who were able to vote that day and put him into office.[10]

The hand that rocked the cradle ruled that election in January 1887. In March 1884 unmarried women and widows of voting age who owned or rented property valued at over $400 had been given the right to vote in civic elections in Ontario. Married women found themselves disenfranchised, but for the first time a solid mass of middle-class women—

more than 2,000 of them—had the chance to swing the result of an election in favour of their candidate.

Election Day dawned clear, not too cold, perfect for sleighing. From early morning every kind of vehicle—hacks, coupes, private carriages—drove to the polling booths decorated with rosettes and ribbons. The women of Toronto went from house to house, doing what they had never done before: bringing members of their own sex to the polling booths, closing ranks to put someone of their choice into political power. As darkness fell, the crowds gathered outside the newspaper offices, cheering or booing as each return was announced from the windows. Upstairs, in the balcony reserved for women in Shaftesbury Hall—women rarely, if ever, attended public meetings and, if they did, they were segregated—Stella watched as the new mayor made his short acceptance speech. "Truly for the Temperance cause," she reported, "it was a famous victory."

The defeated candidate called the decision the result of "concentrated ignorance." Stella quoted the loser's speech in her column on January 8, 1887, and—tongue-in-cheek—called upon the women of Barrie, "our more enlightened sisters, all of whom apparently dwell outside Toronto's environs," to sympathize with "the pitiable state of ignorance" of their Toronto sisters.

Stella's election coverage must have been a great comfort to "Augusta" of Barrie, who, in March 1886, had written a letter to the editor on women's rights both to employment and to the franchise. "Augusta" deplored the press's "dismal homilies on woman being kept in her proper sphere, meaning, of course, the kitchen . . . instead of having a chance with men in the profession of medicine, especially in treating the diseases of women and children, light handicrafts, clerkships . . . she is as justly entitled to the franchise in its fullest extent as a man."

Not only did Stella start to create a network for herself, but she drew other women into the structure she was building—women who were isolated from one another by geography, by lives centred in the home, by the lack of organizations through which they might meet and find out about one another, and by the lack of press coverage given the few events attended and influenced by women. One of the only organizations to give a voice to nineteenth-century women was the Woman's Christian Temperance Union, established in 1874.

To a modern generation the WCTU sounds like a society of prudish killjoys—and some of its members undoubtedly were. But the true story of those early women is one of courage and determination in the face of opposition, ridicule and negative or non-existent press coverage.

The founder of the Canadian WCTU, Letitia Youmans, went on to have a considerable reputation across Canada and the United States, and by 1891 her powerful personality and ability as a speaker galvanized more than 9,000 Canadian women to join the organization. Before that could happen, however, she had to speak before largely male audiences who were hostile to the very idea of a woman doing anything of the kind, let alone a woman attempting to interfere with their personal freedom. After all, it was men she was criticizing, men who had to sit and hear this woman telling them about men drunk in ditches and having to have frozen limbs amputated, men beating their wives and children. And in 1894 there must have been a few anxious moments for many men in Ontario when the Ontario branch of the WCTU threatened to publish the names of prostitutes' clients so that mothers might better be able to protect their daughters from such degenerates.

In its early days the WCTU saw liquor as the root of most evils in a pioneer society and believed that prohibition was the only way to curtail crime, family violence, and even government corruption. As time progressed and they became more politically sophisticated, the members realized their beliefs would mean nothing unless women had some kind of political power, and by 1891 the organization endorsed female suffrage.

If at some point Alice joined the organization, clearly it was not merely total abstinence that was the attraction. There is evidence in later columns by Faith Fenton that she enjoyed a glass of wine herself: she describes looking for some of the famous Point Pelée wine when she visited the island, and she picked up a bottle of port in St. John's, Newfoundland, saying that, "because of certain total abstinence principles," she would have to claim it was for medicinal purposes only.

In December 1886 Stella writes about a Toronto council meeting on the reduction of liquor licences and counsels prudence: "Our temperance friends are zealous, let them also be discreet, and as surely as the sun shines in the heavens, their cause—the cause of humanity and God—shall win." She also remarks on the number of women who stayed to the end of the debate. It was largely through the WCTU that women of the time were able to meet one another without men being present to give them respectability, let alone share their thoughts or learn the skills for a public rather than a purely private life.

The hand that rocked the cradle was beginning to rock local and municipal council meetings as well as municipal elections. The WCTU woman who made her presence known outside the home was far from being a strait-laced spoilsport; she was an explorer into *terra incognita*, a bold adventurer who, although often "swayed as a reed by the conflicting passions of human hate and love," sought to "reign supreme over the surrounding savages."

The quotations are from Stella's column on *She*, by H. Rider Haggard, which was published in 1887, and which Alice read with "laughter, tears . . . terror." She found it "uncanny . . . fascinating . . . one of the most attractive books I ever read." "She" is the beautiful woman who reigns over the lost city of Kor, "the one central figure around which the narrative threads of the story twine." Woman at the centre of the narrative, woman as the power figure—what a revolutionary idea! No wonder Alice, "completely enthralled," could not put the book down; her descriptions mirror her dizzy frame of mind: "grotesquely awful," "uncanny," "almost sacrilegious." In somewhat calmer tones, Stella urged her readers "to purchase a copy and peruse it at leisure."[11]

On December 22, 1887, Stella wrote a Christmas column for *The Northern Advance* about Advent and Christian celebrations, Christmas shopping, children and Santa Claus. It is charming, non-controversial, and it closes: "But my indulgent editor is frowning; his lips are saying 'space,' and I must close. Stella's hands clasp closely the kindly ones held out, while her heart gives grateful greetings to the many friends beyond the threshold of the sanctum." Then there is silence for nearly ten months.

On October 18, 1888, a column entitled "Stella Greets Her Old Friends" makes an appearance and begins by asking "How many fair readers of *The Advance* have forgotten Stella?" It is the last of Stella's articles for the Barrie newspaper.

There is no farewell; it is as though the writer were expecting to be back. The subject matter is far weightier than the Christmas column, and at the core of the article is Stella's anger over "that travesty of justice—the sentence pronounced upon the murderer Buckley."

"Tom Buckley Murders His Paramour in a Whiskey Dive" was the sensational headline that greeted the readers of *The Toronto Mail* on May 15, 1888. The previous day, twenty-four-year-old Bertha Robinson lost her life at the hands of the man she loved.

Bertha Robinson, also known as Bertie Usher, was not a good girl; she was "a woman of questionable repute," said *The Toronto Mail*. In plain language, Bertie was a prostitute. She was a handsome girl—even lying in a black pine coffin in the morgue, "her face and throat swollen and disfigured," the boot-marks of the man she loved still black on her neck, there were traces of beauty left. She was petite, with dazzlingly white skin and masses of wavy, raven-black hair.

Bertie ran away from her well-to-do, respectable Brantford home when she was very young—the reason she did so died with her. She moved around for a while, making her living in Guelph, Chicago and Buffalo as a prostitute, before returning to Toronto with Tom Buckley, whom she had met somewhere on her travels, possibly in Buffalo.

Unlike his paramour, Tom Buckley did not come from good stock; the Buckleys of Brockton were well known to the police. One of his relatives, known as "the Brockton Sykes," had killed his common-law wife in a drunken rage in 1882, and Tom Buckley had a string of crimes to his name—he was, in fact, "one of the worst characters in the city . . . a tin horn of the first water." Among other offences, he had had the audacity to steal a gold watch from a detective in Buffalo, and had nearly bitten through the finger of a policeman during a scuffle at Alice Miller's bawdy-house on Adelaide Street in Toronto; the officer nearly died of blood-poisoning as a result. He, and four other city toughs—Paddy "Rats," "Squib" Mitchell, Tom Jones and "Stoney" Jackson—ran a chain of whisky dives on Adelaide Street, and Elizabeth Street and Victoria Lane slightly to the north of Adelaide, where the corporate towers of Toronto now rise. Bertie was put in charge of one of them, a tumbledown two-storey structure at 72 Victoria Lane.

The partnership was not amicable. About six months earlier Tom Buckley had been shot in the stomach by one of his business partners, Tom Jones, but when he recovered he refused to give evidence against Jones, and the police had to drop the charges. As always, drink was at the bottom of the fight, and it was drink that led to the death of Bertie

Usher. She was habitually drunk to a greater or lesser degree, and was consequently cheated by her customers.

On the day before her death, Bertie borrowed the one good dress owned by a seventeen-year-old prostitute, Lizzie Foster, who used 72 Victoria Lane to entertain her clients. Bertie wanted it to wear in court the next day, to look good for Tom, who was making one of his frequent appearances and who had asked her to get up early and go with him. Lizzie stayed at the whisky dive overnight and went about her business as usual. When she came down the next morning after letting out one of her regulars, Hiram Piper—"who only stayed five minutes"—the little maid-of-all-work, twelve-year-old Annie Palmer, had already lit the fire and was cooking meat over the cylindrical coal stove in the one furnished room on the ground floor. One of the neighbours, a Mrs. Cryor, dropped in for a chat, and shortly after Tom Buckley and Bertie arrived.

At some point the conversation turned to money. The three women remembered Bertie putting her hand down to her stocking and saying, "I've lost my money," whereupon Tom Buckley hit her across the face with his fist, knocking her to the floor; he then kicked her and ordered her to get upstairs. The last thing the three women saw before they ran outside was Bertie crawling up the stairs with Buckley after her.

Seventeen-year-old Lizzie was the bravest. After about five minutes she went back inside and upstairs. There she saw Buckley standing over Bertie, a chair in his hand. The last words she heard her friend say—the last words Bertie said in her life—were: "Don't hit me, Tom, because I love you so." Lizzie ran downstairs and outside for help. When the three women plucked up courage and came in again, Tom Buckley was sitting at the table, eating the meat Annie had cooked, as though nothing had happened.

"It's too bad you have to hit her like that," said Lizzie, who knew the beating was only one of many.

"It's too bad she has to get drunk like that" was the reply. The three women went upstairs. In a room furnished only with a dilapidated bed, a strip of soiled carpet and a washstand, Bertie lay dying; she had suffered her last beating at the hands of the man she loved.

Although at first Lizzie panicked and ran away, eventually she, Mrs. Cryor and twelve-year-old Annie found the courage to stand up, not only to Tom Buckley, but to the thugs who surrounded him and who threatened them with death. The three women testified in a packed courtroom that October, each supporting the other as to what they had seen that day at 72 Victoria Lane.

Chief Justice Sir Thomas Galt[12] directed the jury that, "in justice to the prisoner," they should not consider the crime to be murder, but manslaughter: "Murder is when the deed is committed wilfully with malice aforethought. . . . The evidence does not in any way show any malice on the part of the prisoner. He and the unfortunate woman were living amicably together up to the day of the murder," said Justice Galt, calling the crime what he had just directed the jury not to call it.

It took the jury only twenty minutes to find Tom Buckley guilty of manslaughter; it took even less time for Chief Justice Galt to sentence Tom Buckley to five years in prison.

A cheer went up in court from the likes of Paddy Rats, Squibb Mitchell and Stoney Jackson. Tom Buckley was smiling as he left the courtroom.

Celebrations were held in the whisky dives and saloons of Toronto's underworld that night. At the St. John's Ward Tavern, the business partners of Tom Buckley made merry, *The Mail* reporting the next day that Buckley's boon companions were "in great glee, and they held high revel and made St. John's Ward fairly howl last evening with their rejoicing." They also reported that threats were made against the three women who had testified for the prosecution. Someone at the tavern that night wrote to *The Globe* that he heard the toughs laughing about Chief Justice Galt and one of them said, "I wouldn't be afraid to be brought before Judge Galt for murder; it wouldn't be any worse than stealin' a watch."

Toronto was in an uproar. "Not since President Cleveland's message to Congress asking for increased retaliatory powers against Canada has any question been so widely discussed," declared *The Globe*, wildly juxtaposing international politics and the murder of a prostitute. Five years for horse-stealing, five years for receiving stolen goods, five years for counterfeiting, five years for vagrancy—five years for killing a woman. At an impromptu meeting of the Board of Trade, Chief Justice Galt was called upon to resign. At one of the Congregational churches in the city, the minister unequivocally declared the Whitechapel murders of Jack the Ripper "not so brutal as this murder. He did not mutilate the bodies of his victims until after death. This wretch beat and kicked a woman until she died."

Such was the outcry that, in an unusual legal move a few days later, Tom Buckley was again brought into court, this time to hear his sentence tripled to fifteen years.

Stella, for one, was not satisfied: "Buckley is still accounted a murderer, and the people see no reason why the extreme penalty of the law should not be measured out to him." She compared Bertie's death to that of Nancy at the hands of Bill Sykes in Dickens's *Oliver Twist*, "the worthless man she loved and sinned for," and adds: "Truly woman's love approaches more nearly than aught else the love Divine."

But perhaps the most striking aspect of Stella's article is the profound pity she reflects that was expressed by respectable, middle-class women for a woman who was no better than she should be, a prostitute—"a pitiful bit of straying humanity," as Stella calls her. She describes "a delicate little lady . . . with her brown eyes swimming in tears," saying that she had not been very far away from the scene of the crime and adding: "I might have prevented it, if only I had known."

There is another conclusion that Stella infers from the "travesty of justice." Buckley, she points out, was not a man of position or wealth who could influence the decision, "so unfortunately no such reason could be adduced." "The wherefore," she says, "of so inexplicable a judgement remains unanswered." But by implication Stella gives the answer: Bertie Usher was a woman, and moreover she was a woman without character. Therefore, she was without value in society.

Alice Freeman was to challenge that view. She understood that, if society held one woman's life as worthless, then every woman was at risk; that every woman who was considered inferior because of her sex and for no other reason was worthless. There were hundreds of women who held the same view, but they had few ways of knowing how each felt about the other in their isolated lives—as the little woman with brown eyes had said, "If only I had known."

There is a common misconception about the Victorian era that middle-class women knew little, if anything, about the Jeannie Gilmours and the Bertie Ushers of the world, and that they were "protected" by a patriarchal society from information that would offend their delicate sensibilities. It is clear from the newspapers of the period that society was as fascinated then, as it is now, by acts of violence—particularly if there was a sexual angle—and that the fourth estate obligingly fed that frenzy.

Of course, women were not supposed to read newspapers, and if they did, they were supposed to stick to the women's pages. Maybe in some households, protective husbands handed out just that section to their sensitive wives. It would be as foolishly naïve as the Victorian husband hoped his wife was, to believe that no Victorian woman ever picked up the rest of the paper when her husband left the house.

The middle-class woman of Alice's world was not so much protected against the harsh truths of society as restricted from breaking the rules made for her by law and custom to do anything to change those truths. She knew every clinical detail of Jeannie Gilmour's botched abortion, the mutilation of that young woman's internal organs; in her daily newspaper she read about a twelve-year-old servant-girl and a seventeen-year-old prostitute witnessing an act of savagery; she was given a precise description of what Bertie Usher's corpse looked like as she lay in the morgue. She could follow the story of the seduction of a sixteen-year-old by her headmaster, the abandonment by this pillar of society of the mother of his seven children.

Certainly, the press reflected the deep concern of the male population over Tom Buckley's sentence. In all the coverage given the case, however, it is only in Stella's column that one finds a reflection of the feelings of women about the death of Bertie Usher. Contrary to what might have been expected of women who were reared to accept only a narrow range of human behaviour, they did indeed care about each other, even about a pitiful bit of straying humanity—if only they knew.

Something extraordinary was happening. Alice Freeman was one of a handful of women stepping through the looking-glass and into the mainstream of life. She, and others of her sex, were on a ground-breaking journey. She would be one of the first tellers of the story—of motherhood, of sisterhood, of womanhood—only it wouldn't be Alice, or even Stella, telling the story. Stella was about to disappear.

VI

Canada's Dear, Far-off Women

> . . . the little women in the country whose books are few
> and opportunities of culture rare, and yet who do so
> long to know of people and things in the great world's
> standing places; women in villages and towns who have
> their weekly chautauqua circle and are eager to learn;
> women upon our great prairies to whom such chats
> come like ringing bells of the far-off days before prairie
> life began . . .
>
> Faith Fenton, "Woman's Empire," 1893.

THE NINETEENTH-CENTURY TORONTO NEWSPAPER world was a jungle, with editors, reporters, columnists, all at one another's throats. The struggle was over territory—readership—and it was fuelled by politics, particularly the debate over annexation with the United States. The incendiary political act of the 1880s, however, was the hanging of the Métis leader, Louis Riel, in November 1885.[1]

At the time Alice Freeman was entering the jungle under cover of her new pseudonym, Faith Fenton, there were at least four principal daily newspapers fighting for readership in a city of around a hundred thousand people: *The Globe*, edited by John Cameron, was the leading Liberal newspaper, and its chief rival was *The Mail*, under editor Edward Farrer, which had moved from its Conservative roots by 1885 and was espousing annexation. E.E. Sheppard's *News* and John Ross Robertson's *Telegram* both held independent positions, with the

Telegram taking a special interest in municipal and provincial concerns.

The News, printed on pink paper much favoured by small boys for their kites, was the most sensational. It ran a gossip column called "Peek-a-Boo" and favoured an elective Senate, among other radical suggestions. After the Riel Rebellion in 1885, one of its columnists claimed that the 65th Rifles of Montreal had shirked their duties in suppressing the uprising, and the regiment sued. E.E. Sheppard found himself saddled with huge legal costs, and a court order that prohibited him from engaging in daily journalism. Around the time Alice became Faith, *The News* was sold, and Sheppard and Walter Cameron Nichol, a twenty-one-year-old writer of verse and skits for *The News*, founded a weekly magazine that would become highly successful, *Toronto Saturday Night*.[2]

"Faith Fenton" made her first appearance in the ten-month hiatus of 1887–88, when Stella temporarily disappeared. At some point in that year, a new writer took over the children's page in *The Globe*'s weekend edition, *The Weekly Globe and Farmer*. Few of these editions have survived, and those that have are often incomplete. The only children's columns of Faith Fenton's that exist are among private family papers, and those can be dated because, in one of them, she tells children about the re-formation of the Toronto Humane Society, which occurred towards the end of 1887.

The column is called "Our Young Folks," and under one heading Faith Fenton requests contributions, "preference being given to original communications etc. from the Young Folks themselves." The subject-matter is what might be expected—birds, pets, fun in the snow—but in one Faith talks of visiting a shelter for immigrants and holding "a baby Arab. Not what we call a Street Arab, understand, but a real, little, live baby, from the far-off country of Arabia."

"Our Young Folks" contained stories, gentle moralizing and poems about winter and Christmas—some or all of which are probably Faith's. Already in this early incarnation, some of her favourite themes appear: her fascination with exotic and distant lands and their peoples—"the perpetual summertime of Arabia . . . dwellers in tents, sojourners, wanderers to and fro"—her love of babies and small children, her visits to shelters for "very poor people, who are destitute or friendless," and her use of her columns to beg others to find sympathy for them—"a language that is understood in every country where human hearts beat."

Since the columns that survive are about the cold, snow, the New Year, Santa Claus, it appears that they were published during the winter of 1887–88.

There is a glimpse of an anonymous teacher and her class feeding the birds "round about the cornices of a certain Toronto school building" every morning, spreading out the crumbs they bring from home on the broad window ledge, "watched with keen interest by the bright bird-eyes that peer from the crannies above." Again, it is the bird as a traveller that fascinates her, coming "from lands far over the sea . . . warm Eastern countries where the sun shines with an intense glow, where frost is unknown."

Fortunately, "Our Young Folks" did not call for any political views to be aired. The Liberal *Globe* attacked Sir John A., Alice's hero, at every possible opportunity.

By 1887 *The Mail* was in deep trouble with the Conservative party, because it had questioned the behaviour of the government over the hanging of Riel. It was not so much the hanging itself it attacked as the government's failure to address the conditions in the Northwest that had led to the uprising: "The Metis population on the Saskatchewan was in fact so much tinder, but the Government itself supplied the match," said an editorial in May 1887; "petitions, letters from the missionaries and deputations had been consistently ignored for several years. . . . Had the Commission been appointed in the summer of 1884 when Riel arrived from Montana, all might have been well; but the policy of procrastination, the curse of our public service, supplied him with a text from which he preached with only too much success."

The Mail accused the government of alienating not only the Northwest, but Quebec also, and went so far as to suggest that Tory ineptitude and the railway monopoly might well lead in Manitoba, for example, "to a closer alliance between her and the territory immediately to the south," adding: "we have created a situation up there which, if it existed in any other country, we should regard as dangerous. But as it exists among ourselves we treat it lightly. We have grown so familiar with provincial discontent in its various forms that we are not to be disturbed by a trifle."[3]

Even more surprising than the general questioning of Tory policy is the specific criticism of John A. Macdonald himself: "It is probably useless, whilst Sir John Macdonald remains at the head of affairs, to urge the reconstruction of a system which has been of so little benefit to all concerned. Sir John's theory . . . is that whenever anything goes wrong the fault lies not in his management but in the want of patriotism of his opponents."

An enraged John A., not in the least mollified by *The Mail*'s special offer earlier in the year of "an admirable Terra Cotta bust of the Premier which has been specially prepared for . . . any person sending six subscribers to *The Weekly Mail*, with six dollars. . . . It should be in every Conservative household in Canada," set about making sure there was a newspaper in Toronto that supported him without question at all times. It was a decision that would change the life of a thirty-one-year-old teacher at Ryerson School.

The headlines of 1887 are uncannily familiar a hundred years later. "What future do you wish for Canada?" was the question *The Globe* asked its readers to answer in September 1888, and the opening sentence reads: "The future of Canada is being discussed in almost every household and every journal in the land." The fledgling Dominion was shaken by religious animosity, by what was perceived in English-speaking Canada as French-Canadian nationalism, and the anti-Catholic stand of *The Mail* threatened the Tory party's reliance on the Roman Catholic vote. "It is not improbable," said *The Montreal Gazette* in 1887, "that the people will . . . be called upon to determine whether the work accomplished in 1867 is to be undone."

Even Stella of *The Northern Advance* had said to her readers the previous year, "The Provinces of our Dominion are not in a very desirable state of harmony just at present. . . . the real difficulty is the one that lies at the root of all inter-state disturbance—the old, old conflict of race and creed," adding: "When will the time come, I wonder, when we shall have neither French-Canadians nor English-Canadians, but Canadians pure and simple. . . ?"

The answer, as Macdonald saw it, was a newspaper devoted to the ideals of the Tory party, and during the summer of 1887 he and D'Alton McCarthy, a distinguished lawyer, member of Parliament and close personal friend, set about founding *The Empire*. As managing director they chose David Creighton, who had edited a Conservative weekly paper in Owen Sound and been a popular provincial member of Parliament for North Gray in the same area.

The staff Creighton chose reads like a Who's Who of nineteenth-century Canadian journalism: Arthur Colquhoun as the managing editor, a first-class journalist with long Tory associations in Montreal who later became Ontario's deputy minister of Education; Harry Good, ex-manager of the great oarsman Ned Hanlan and father of sports-writing in America; John Bayne McLean as the Commercial–Financial editor; and, as news editor, Louis "Pica" Kribs, one of the best-known journalists of the day, whose articles were reproduced all over North America.

On December 27, 1887, *The Empire* entered the jungle world of journalism. Considering itself a cut above what it called "the reptile press," it proceeded to advance the aims and policies of the party that had created it, earning the retaliatory barb of "fossil toryism" from the other denizens of Toronto's newspaper world, and the characterization "hobbled journalism" in the memoirs of its theatre critic, Hector Charlesworth, who wrote under the pen-name "Touchstone."[4] In January 1888 a column was added especially for women readers, the first of which was untitled. The second was called "Woman's Empire," and the first column edited by Faith Fenton appeared on February 4 of that year.

Garth Grafton of *The Globe* led the way in 1886—having had to prove herself first in the United States—but Faith Fenton of *The Empire* predated all other women columnists—Gay Denison, "Lady Gay," of *Saturday Night;* Jean Blewett, of *The Globe*; and even the better-known Kathleen "Kit" Coleman, who is often called the forerunner of Canadian women journalists.

A pseudonym, of course, was necessary. For her surname Alice went back to her British roots, a move that was to prove useful when it came to concocting a family history that would give her entrée into circles coolly disposed to the daughters of tradesmen. "Faith" appears to have been chosen from a poem that appeared in *The Globe*.

> She kept her lamp still lighted
> Though round about her came
> The throng whose faith was blighted,
> To laugh at her poor flame.

She kept her sacred altar
Lit with the torch divine
Nor let her purpose falter
Like yours — O World! — and mine.

And they whose cold derision
Had mocked her came one day
To beg of her the Vision
To help them on their way.

And barefoot or in sandal
When forth they fared to die,
They took from her poor candle
One spark to guide them by.

The poem, clipped from *The Globe*, has survived a hundred years or so, stuck in a small notebook of Alice's that contains little else apart from some autographs of John A. Macdonald, Emma Albani[5] and Charles Tupper, among others.[6] "Faith" is the title, and the poem abounds with the symbolism beloved of Victorians in prose, poetry and works of art. Even the much-reviled early realism of the Pre-Raphaelites had by now turned to more acceptable and financially rewarding work, and the poem's imagery is reminiscent of Holman Hunt's *The Light of the World*, in which Christ, lantern in hand, knocks at a heavy wooden door.

The editor of *The Northern Advance* said of Stella in December 1886, with some prescience: "We predict for this lady a prominent position among our coming periodical writers." How did Stella transform herself into Faith Fenton so effortlessly? Why did she end up at *The Empire*?

Louis Kribs had been editor of *The Northern Advance* in the late 1870s and early 1880s. Famed for his practical jokes as well as his journalism, he once had half the population of Barrie traipse out to view the body of one T.H.O. Mascat on the railway line, only to find the remains of an unfortunate tabby cat. Stella had praised his journalistic skills in one of her columns, although at that time she had not met him.

She may well have met D'Alton McCarthy, however, through her father's Tory connections in Barrie. McCarthy was a local boy, born and educated in the area, and his father practised law in partnership with one of the most influential members of the Family Compact, D'Arcy Boulton. Although defeated three times at the polls, McCarthy became the riding association president for Simcoe, and finally won office in a by-election in 1876, and again in the Conservative victory in 1878. For the remainder of his career, Simcoe North re-elected "the Simcoe Boy," and he never gave up his ties with the area. Linked by marriage to Sir John A., he was his protégé and right-hand man and viewed by many as the old chieftain's eventual successor. Faith's early connection with D'Alton McCarthy could well explain her access later on to both Macdonald and his wife, Agnes.

There was no question of Faith giving up her day job. There are no records of what she was paid, but it can be estimated from what is known of the incomes of other journalists.[7] The annual salary of *The Empire*'s Commercial–Financial editor, John McLean, was $1,200. In 1887 he was paid $14 a week by *The Mail*, and his freelance articles fetched about $4 for a single column—this for a writer who was top in his field, and male to boot. A printer's devil, as an errand-boy in a newspaper office was known, earned about $2 a week on a country newspaper, a journalist $3. It seems likely that the salary for a weekly column by an unknown woman was around $2. In 1888, when she joined *The Empire*, Alice Freeman's teaching salary was $586.89: $11.29 a week. The extra dollar or two must have been more than welcome, but there was no way she could stop being Miss Freeman of Ryerson School. She would have to remain both Alice and Faith.

Grand Opera House Lane: what an apt place for the granddaughter of lyricist and playwright W.H. Freeman to start her Toronto career! The first offices of *The Empire*—business office, editorial rooms and composing room—were part of the building that housed The Grand Theatre on the south side of Adelaide Street, west of Yonge, the focus of theatrical activity in Toronto for the last twenty years of the nineteenth century. Built in elegant Second Empire style, with a mansard roof and a tower topped with the royal coat of arms, the theatre had reopened in 1880 after a fire gutted the interior. The stage and the domed auditorium were the largest in Toronto, with a seating capacity of 1,750, and on that stage the stars of the era would shine: Emma Albani, Sarah Bernhardt, Lillie Langtry, Henry Irving. Eventually *The Empire* would move to a warehouse on Adelaide Street West, not far from the theatre, but, at the beginning, Grand Opera House Lane was home. For the granddaughter of a playwright and an actress it was paradise.

How different those two worlds were. Perhaps that made it easier for her to separate the two women she had to be, but she was going to need the skills she had inherited from her actress-grandmother for this dual role she would play night and day for the next seven years. It was a task that would demand that she assume two vastly different personalities, and that one of those personae remained hidden from the world in which the other lived.

When Miss Alice Freeman saw her class out the door at the end of the day and made her way to Grand Opera House Lane, she left behind the averted gaze and passive disposition essential to her survival as a female teacher in what had formerly been an all-male profession. As she walked along Adelaide Street and turned onto Grand Opera House Lane, she took on the personality that would assure her success as Faith Fenton, a woman in a field formerly reserved for men: independent, unconventional, a woman who not only spoke before she was spoken to and looked you straight in the eye, but also asked questions and offered her own opinions.

Perhaps she paused next door to peek into the auditorium of The Grand to catch part of a rehearsal. Later columns show that she knew the back-stage areas, the dressing-rooms and the corridors quite as well as the auditorium and front of house. As she walked through the corridors she may well have seen members of the cast running lines or having a costume repaired. Perhaps she exchanged a word with the little soubrette sitting on one of the big cabin-trunks waiting her turn to go on, before climbing the stairs to the newspaper office.

Like the soubrettes and the stars of The Grand, night-time would also have been Faith Fenton's time to perform. She would have written and delivered her articles at night, or at the weekend, staying to discuss the space available—her "weekly budget"—or to watch them typeset, and see her byline appear on the printed page of a major newspaper.

She would certainly have run into David Creighton, padding up and down the stairs in his socks—a habit he had acquired as a country editor and kept in Toronto. An eccentric, kindly man, he made sure he kept a personal eye on every department of the paper. Toeing the party line and pleasing everybody, however, was to prove next to impossible, and Faith Fenton would see the head of many an editor rolling around *The Empire* offices.

As she left to hurry home through the dark empty streets, sometimes with an escort—one of her colleagues, perhaps the crime reporter—but often alone, she would have heard the melancholy sound of oboe and trombone wailing softly from the offices—Louis Kribs, who had played oboe for the Waterloo town band, and one of the other editors, James Curran, who had played trombone for the Orillia town band, playing impromptu duets to while away the night hours.

For a woman of her time, Faith Fenton kept very odd hours. She also led a liberated life. She met men to whom she was not related or to whom she had not been introduced, worked in an office surrounded by men, asked men to escort her on the occasions that demanded it—without waiting to be asked first by them. She sat in Emma Abbott's dressing-room, chatting to her between acts, and then watched her death-scene from the wings.[8] The only people who knew for certain that Faith and Alice were the same woman were her family—particularly her brother Fred and his wife—and it was to her family's lodgings the journalist returned in the small hours. They could be trusted to keep her secret.

From time to time Faith Fenton would take others with her on assignment. Her usual practice was either to change the name of her companion or to omit it, but on most occasions the person with her is one of her younger sisters. If an escort was required, she usually prevailed on one of her male journalist colleagues to accompany her. There is no evidence of her taking any of her teaching colleagues with her, nor does she talk of any particular female friend who can be identified as someone from Alice's world. There may have been teachers who knew, or guessed, that the Junior Book Classes teacher at Ryerson was Faith Fenton, but Faith herself seems to have made every effort to keep her worlds apart.

It was essential that the woman who was Alice and Faith never confused her roles, and this she managed to do for the next seven years. Her double life was a skilled performance and not the product of a disordered mind. Alice and Faith knew of each other's existence, and the vital

importance of each staying away from the other's sphere. That the existence of Faith contributed an element of danger to Alice's narrow world
would only have added zest to the enterprise.

It is not gentle Alice Freeman the teacher in the studio portraits of
the early 1890s, looking straight back at the photographer and the world
with her bold dark eyes in that strong face. It is another woman, released
by a name and a space in which to air her views, views whose growing
boldness and originality would surprise, not just her readers but quite
possibly the woman herself.

Faith Fenton began in a small way, with a column of her own among
the syndicated pieces from other papers, such as *The Buffalo Courier*,
under a general heading, "Woman's Empire," and the subtitle "Prose
and Poetry to Interest the Ladies," which she herself used later on. Her
first column, "Concerning Sleep," engages the woman reader in the
opening paragraphs by setting up a scene with which she can immediately identify—although the subject is abstract, the setting is not:

> We sat together in the early winter twilight, watching the
> crimson flush fade away in the western sky, and talking
> together with the easy confidence that evening and firelight
> always give.
>
> Our conversation had been at first of housekeeping and
> home making, for my little Dame Durden reigned queen in a
> certain small stone cottage, within whose four walls lies the
> limit of a woman's world—husband and babies and home.
>
> We talked of pickling and preserving, making and mend-
> ing, of Jack's school successes, of baby's budding wilful-
> ness, of the new stitch in crochet, and the latest books.

"Faith Fenton" is the signature at the end of a column and a half; by
the next column on February 11, the signature is in print twice the size of
that of the previous week, and the quotation marks have disappeared.
Already it would appear she had made an impact; she had drawn women
into her wider world by understanding theirs. Faith's instinctive ability to
reassure her middle-class readers of the acceptability and "respectability"

of unconventional and challenging new ideas, while at the same time showing how much she valued the traditional woman's sphere, would be one of the prime reasons for her success.

By the end of her first year with *The Empire*, the readers of Faith Fenton's columns have shared with her the major celebrations of the Christian church—Easter, Lent, Christmas—read about some of the churches in Toronto—St. Andrew's and St. Michael's—and been introduced to some of the most celebrated preachers of the period.

They have also heard about Professor Pundita Ramabaia, who came to one of those churches to tell the congregation about the plight of women in India: ". . . the popular belief is that no woman can have salvation unless she is married. . . . a woman's religion is to worship her husband and cook for him. If a woman obeys her husband she will have the honour to become a man next time she is born. If a man is much too fond of his wife he is sure to become a woman next time he is born. That would be a degradation . . . so he takes care he does not too much love her." The lady professor from India was a specialist in Sanskrit at Cheltenham Ladies' College in England.

The situation may have seemed familiar to some nineteenth-century wives reading Faith's columns. Certainly it will have provided food for thought, as will the visits by the end of that first year to the Aged Women's Home, the Hospital for Sick Children, a Toronto kindergarten, the Protestant Orphans' Home and the Mercer Reformatory for Women.

As early as her second column, Faith Fenton takes her readers on a visit to a crèche run for women who have to go out to work to support themselves and their babies, and urges her readers to contribute old toys, cribs, anything they can: ". . . bring down from the garret the cradle and small chairs so long since fallen into disuse; brush the dust away and send them, with old lullabies clinging about them. . . ." Faith could even make an appeal for charitable donations sound gloriously romantic. And those appeals had results, as the following letter shows:

> Dear Editor of *Woman's Empire*: Your article about the Night Shelter seems to have touched a good many hearts. The first gift was a sack of potatos [sic] from a kind Scotchman, then ten dollars from a little band of working lads, "God bless them," to help the poor girls, they said; ten

dollars from a Brantford merchant; five dollars from an unknown friend in Parkdale, "to be used for some girl without a home." Five dollars was brought this evening by a gentleman who read of the work. A physician has also promised to do all he can for the work in the way of medical attendance. Two young girls have been brought to us with such pitiful life stories that I dare not even tell you. . . . Please acknowledge through your paper these gifts.

What is clear from this letter is that, although some men were obviously being informed by their wives, others were reading Faith Fenton's column themselves.

Faith always did her research and made it her business to know the facts and figures, but what gave impact to her accounts was her ability to provide the telling detail from her visits to institutions, to create a poignant image that brought the scene to life and, more important, the human beings within those institutions. Here is a moment from her column on the Aged Women's Home: "A thin, frail hand lifted itself to mine, and a pair of wandering eyes were lifted. 'I want to go to Dublin,' said the quavering voice. 'I want to go now.'" A hundred years later the pain of the old Irishwoman's homesickness is still palpable.

Her trip to the Mercer Reformatory for Women on King Street West, then surrounded by fields, with only the lake to the south and the railway tracks to the north—"that readers of *The Empire* might know something of the daily lives of those restless, broken-winged birds, the imprisoned women of Ontario"—must have been an eye-opener for many of her readers.[9]

Faith describes for them the tiny cells of the more privileged prisoners who have been rewarded for good behaviour, each with a separate window, a chair, a box, a bracket shelf and a small iron bedstead. She takes them through the sewing-room, where she examines the piles of underclothing, "neatly made of factory cotton," and details the inmates' uniform "of blue denham [sic], a material much the same as that used for shirting and overalls. On Sunday each woman is given a long white apron and a linen collar. They are allowed the privilege of dressing their hair, which is not cut upon entering the institution, in any neat method."

Then she tells them of "the dungeon," the solitary-confinement area, and "the Iron Corridor," the three tiers of cells where the prisoners are housed each night. She learns that there are no printed rules and no classification for prisoners. No parameters are set for how the inmate should behave, and the most hardened criminals mingle freely with the young girls who may have come in for a comparatively trivial offence:

> No classification: I wish that I could "write it large—very large." I would that it could be written in great crimson capitals that would burn and brand themselves into the hearts and consciences of those officials who are responsible for this terrible state of affairs. . . . A young girl is sentenced to the Mercer for larceny or assault, or it may be her first offence. How is she likely to come out after associating with confirmed drunkards and prostitutes? And yet this institution is termed a reformatory.

"Let me tell you . . . ," she continues, and goes on to quote facts, statistics, costs:

> . . . the institution costs over $26,000 yearly, the average daily cost per inmate being 57.98 cents, or $4.05 per week.
> How many respectable working girls are there in Toronto who are compelled to live on less than that amount?
> Out of 142 inmates committed, 77 were sentenced for six months, 24 for twelve months and the remainder between one and two years. Of these 46 were under 26 years of age, 50 between 20 and 30, 38 between 30 and 50, and the remainder over 50 years.

Faith points out that over a third of the women were there for "personal immorality in various phases." Most of her women readers would already have been brought up short by the word "prostitute." Not for Faith "fallen woman," or even "a pitiful bit of straying humanity."

Not every column was of such serious stuff. During the summer months Faith took her readers with her on trips to the Niagara Peninsula, sharing with them her delight in travelling "Across the Lake in the *Cibola*" and listening to the Italian string band playing for the passengers, or boarding "one of those cheery, fussy little ferries" at the Church Street wharf for a trip to the Toronto Islands and a ride on the Coney Island Carousel with her little sister Gracie—who is not identified as her sister, just as, in her first column, Jack is not identified as her nephew.

Modest outings these, but the beginning of a pattern that was to carry Faith Fenton across the face of her country from east to west, taking "the little woman in the country" along with her—that same little woman who wrote that she was "green with envy" when she read of Faith's visit to Niagara Falls, the little woman of the new Dominion whose only voyages were when she sat in her chair by the hearth and travelled with Faith Fenton.

There was yet another woman for whom Faith Fenton was to be a lifeline. This was the woman who had gone on great journeys, travelling hundreds of miles with husband and family to open up the new west, and then found herself on her own in the midst of a loneliness and isolation she could never have imagined. She would feel again through the "Woman's Empire" columns the companionship and closeness she had left behind in the cities and towns of eastern Canada, a sense of belonging once more to a community she thought she had lost for ever.

"Wildflower" was such a woman. She, and "Bent Face," and "Iceberg," and many others, would correspond regularly with someone they would feel they knew as well, or better, than those around them. Faith understood; she listened; she reminded them that life was often difficult, even in the cities and towns they had left behind. As she told "Prairie Lily," who, in Faith's words, was "a young girl transported from an Ontario town out to the great North-West, away from her books, her friends, her classes, into the heart of pioneer life": "You need not envy me my lot, Prairie Lily—it is full of perplexities sometimes. Nevertheless," she admits, "I would rather live my own life than any other."

Faith Fenton gave those women back a sense of their own worth and the identity they had lost in the endless, terrifying emptiness of a new land and a new life; she was also starting to realize that it did not necessarily take a great journey to experience a terrifying emptiness. The letters that began to pour in to the office told her that there were women everywhere suffering "a perpetual discontent because of the narrowness of their limitations . . . sometimes it is an open irritation that betrays itself upon the surface. More often it is hidden, a secret sore—that none save a heart friend may guess at." Her relentless optimism may have irritated some whose lives were "a chafing and a fret," but there were many more who wanted to hear that "there is always a way out—I am sure of it. There is a way of escape for every woman—a door into the larger life, of which she alone holds the key."

Faith Fenton was to be that "heart friend." The women who were her audience were not necessarily Conservative, not necessarily Protestant, not necessarily Anglo-Canadian. They wrote to her from the East Coast, from the Prairies, from Montreal or Belgium or Britain, from wherever they had had Faith's column sent to them. They were homemakers, clerical workers, lady's helps, teachers, missionaries or missionaries' wives, farmer's wives. They were everywoman.

Never would they become for her "that mythical creature of the syndicate letter or magazine article, who serves well enough as a dummy for needy writers to trick out in feminine apparel." Never would Faith see her women readers as "that composite creature—an average woman." As she told them: "I speak as a woman to women. I know, for you have told me, in often unconscious plainings, of your searchings, your restless questionings and blind outreachings towards the far-off thing that seems always a greater good."

However different her life from theirs, she and they were doing what had not been done before: "That a woman should criticize the law and the prophets, with a view to acceptance or rejection of the same, was a quarter of a century ago an unheard-of thing. Whatever of injustice or heart-break entered her life yet her lips were mute—or parted but to murmur a dumb submission."

There would be a price to pay for such "restless questioning," and Faith knew it better than most. Her readers, like her, were "in danger of losing their happiness in the sudden growth of a critical faculty which introspects, analyzes, dissects and refuses utterly to accept the old, simple pleasures in the old, simple way." Yet there was no question of going back: "We say not now: ' 'tis the will of Allah,' and cover our heads in harem seclusion; but we enter into the world's arena, and in critical debate argue the pro and con, or in open revolt fight it out."

Calling a prostitute a prostitute was one thing; using such jolting language to encourage her middle-class audience to revolt, or merely to criticize, would have been counter-productive. Faith was enough in touch with the society she addressed to know that the best way to engage them was to make them feel comfortable, at home with the unfamiliar—and possibly she needed to reassure herself too.

Over the six years of "Woman's Empire" Faith saved her softest language for her most provocative columns. The articles in which she challenged traditional female roles are awash with words from the heart of the nineteenth-century woman's vocabulary: cosy, bright, pretty, womanly, gentle, tender, dainty—the last above all. It was clearly a word she loved, but it was also a word she produced automatically when reassurance was needed. She was not unaware of its manipulative qualities, and she used it to great effect in some of her satirical pieces:

> I was somewhat amused and a good deal disdainful concerning the plaint of a Canadian young man in the August number of The Canadian Monthly. Mr. J.L. Hayne cries woe, woe, woe, through several pages of print, because he believes that, in view of the greater skill of girl clerks, male clerks are doomed to extinction. . . . This same profound thinker desires that 200 girls should withdraw from clerical positions they occupy in Ottawa in order to "create an opening" for the same number of young men, "for there are at least that number of girls in the capital who have no other excuse for working than comes from considerations of cupidity, selfishness and pride." . . . O, you clever Canadian girls, what terrible wrong you are doing these young men in Ottawa! . . . There's room and work for a man all the world over, but he's got to be a man and not a delicate creature, who sighs for clerical work and the Civil Service, and who urges the deposition of those whom he acknowledges to be superior in the work in order that 200 of his kind may step daintily in. And failing to do this, O you bright Canadian girls, your punishment will be a terrible one—these dainty Jeremiahs cannot marry you.

Faith Fenton saved her anger for the abuses of society that caused real human suffering; she rarely wasted it on the J.L. Haynes of the world, or on politicians. In March 1889, the beginning of her second year as Faith Fenton, she took her readers along with her and a young woman friend, whom she reassuringly describes as being pretty—no dour old maid this, not a grim suffragist, "with blue eyes, fluffy hair, and a small piquant face"—on a revealing visit to the Ladies' Gallery of the Ontario Legislature.

She opens the column by reciting the nursery rhyme about Humpty-Dumpty and then states: "Mother Goose evidently knows what it is to mourn a shattered ideal, and tonight her despairing wail finds a sympathetic echo in two foolish feminine hearts at least." "The shattered ideal" of the column is the high expectation of the two women, particularly about "the Doversville member," whom Faith's friend had come to see, but in fact their disillusionment is all-embracing. Faith described the appearance of the House:

> The members are arranged, sheep and goat fashion, on the right and left of the Speaker, a portly old gentleman who seems somewhat affected by the somnolent atmosphere of the Chamber. His duties seem to be chiefly to mutter an occasional indistinct sentence and to help the House adjourn. In place of the immaculate broadcloth and oratorical pose, we discovered the majority of the members in tweed suits, somewhat the worse for wear, with shapeless felt hats tipped at a "jolly-good-fellows" angle over forehead and nose. . . .

During their visit the member from Doversville let the side down badly, to the chagrin of the young woman—"He never says anything about sleeping or newspaper reading when he comes home. . . . I suppose it wouldn't be parliamentary."[10]

Faith concluded: "There is one thing our Ontario Legislature can do well, and that is—adjourn. The placidly-reposing Speaker jumps up, mutters a few indistinct words, pops on a queer-shaped hat: the sergeant-at-arms rushes forward, seizes the mace, precedes the Speaker, and the two vanish out of the Chamber in the twinkling of an eye."

Added her young friend: "When women enter Parliament the men will take their hats off, and set up straight, and keep their eyes open and look as if they knew something . . . and then think how nice it will be to receive $600 for thirty days' work—just to look wise and adjourn."

In April 1889 Faith Fenton made a return visit to see a matinée performance by Mrs. Scott-Siddons, whom Stella had seen one rainy day in 1887. The column reveals that there was yet another theatrical portrait on the walls of "the family sitting room of the home I left so many years ago"—that of Mrs. Siddons. It also reflects a certain licence afforded the Freeman children, because the woodcut had been put there by one of them, "a household aesthete," in place of the portrait of "the Rev. Morley Punshon, or some other equally eminent divine," and it was still hanging there "above the little old piano, looking down on many a family gathering."

Faith opens by repeating a "current statement," that Mrs. Siddons is retiring, and speaking with the nostalgia and affection of a true fan of the actress "who now withdraws from the glittering footlights as she first stepped before them—a rarely beautiful woman." She describes in detail Mrs. Siddons's fabulous dress created by the great designer Worth—"wine color velvet, embroidered in silver, with fuschia buds and leaves"—and, having paid homage, then proceeds to suggest that retirement is probably a good idea: "Possibly as Mrs. Siddons purposes retirement from the stage she has not thought it worth while to add to her repertoire. This fact may also account for a hurried delivery and a disregard for detail. . . . It is well, I think, that Mrs. Siddons has finally elected to retire in the full flush of matured womanhood." The bloom is sadly off the rose, the illusion gone; Faith's childhood idol has feet of clay.

Three days later a letter from Mrs. Siddons herself arrived at the offices of *The Empire* from Boston, Massachusetts. It is five pages long, written in her own hand, denying the rumour of her retirement from the stage: "I have always detested the catch-penny trick of announcing as 'farewells' the appearances in the latter part of an artist's career. I quite agree with you as to the fitness of retiring before the powers begin to wane & trust I may never have to outstay my welcome. . . ."

Mrs. Siddons then goes on in some detail as to why she was (quoting from a play of the period) "all loose and quivering inside & out." It seemed she objected to performing on Good Friday, and had also mislaid her copy of *The Execution of Montrose*. Her agent managed to find one in Toronto, and she had to sit in her dressing-room copying out the pieces she required for the performance—"You will not be surprised *now* at my not receiving you that morning. I did not know then who you were or that 'The Empire' had a rather disagreeable article on my recitals of the previous night."

Poor Mrs. Siddons! Faith had apparently even got the description of her dress wrong—"The light must have been very poor in the Hall, for there is neither pink nor blue in that gown I wore"—and the jewellery—"The bracelet on my right arm is the one Her Majesty gave me, gold set with rubies and diamonds, & on the other I wore a bangle with six tapering diamonds and a ruby in the middle. I have never possessed an opal and yet have had perhaps more than my share of 'mischance & woe.'"

She ends by saying she will call on Faith when next she is "appearing in Toronto again when Toronto wants me." There is a long, expressive squiggle from the "n" of the word "when." The letter ends with a page-long postscript, again about her supposed retirement, adding: "This is intended as a purely personal letter, but you are welcome to make use of it if you wish," and asking Faith to let Toronto know, "in your own delightful manner," that—contrary to popular belief—she may well be back.

Faith Fenton would often print extracts from letters she had received from politicians, politicians' wives, actors and actresses. Copies of their signatures were reproduced in the columns of "Woman's Empire": Emma Albani, Wilfrid Laurier, Lady Agnes Macdonald. She never used Mrs. Siddons' letter or alluded again to the mediocre matinée. Yet the letter is one she kept with her papers for the rest of her life. For that reason alone it is obviously a significant letter, because so little remains of the huge correspondence she received during her years as Faith Fenton of "Woman's Empire."

One of the great actresses of the period—albeit past her prime—had thought her important enough to write in haste and at length to justify an off performance, to flatter her—"Your discrimination . . . pleases me more than the undeserved praise of the press in general"—to excuse herself for having refused an interview, and to ask Faith to lay an unfounded rumour to rest. What is more, she had suggested she might call on her—not that it would have been possible. Faith Fenton existed only on assignment, in the office, in newsprint. A dazzled Alice Freeman, standing in front of her class at Ryerson School, must have found it very hard to believe what was happening to her.

Perhaps it was this letter that first made Alice Freeman aware she had arrived. Mary Frances Scott-Siddons, the star of the woodcut in the old family parlour, believed that she—Faith Fenton—existed.

VII

The Spirit of Vagabondia

Have my readers wearied of them, I wonder . . . these summer saunterings, these wayside chats of sunshiny hours? . . . if through them Canadian women have gained even in slight degree a further knowledge of their own beautiful country, I am content.

Faith Fenton, "Woman's Empire," 1889.

Our charming summer idyll is over, and we must write "finale" even as it must be written sooner or later to every journey. . . .

Faith Fenton, "Woman's Empire," 1889.

MARY KINGSLEY WENT TO WEST AFRICA to die and found a reason to live; Isabella Bird went to Australia and Central Asia to find better health and found fulfilment; Gertrude Bell went to Arabia and found political intrigue; Margaret Fountaine went to Siam, the West Indies and the Amazon, chasing butterflies and love: they, and a handful of other nineteenth-century women, defied convention and set out to explore the world. Sometimes their motivation was missionary zeal, sometimes it was wanderlust, but, to a greater or lesser degree, they all had the independence money brought.[1]

Faith Fenton, dependent on the salary of a female public-school teacher, was not in such a fortunate position. So, when she set out in the summer of 1889 for a six-week trip on the lighthouse supply boat the *Canada*, it is more than likely that some, or all, of her expenses were paid by *The Empire*. Faith's first major excursion may seem mundane when compared, say, with Mary Kingsley's to West Africa, but it took her and her readers on a seven-hundred-mile voyage of discovery—"a far journeying for a summer outing, especially when we remember that it has been confined to the bays and lakes of Ontario." More significant than the distance was the company she kept, for her readers went along with her, following the ten articles she wrote on her trip, and by the end of her journey she was a celebrity.

In the nineteenth century there were hundreds of lighthouses scattered the length and breadth of the St. Lawrence and the Great Lakes, forming a vital network for the safe navigation of treacherous and busy waters. During the summer months they were supplied with the goods that would hold their keepers through the gales of autumn and, in some cases, during long periods of winter isolation. Besides food, the *Canada* carried oil, coal, white paint, brushes, lamp glasses, and even small boats, to serve just under two hundred lights. This particular boat took a crew of twenty-two, and twenty-eight passengers, a surprising number of them women travelling in groups. Though Faith gives the impression that she was alone this time, clearly a trip on the lighthouse supply boat was considered acceptable for females.

How gloriously the summer must have stretched ahead of Faith as she put Miss Freeman of Ryerson behind her and boarded the *Spartan*, the boat that took her down to Montreal and the beginning of her adventure! Passing rapidly over the beauties of the Thousand Islands, "too often described to require a word from me," Faith transferred herself, her bags and her readers to the *Canada*, with a sigh of relief at a chance "to get a nice cup of tea, unlock valises and settle down into the cosy stateroom of my water home." From her berth that night she lay and watched the fire-lit windows of the great iron works, from whose towering chimneys huge flames shot upward, "like the belching of some great dragon," until she fell asleep "to the clank of a thousand hammers."

The next day there was time for a brief guided tour of Montreal. The main excitement was that she left her purse on a gravestone in Mount Royal cemetery and had to go back for it. She spent as much time on the tour guide's quaint comments and the inscription on the gravestone of an old sailor called "Joe Beef" as on descriptions of the city.

Already Faith Fenton was demonstrating what would be one of the hallmarks of her journalism: a preference for scenes in which human beings play a central role—"the one central figure around which the narrative threads of the story twine"—rather than the description of scenery for its own sake. She set her readers straight about her priorities in her very first "Among the Lighthouses" column: ". . . though the study of Canadian scenery is delightful, the study of human nature is much more so. . . ." It would be the lighthouse keepers even more than the lighthouses that would fascinate her.

By the end of the first two days, the *Canada* had served nearly a dozen lights in Lake St. Louis and Lake Francis, and had then bumped its way through the Beauharnois Canal, almost touching each bank and close enough for Faith to watch the *habitant* farmers working in their fields, scattering seed "even as it was sown in Bible days." In Lake St. Louis, Faith took the opportunity to row out with the inspector and some of the crew to the Port Louis light, which was kept by a woman.

They were greeted by the lighthouse keeper with her two daughters, who shared her isolation. Her husband had died a month after he was appointed to Port Louis and she had stayed on: "for thirteen long years she has kept and trimmed her light," Faith told her readers.

Seeing another woman was obviously an unexpected pleasure for the keeper of the Port Louis light, for she showed Faith around her lonely domain, including her "little bedroom in the tower with its one window looking across the lake waters, and I thought of the stormy seasons, of the rain and the wind with its bitter autumn moan. . . ."

Then it was on to serve the multitude of lights around Cornwall, Prescott and Brockville—"in rapid succession . . . each serving means a scramble upon the dock or a bigger scramble down the ladder by the vessel's side, to be rowed ashore over shoal water to the tower that stands, perhaps, half a mile away. Today," Faith told her readers, "we have paid several such visits, and each one means much muscular exertion."

Thence to Kingston, past the martello tower on Cedar Island and Dead Man's Bay, where the bodies of the drowned often washed up on the shore.[2] It was evening when they arrived, and the military college and the citadel were a dazzling white in the setting sun. They were to spend six hours in Kingston, and Faith Fenton's sightseeing trip—apparently in the company of some other passengers—would be to the Kingston penitentiary over terrible roads that had her exclaiming: "O, dear! I shall never grumble about Toronto roads again."

At that time one prison housed both male and female prisoners in separate areas. When Faith visited there were only about twenty women in accommodation that could hold eighty, and between five hundred and six hundred men. Before she could see over the prison, however, the lady journalist ran into a problem; she had not set up her visit in advance with the special permission required. Fortunately, the female guard knew of Faith Fenton and agreed, saying, "We will do what we can for *The Empire.*" In preparing for her trips from then on, Faith would always secure the necessary letters of permission from the correct authorities, or personal letters of recommendation from those in high political positions.

Miss Fahey, the matron, showed Faith around the prison, starting with the sewing and laundry rooms, where the women were working. Faith was impressed by their outfits of "dark blue and becoming little white caps," but shocked at the size of the cells: "No woman, be she ever so guilty, should be walled up in a dark closet that gives so terrible a sense of confinement as these do. The wickedest woman is entitled to light and air. . . . If she be emotional or imaginative, and most women are in a greater or less degree, in such a cell she will suffer a torture inconceivable to men."

Like most of her nineteenth-century contemporaries, Faith thought that women were more affected by their physical surroundings than were men, and saw it as the reason why they took such pains to arrange and adorn them. Certainly the cell she was shown by the matron belonging to a French-Canadian woman serving a life sentence bore striking testimony to her theory:

> She is a French woman and very dainty in her ways; perhaps you would like to step inside." We stepped inside the iron-barred door and viewed the apartment, spotless in whiteness. Bits of snowy towelling upon the floor, bright little cards on the box table, a gay log cabin cushion on the chair, numerous devices of ornament about the dimly-lit walls; it was a room made pathetic in its womanliness, yet the dwelling-place of a murderess.

Miss Fahey then handed Faith and her party over to one of the male wardens, who showed them around the men's prison where, "in view of the recent outbreak, our impressions were ten-fold deepened." Before she took on more weighty matters of non-classification and, again, "the torture of these coffined cells," Faith had some observations to make about the male prisoners' looks: ". . . most of them [are] young men, and many of them very nice looking. I was surprised at the predominance of intelligent faces, indicative of well-trained intellects. The heavy, brutal cast of countenance so common in our police courts, was an exceptional sight." Whether it was in prison or in Parliament, Faith always had an eye for a good-looking man.

She concludes her account of the visit by criticizing the system rather than the individuals whom she had met that day: "To me it seems that our whole penal system is wrong. Criminals should never be massed together by the hundreds, and until the ward system is introduced the work of reformation must be sadly slow, and insurrections will occur. Men and women must be individualized, not massed." Here was one Victorian who believed that incarceration should not be solely a matter of retribution.[3]

A busy day was ended by a visit to the Rockwood Insane Asylum—"floors stained and polished, bay windows and flowers, artistically painted ceilings and walls, pictures and cabinets and an in-blowing breeziness from the grounds around; a delightful home for the marred human lives." Again, not the picture usually conjured up of a Victorian mental asylum—"The asylum owns a really fine brass band, composed of inmates and officials. We saw the instruments lying in the music room. . . ."

The company lingered over a late dinner that night to discuss the events of the day—"the sad problems of life"—the table decorated, as always, with flowers: "Sometimes from the carefully tended garden of a lonely lighthouse the Inspector will bring us late roses or sweet peas; occasionally it is a bunch of thorny blue-bells gathered from sandy shores, or field daisies and buttercups . . . and when all these fail we do not by any means despise red and white clover and wavy wild grasses."

Faith was one of the first to leave to write up the day's events. Looking longingly at the easy chair on deck, the hammock swinging invitingly close by, the last rays of the sun on the water, she took herself to her stateroom. Outside she could hear the women's laughter, the sounds of the piano in the saloon, the shouts of the men as they lowered the boat, and the shrill note of the ship's whistle hailing a lightkeeper or greeting passing vessels.

As she sat transcribing from the shorthand in her notebook so that she could mail off her column to *The Empire* at their next stop, did she think back to the little girl Alice on that steamer long ago? The memories always came back to her "with the jingle of a state room key"— memories not just of the ten-year-old weeping on the life-preservers, but of the thirteen-year-old sitting alone in the big saloon. That "solitary but intrepid young traveller" must often have been in Faith Fenton's thoughts that summer of 1889.

From the St. Lawrence to Lake Ontario again, serving lights by the score: Burnt Island, the Outer Drake, False Ducks, Point Peter, Scotch Bonnet. At Port Hope they held an impromptu concert on the deck, singing to the sound of a guitar, played by "the merriest little lady of our party . . . with no harsher critics than the mate on the pilot deck and the man in the moon." On to Gull Isle, Port Darlington—so close to where Alice Freeman was born—and Frenchman's Bay. Then the *Canada* put on full steam for Toronto, where Faith tried to view her city "with a stranger's unbiassed eyes," but gave up trying, agreeing with the Ottawa citizen standing next to her that it was "the finest city in the Dominion."

Every light along that winding coastline was served until "the green variable waters of Lake Erie lay before us . . . as cranky and moodful as a man—some men I had better say. . . ."

When they reached Port Dover, Faith Fenton found there was a deputation on the dock to greet her—"'We saw by the paper that the Woman's Empire was making the trip and thought we would like the pleasure of shaking hands with her,' they said, with cordial laugh, adding many pleasant things about the journal and its success." Faith's first reaction was to wish she had worn her best bonnet instead of a big sunhat trimmed with tarletan, a light open-weaved muslin, without ornamentation.

Three or four hours on from Port Dover, the lighthouse keeper's wife at Long Point Island wanted to do more than shake the lady journalist's hand. From her collection of stuffed birds and animals—all of which she had "set up" herself in her "little low-ceilinged apartment . . . filled with blinkless eyes, spread wings and soft feathers"—she gave Faith a large brown owl for the offices of *The Empire* "wearing an expression of utter knowingness. . . . Some one remarked that it was a really striking likeness of the Premier."

The first columns covering Faith's trip had just appeared in *The Empire* and already she was discovering that she could reach her audience.

The *Canada*, with crew and passengers, continued on its appointed round, through Lake St. Clair and the St. Clair canal into Lake Huron, Georgian Bay, and on to Lake Superior, their progress always halted for church on Sunday, wherever they might be and in whatever church was available. The gifts and the recognition continued along the way, and "Woman's Empire" readers were introduced to a striking range of personalities.

On Lonely Isle, in Georgian Bay, the lighthouse keeper and his family lived a life so isolated that "the poor woman had forgotten the ages of her children and knew neither the days of the week or month. The children—little wild creatures with superb eyes—ran like frightened fawns. . . . it is to its dreary banks that most of the victims of Georgian Bay's wrathful waters float. . . ."

Somewhere in Lake Superior a lighthouse keeper gave Faith a tiny slip of geranium that she managed to keep alive and planted in her Toronto window-box. Its story would come in useful for a column on her little window garden six months later, when she told of how "the solitary keeper with infinite pains had scraped together sufficient soil for a garden plot, and a few red geraniums and yellow marigolds bordered the little patch of peas and potatoes. 'Rocks is all right, but you can't eat 'em . . . and a bit of green as is some use . . . is comfortin' to one's eyes.'" Before she reached Lake Superior and the gardening lighthouse keeper, however, Faith ran the rapids at the Sault.

Sault Ste. Marie was a growing town of about 3,500 people, with one long business street running parallel to the river and several side streets "on which the buttercups and field grasses still contend for possession with newly constructed pavement and roadways." There was already an American ship canal which Canada had used without incident until 1870, when the Americans refused access to the steamer *Chicora*, which was on its way with troops, munitions and supplies to help quell the Riel rebellion. In 1887 construction had finally begun on a Canadian canal and lock system, to provide an all-Canadian route from the Atlantic Ocean to the head of Lake Superior, and at the time of Faith's visit there were two hundred men employed on the project.[4]

Faith took herself along the canal bank until she found a father-and-son partnership—native Indians—who agreed to take her out on the river for fifty cents. The father asked her why she was all alone, and Faith told him that no one else would come with her.

"If you drown, no one else will come," he told her, apparently amused by the thought. Faith agreed emphatically. "Then you must not drown" was his reassuring reply.

Seated on a block in the middle of the canoe, with the father in the bow and the son at the stern, both with long poles, Faith Fenton took "Woman's Empire" on a wild ride between the great boulders and white-capped waves of the rapids, the poles bending double with the strain, and she confesses at this point that she "just for a moment felt queer." When the pilot asked her how much she weighed and, on discovering that she was light, suggested, "You like to go out far?" speechless Faith nodded her assent. Her guides then changed the long poles for small paddles, and the older man took off his moccasins, wet the soles of his feet and placed them firmly on the cedar slats.

Her description of the old pilot breaking into a wild peal of laughter as they hurtled down the tumbling mass of water catches the giddy euphoria of the moment. So fast had been their movement down the rapids that for a while the houses and bridges all seemed to be in motion to her baffled eyes. "Altogether," says Faith, "it was an exhilarating experience, and I felt well repaid."

Just over fifty years earlier another enterprising woman writer, Anna Brownell Jameson, had been the first white woman to shoot the rapids—"and assuredly I shall not be the last."[5]

The Indian and his son were not Faith's first meeting with the Native peoples of the region on her trip. She described her visit to the Indian village of Kergawan, near Manitoulin, where there once was a great fight between the Huron and the Ontario and how the Huron were saved by the arrival of allies in canoes—hence "Kergawan," which means: "Canoes are coming."

She spoke of the Indian burial ground Kaskawasong, on St. Joseph Island, and the offerings they brought their dead—first fruits, maple sugar in bark boxes, pipes and tobacco—offerings then stolen by the Europeans, so the lighthouse keeper there told Faith. When she asked him his opinion of the Indians as individuals, he said, "About here I have found the pure Indians indolent, but very faithful and honest. Where they are of mixed blood the treachery comes in." Faith presents the keeper's remarks without comment, as she does his story about the graveyard thefts, leaving her readers to draw their own conclusions about where dishonesty may be found.

The final destination of the *Canada* was Port Arthur, now known as Thunder Bay, and the tenor of Faith's writing changes as they cross Lake Superior—"the greatest of our inland seas—the lake whose gray, cold waters [do not] yield up their dead, but hold them in unsounded depths until the Ruler of the waves shall command their upgiving . . . fog broods over its surface almost constantly, and in many places ice lingers throughout the summer days."

Faith, in fact, devotes an entire column to the difficulties and dangers of serving the lights of the Great Lakes, quoting statistics, giving examples of how the private operation of the lighthouse supply boats for profit makes the captain take unnecessary risks in bad weather while carrying "a cargo so inflammable that but a falling spark would be needed to convert the boat almost instantly into a burning mass . . . in speaking thus I under-estimate rather than over-estimate the danger as anyone who has taken the trip can testify."

Dense fog brings an unexpected bonus: an impromptu dance held in the wharf warehouse on Michipicoten Island, a deserted mining property in Lake Superior. Once there had been a small community on the island, and the cottages were still there, "left with their household furnishings, no one in them—no one on the island save the lonely light-keeper."

The dance started at around three o'clock in the afternoon and ended late at night:

> Over the wharf and up the steps we climbed into the snuggest place; the floor was of hard smooth wood, and nail-kegs and boxes . . . were ranged round for seats. One of the crew, a fine piccolo player, supplied the music—as perfect in time and tune as any orchestra could furnish. We had Lake Superior lancers, Michipocoten [sic] quadrilles, Lonely Island clog dance, Colchester Reef waltz, and ever so many more. . . . We had a chairman most dignified and programme most varied; we had solos and choruses, speeches and recitations, interspersed with dances. We wore our prettiest dresses, curled our hair and donned our badges. [Presumably some sort of name-tag: Hello, my

name is . . .] Our ballroom was lighted with the ship's lanterns and presented quite a fantastic appearance especially when between dances we sat perched upon the nail kegs round about. . . . I don't suppose the Michipocoten Mining Company will ever know what means of grace that storehouse provided for us—a safety-valve for escape of superfluous energy—but the directors may wonder, if ever they return, how those nail kegs came to be so disturbed.

Four days later, at Port Arthur, she and a few other hardy souls, "being skilled in steep ascents of lighthouse towers," climbed to the top of one of the largest grain elevators in the world, the CPR's on the Kaministicwia River:

Steadily upward we travelled, gathering our breath afresh at the foot of each ladder flight. The grain dust powdered our hair and smudged our faces; the big, broad revolving belt puffed quivering air about us, but we travelled on, leaving laughter and speech at the lowest stairway, and devoting all our muscle and energy to the task until we stood at last beneath the slanting roof and gazed from the narrow, dirty windows over the town, over the broad, winding river, over everything save the solemn, misty mountain tops above us.

Here was a thirty-two-year-old woman talking about muscle—not just energy, but *muscle*—and climbing in long, cumbersome skirts up ladders to dizzying heights "equal to half a dozen lighthouses rolled into one." Women like the correspondent who was "green with envy" at Faith's visit to Niagara Falls would have seen another woman who was not afraid of her physicality.

Then it was back to Montreal, with the *Canada* loaded with grain for the return trip, sitting "low and steady in the water, to the great satisfaction of those of her passengers who do not appreciate a toss."

(PHYLLIS MacKAY)

Faith Fenton's grandmother, Miss Lardner, the opera singer whose charms lured William Henry Fenton into marriage, and a change of name and career. A photograph of the painting that hung on the Freemans' parlour wall. The original portrait has disappeared.

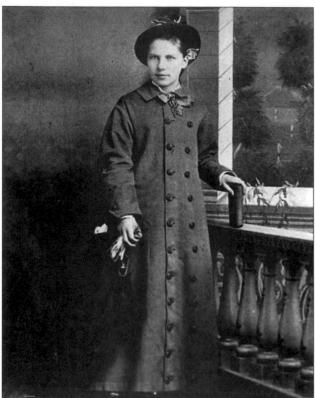

Faith, aged about seventeen, about to begin her teaching career. Perhaps the elegant outfit was her first professional ensemble.

Faith, in her mid-thirties, during her "Woman's Empire" years. The portrait catches perfectly the direct gaze that was considered too forward for a woman of her time—and that Alice Freeman would have struggled to suppress.

The Sage of the Grange. Goldwin Smith in his library, with the accoutrements of the Victorian aesthete: smoking-jacket, skull-cap and books.

Slum dwellings. Virgin's Place, Toronto. Although this photograph was taken in 1912, little had changed for what Faith called "the submerged tenth" of the population, at the other end of the social scale from the Sage of the Grange and his peers.

A signed photograph of Wilfrid Laurier, given to Faith Fenton. The signed photograph of John A. Macdonald that stood on her desk has since disappeared. Perhaps the picture of the Liberal leader had to remain hidden.

Covers of the *Canadian Home Journal* for June and December 1896. Both these illustrations were used again, but most covers were different. The list of contents is typical: for example, the coverage of the Montreal Conference of the NCWC in the June issue, and the December article by the former "Touchstone" of *The Empire*, Hector Charlesworth, who gives Faith only a passing mention in his memoirs.

...Christmas, 1896...   PRICE TEN CENTS

December 1896 ❧ ❧

Home Journal Publishing Co., Ltd., Toronto.

Faith's last column in the series is gentle, nostalgic, "an unsensible one," as requested by one of the women passengers.

Back in Toronto again, sitting once more in "the night-stillness" of her quiet room, Faith could still feel the movement of the boat, hear "the soft swish of the cleaving waves." She had a store of priceless memories, but the deepest satisfaction of all was the recollection of "THE EMPIRE's many friends, and delight in the kindly memories they afford."

The columns of "Woman's Empire" that bridge 1889 and 1890 follow the pattern Faith Fenton had already established: reports on visiting speakers and preachers—"'I am going to hear Miss Nora Clench, the lady violinist tonight,' I remarked to the old Scotch lady at the tea-table. 'Fech then, I wouldna' care to hear her; fiddlin' is man's work'"—a return trip to the Mercer Reformatory, and a visit to the Woman's Medical College that begins defensively, "I do not propose discussing the neccessity for such an institution. . . ."[6] There are columns of local interest such as a discussion on problems with Toronto streetcars, largely in defence of the driver—"But of all things most irritating is the habit certain elderly members of my own sex have of opening the door and prodding the driver with an umbrella . . ."—and, with the approach of winter and the final decade of the century, a more personal and revelatory column, "The Art Of Growing Old."

A melancholy mood—perhaps engendered by Alice's return to the classroom—and a chance meeting had made Faith's thoughts "age-haunted." The week before she wrote the column, she had run into "a fair-haired, sweet-voiced songstress, an idol of childhood days whom I worshipped from afar." Shocked by the heavily powdered and rouged face beneath a coquettish veil, topped by a wig with "a dead yellow tinge," she was driven to ask the question: "Why is it that there are no teachers of the art of growing old?" Yet it was clearly her own ageing that haunted her, and the actress's appearance had merely driven home to Faith "the years of the first wrinkles and the first gray hairs . . . the nondescript years of a woman's life when she ceases to win interest as a young woman. . . ." Even in the predominantly light-hearted article on streetcars she decried the men who only give up their seats to pretty

women: "Oh, you foolish men! . . . a woman knows that were she sufficiently attractive, were she young and pretty and fashionably attired,
half a dozen seats would be promptly placed at her service."

As she approached her middle-thirties, Faith was becoming more
and more aware, not just of the passing of time, but of time spent alone:
"A woman's bitterest moment, I think—especially if she be a woman
unloved and therefore lonely—is when she turns from the mirror realizing for the first time that the fair flush of youth has vanished, that the
sun of her years has reached its meridian. . . ."

The looking-glass no longer reflected only happy images, the lady
journalist swimming confidently on the broad stream of life; it mirrored
her grey hairs and, more poignantly, reflected her solitary state. Whether
the chance meeting in the street and her teaching duties were the sole
causes of her unhappiness can only be guessed at, but something had
made Alice painfully aware that she had passed the first flush of youth
and was unloved. Despite the success of the summer and the sense of fulfilment it had given her, Faith Fenton was clearly finding it difficult to
comfort herself with "the honors of true friendship . . . [and] greater liberty of action."

But the final paragraph of her column is characteristically positive:
"Yet it is a beautiful journey if we choose to make it so. . . ." It was a
theme to which Faith would return again.

After a period of some depression, Faith's encounter in the last
month of 1889 with a seventy-one-year-old woman who had devoted
over forty years of her life to the cause of women's suffrage set her on
the path that would put an end to her loneliness, and would lead her—
paradoxical as it may seem—to "that one greatest love that is present in
every woman's thought."

Scorned, reviled, ridiculed, undeterred by obscenities in the press and
rotten eggs on the platform, Susan B. Anthony, legendary leader of the
women's suffrage movement in the United States, marched on to the
sound of a different drummer, fighting for the enfranchisement, not only
of women, but of black Americans.[7] Wearing on her dark dress the
emblem of women's suffrage, the knot of yellow ribbons that symbolized

the wild Kansas sunflowers that never grow "save where the ploughshare has upturned the sod," she walked onto a Toronto platform for the first time before a sparse audience after travelling night and day from the Dakotas, where she had been lecturing five nights a week.

She spoke for two hours without a break, and at first Faith was disappointed: there were no fireworks, no histrionics, no panache. With her narrow face and deep-set eyes behind spectacles, her hair draped over her ears in an outmoded style, her sharp nose and chin, her lips set in a hard line, Miss Anthony did not even appear particularly prepossessing. But Faith recognized a fighter when she saw one, and two hours of "pungent reminiscing," and a torrent of facts, figures, experiences, delivered rapidly without a break and with "a touch of bitterness and aggressiveness," left Faith marvelling at this woman "who at 71 years of age— the age when most of us are willing to cease our fighting and fold our hands . . . travels and lectures five nights in the week, not for pecuniary profit but for the advancement of a cause."

Faith's coverage of Susan B. Anthony's first appearance in Toronto was more detailed than that of other leading newspapers, who noted the visit without much comment. Most of *The Globe*'s column space on the event was taken up with the names of those on the platform, but the reporter couldn't resist adding: "The Mayor's opening speech was as smoothly eloquent as usual but he very coyly avoided committing himself, in the midst of his complimentary sentences to the woman suffrage movement."[8]

Above all, Faith's columns were the only coverage by a woman of an event of vital importance to women, and she went further than the platform speeches and presentations. She obtained a private interview with Susan B. Anthony afterwards. Her first question was, in effect, "Would you do it again?" The answer was an unequivocal "Yes." When asked if she had any regrets, Susan Anthony replied that she would have wished "a speedier completion . . . but considering where we have started, we have done well." To Faith Fenton's third question—"Do you think the possession of the franchise will cure every evil?"—came the answer: "No, indeed; but it will place us in a position to say what remedies shall be adopted"—a response that would have struck home to her interviewer.

Susan B. Anthony's time projection for the enfranchisement of women was "in less than one [decade] in Canada. . . . In America the work will be more prolonged, for we have to attack each state separately.

I think Great Britain and Canada will grant it simultaneously." Canadian women would, in fact, be enfranchised before both their American and their British sisters—except in Quebec—but it would take, not one, but another three decades.

The conclusion of the column is Faith at her most optimistic: "The day when the question of woman's rights served as a subject of scorn or ridicule has passed, and the nineteenth century belongs most truly to woman . . . and when the records of all battles be searched none will be found to have fought more bravely than Susan B. Anthony." Faith had found a new heroine.

It is possible she also found two other heroines during this period, but she may have met them earlier. Before Faith attended Susan B. Anthony's lecture, she met with Dr. Emily Stowe, first woman public-school principal in Ontario, founding member and president of the Dominion Women's Enfranchisement Association, and the first Canadian woman to practise medicine in Canada.[9]

It was probably Emily Stowe who arranged the private interview afterwards. This extraordinary woman was the mother of an extraordinary daughter, Augusta Stowe-Gullen, the first woman to graduate in medicine from a Canadian university. It may well have been this Augusta who had written so passionately and so articulately to *The Northern Advance* in 1886, decrying the perception of women as slaves of the kitchen, "instead of having a chance with men in the profession of medicine." Slowly but surely Faith was building up her contacts with ground-breaking women in both Canada and the United States, contacts that would take her into a world of power and privilege.

The year 1890 saw Faith Fenton and "Woman's Empire" in all the usual places: at the theatre, with the homeless—"the Other Half"—and attending lectures. Faith often found the speakers whose writings she had read a bit of a let-down: Stanley, the fearless explorer of darkest Africa, was not an entire success as a lecturer "from the fact that his voice is unequal to the demands made upon it [and] the Auditorium was very still; a clock tick would have been audible in every part"; Dickens's son was a pedestrian reader of his famous father's writings, and the great Siberian traveller

George Kennan was best imagined from his daring accounts of those travels: "Upon the stage in that conventional evening dress that does so destroy the individuality of the sterner sex, Mr. Kennan appears just an ordinary manly man . . . ," wrote a disappointed Faith.

But one lecturer in town gave Faith a chance to take on that pillar of Toronto society, Professor Goldwin Smith, the seer of The Grange. Armed with a January 1890 copy of Goldwin Smith's magazine, *The Bystander*, in which he had attacked the women's rights movement, and Susan B. Anthony in particular, Faith went to interview the Reverend Anna Shaw, an American suffragist who was in town.[10]

Having first explained "who Prof. Goldwin Smith is, what he is, and why he is what he is. Think of having to summarize our eminent litterateur in that impromptu manner"—she then went through the article with Anna Shaw.[11] The whole of Faith's column is a line-by-line critique by Anna Shaw of one of the doyens of nineteenth-century Toronto, made all the more devastating by its quiet scorn, gentle wit and, above all, Anna Shaw's knowledge of her subject:

> Prof. Smith starts out with a mis-statement. He says that Miss Anthony proposes to regenerate society by turning over the government to the ladies. Now, Miss Anthony does not propose to do anything of the kind . . . he says: "Women, instead of being degraded, are in the enjoyment of oppressive privileges." Then again, he does not state what these "oppressive privileges" are. An indefinite statement is a very convenient refuge, but a poor prop in an argument. "Miss Anthony assumes that women are an unenfranchised class. They are not a class but a sex"— Humph; well I don't see that it makes an inch of difference to the argument whether women are a class or a sex . . . but we'll use the word sex if the gentleman prefers. . . . "The reason why men have made and must make the law, is that they alone can enforce it." . . . That's very weak . . . as weak as the laws must be that require muscular force behind them to enforce them. . . .

For just over three columns Anna Shaw tears the professor's paper tirade to pieces.

The last two paragraphs of "Woman's Empire" give a clear idea of the impact Faith's increasingly radical views were having back at the office:

> "In Massachusetts [said Anna Shaw] there are 70,000 sur-plus women; yet the proportion of male prisoners to female is as 10 to 1; of paupers 8 to 1, and of idiots 7 male to 1 female."
>
> I quoted this statement very triumphantly upon my return to the office; but it was met by the crushing reply that "with such a surplus of women it is a wonder that the proportion of men who are paupers and idiots is not greater, and as for prisons—the poor fellows need some refuge."

Not only was she surrounded at the office by men who resented her views and, quite possibly, her ever-increasing popularity, but she made no attempt to conceal her feelings from them. Attacking Goldwin Smith's pronouncements was a little like attacking a papal edict, and a woman's doing so was tantamount to blasphemy.

Faith continued to write about the plight of women. Among light-hearted columns on her book-shelf and her window-garden, passionate pleas for a break for working women in their everyday expenses, such as streetcar fares—"Sometimes when I have seen the worn, slim purses opened and the silver bits reluctantly parted with, I have thought a working-woman's small change to be a very sacred thing"—interviews with actresses, visits to more institutions such as the Hillcrest Convalescent Home and the School for the Deaf,[12] there is a stunning column on Les Soeurs Missionaires, fresh in from the headquarters of their order in Carthage (modern-day Tunis), where they bought slaves from the Arabs and then freed them. Speaking through an interpreter—Faith's halting schoolgirl French was not quite up to the occasion—they told her of their lives: "A woman's life is nothing, nothing. It is no more wrong to kill a woman than to crush a spider. The men at least are free until they have been conquered, but the women are born slaves. . . .

Only recently a priest of our mission was invited to the dwelling of an Arab chief and informed that in honour of his visit the chief would burn eight of his prettiest wives. . . ."

At the end of the interview, Soeur Marie Caroline had a request: ". . . we would be so pleased if you could send *The Empire* to Carthage. . . ."

Faith Fenton was what she was without apology and without subterfuge. If her colleague Hector Charlesworth's memoirs are a true reflection of the time, the few women journalists there were—Grace Denison and Kit Coleman, for instance—seem to have used what once were called "feminine wiles" to get by. Perhaps that is why he gives Faith only a passing mention—or perhaps it is because by now the lady journalist was quite as well known for her writing, and her theatrical writings at that, as was *The Empire*'s theatre critic, Touchstone.

There was, however, at least one editor at *The Empire* secure enough in his own talent to admire Faith Fenton. At the beginning of July, when Miss Alice Freeman was let out of school once more for "two long lovely months," "Woman's Empire" was off again "far away by the wide Atlantic, watching the great salt waves that wash the shores of Canada's maritime provinces." Faith was taking her first look at the ocean, and the editor to whom she was reporting was Louis "Pica" Kribs.

The sixteen columns sent from her trip out east were placed in the main section of *The Empire*, and not in its lace-collar ghetto, "Woman's Empire." All were signed with her name, and some began with her name incorporated into the heading. This was journalism of interest to everyone, and the fact that it was written by a woman was not a handicap; the fact that it was written by Faith Fenton had become an asset.

A light-hearted opening column on nearly missing the boat in Quebec City is followed by two more weighty columns on the closing of some lobster factories in Newfoundland, apparently by orders of the French commander on the then French-controlled portion of Newfoundland's shoreline. They are well informed, full of direct quotes transcribed from Faith's shorthand, and devoid of the usual sentimental touches by now associated with Faith Fenton. The French Shore question was uppermost in the minds of both Newfoundland and Canada, and obviously these articles are meant to convince the male audience that they were going to get facts and figures, and not be deluged by frills, furbelows and frou-frou.

Faith returns in her third column to a stop made on her long journey before taking the train to Halifax—a stop that was short in duration, but long in significance. Under the heading "Visit to the Premier at Rivière du Loup," Faith Fenton describes her visit to John A. Macdonald's summer home, "Les Rochers"—her first, but not her last.

Surprisingly, there are no great insights, no wise words from the great man; in fact, most of the column concerns the problems of getting to Rivière-du-Loup, the nature of the terrain, a description of "Les Rochers" as "big and breezy and rambling and irregular, part old, part new, a quaint white farmhouse with a modern addition." What is interesting is the informality of her arrival—a gardener who was clipping the grass carried in her card—and the description of Sir John A.'s study: "A plain room with whitewashed, dusty walls decorated only by a few odd scrap pictures, a bookcase containing a few official volumes, a table covered with letters and papers, one or two office chairs, newspaper files, a trunk marked with a big 'M,' windows looking away out over the river and the hills beyond. . . ."

She watched the prime minister's pen glide over the paper; she noted his alert, vigorous movements. They appear not to have discussed anything of any import. But whether "his kindly attention" included any words of wisdom is not important. All that mattered was that Faith Fenton had gained access to Canada's great man, and she would build on that brief moment in the summer of 1890.

She also made the acquaintance of Macdonald's private secretary, Joseph Pope, while she was there. At that time he was still in his thirties, only three years older than Faith herself, but he would go on to have a distinguished career as under-secretary of state for Canada and under-secretary of state for External Affairs. Born on Prince Edward Island, he was the son of William Henry Pope, one of the Fathers of Confederation. It was another powerful connection for the lady journalist.

The series of articles on Newfoundland under the heading "The Land of Fogs and Fishes" are classic Faith Fenton. After the uncharacteristic opening articles she returned to her preferred technique of building up a picture of a community at a certain time and in a certain space by portraying the people, rather than by delivering facts and figures. As she herself said, she would create for her readers "a sketch which I hope to fill in week by week with many details, but now I shall draw a pencil through those tiresome figures in my note book and trouble you with them no more."

Faith always made it her business to know "those tiresome figures," but without the central *human* figure to live and breathe them, she had little interest in them. She was particularly adept at focusing on a single person to illustrate a larger picture. Here is her biting portrait of the scion of one of the wealthiest families in St. John's:

. . . a young man of superb physique, auburn hair and beard, and full brown eyes, a complexion of rich, warm coloring that I have found common to Newfoundlanders, but that I have seen nowhere else: a rich, peachy tint suggestive of sunshine filtered through crimson glass. His face was not intellectual and his manners were atrocious. A discussion arose at the dinner table about pretty girls, Newfoundlanders being somewhat noted in this respect.

"Pretty," he said, pausing in his occupation of going through the menu, a tri-daily undertaking he performed with great zest; "pretty, I should hardly call them so—fine-looking perhaps, that is all." Being informed by the chief officer that I was a newspaper correspondent who purposed visiting the Island, he looked superciliously at me and remarked: "Well, I suppose it will put a few dollars in the firm's pocket."

I have met with self-satisfied people in my life, but never one to equal this young Newfoundlander. He was not assertive; he did not consider that necessary; he was simply serenely unapproachable in his own esteem, and walked about with an air of owning the world and carrying the key in his pocket.

From this satiric portrait Faith moves into a broader discussion of the inertia, self-satisfaction, and what she calls "the extreme conservatism" that had become in St. John's "a chronic disease . . . in politics, in civic government, in education." The lack of sanitary systems, for example, have brought about serious epidemics of diphtheria—"The ground is saturated through and through with refuse," she was told. When she asked why nothing had been done about it, the reply was one she would hear again and again: "It has always been so." Faith concludes that this inertia "among the lower class . . . a natural result of ignorance and toilsome industry: among the wealthy . . . the result only of exclusiveness" is "exasperating beyond measure."

Politics in St. John's, as Faith saw it, was "one of personalism alone. . . . There are two parties in this bitter warfare of personalities, but neither have any clearly defined platform save that given me by an astute old citizen: 'Them that's out wants in, and them that's in wants to stay there.'" This caused her no end of trouble with her letters of introduction to prominent citizens: "A clerical gentleman on the passage over gave me a pointer. 'If you meet Sir Stephen be sure not to mention the fact that you have a letter to Sir Simon; it would be like a red rag to a bull,' he said, with amused laugh. So I reserved my letters for a few days until I had grasped the situation. . . ."

Faith gave her readers in Ontario and the West landscape, seascape, the appearance of the Newfoundlander—the fog and the icebergs drifting in the harbour, the rosy-cheeked pretty girls—and the sound of the Newfoundlander, as sharply differentiated as the two distinct classes she found, particularly in the outports:

> Yesterday I enquired my way to church of a pedestrian.
>
> "Jurdge; eh then, its t'jurdge ye be's wantin? It's up t'hill—tur' all up t'hill. It's plenty of jurdges we got."
>
> The direction was not very explicit, so I enquired of a gentleman immediately following him.
>
> "The English cathedral! O certainly, with much pleasuah. It is up the hill awound the first cohnah. You are a strangah heah, I presume."

And it is on her trip to the outports on the steamship *Volunteer* that Faith finds the most powerful images of all for, as she herself said, "Seeing St. John's is not seeing Newfoundland, but only a very small part of it."

With Captain Delaney at the helm, a Newfoundlander back to his great-great-grandfather, singing in a superb baritone "that would have made his fortune in concert halls," Faith visited a seal-oil factory, where she watched "the pretty piteous-eyed creatures" being tossed overboard from a newly arrived vessel; climbed three hundred feet up the steep yellow hills of a copper mine in Till Cove, the main settlement in Notre Dame Bay; and was roused from her bunk in the small hours of the morning when the *Volunteer* got stuck on the rocks while steaming across Belle Isle Strait to the Labrador shore past a two-mile long iceberg.

The icebergs inspire Faith to lengthy Tennysonian description: ". . . very beautiful they were, with a weird majesty all their own . . . opal pyramids beneath the sun's caress. . . . One stood a high cathedral mass . . . another lay a marble ship upon the blue water. . . . We looked long at the lovely vision till the sunset flush crimsoned the waters, and this pure Lily-maid moved southward through the rose waves. . . ."

But the most riveting images are far from romantic. On the "peculiarly desolate and poverty stricken" north shore of Newfoundland, Faith stopped off at the tiny settlements of Englee and Conche, "the most barren of barren regions. . . . No cattle, save an occasional goat, no poultry, no cellars stored with vegetables . . . [a] few pathetic little garden patches fenced crookedly between the rocks. . . . These fisher folk have no resources save the one." One poor woman of haggard feature and hard-worked frame speaks directly to the reader:

"You see, ma'am, we has to get all we wants in the fall before the boat stops runnin'. If the fishin's real poor maybe we don't catch more'n one quintal through the summer. (A quintal is a cwt of cod-fish and is worth about $20.) That don't bring us much in trade when flour is $6 a barrel. . . .

"I was better off than the rest . . . because my husband is a salmon fisher, and they generally makes enough, but the cod fishers have been making nothing. I never want to see such another winter . . . every day women came into my house with seven or eight children crying with hunger and we made a meal for then as best we could with tea and dried fish. Our men went up into the country . . . to try and catch deer, and we had nothing to give them to take along except a few frozen potatoes. . . . if it hadn't been for the French vessels, who were the first to get in last Spring, there wouldn't have been a child left alive. . . . No, we haven't any hard feelings against the French; they help us in many ways.

"Last March we was three and four days without food. In April our men chopped the ice and got out some mussels, and we lived on them for a few weeks till help came."

As the women gathered about Faith and shared with her "their bitter experience in an uncomplaining way," she showed her readers in prosperous Ontario lives of unremitting hardship on the edges of civilization, a reality without easy answers.

Of course, being Faith, she tries to come up with some practical solutions to the poverty: "Broom or brush making, rope making, wood carving, chair caning—anything for which material could be supplied and a market found." Succumbing to the demands of journalism for a happy ending, her final column from Newfoundland is upbeat:

For those who love adventure, a coastal trip about Newfoundland will prove novel and exciting, and if taken in the *Volunteer* a pleasant trip is ensured . . . my sleep was filled with dreams of lobsters and men-of-war, who danced about upon the wave-tops to the tune of an absurd little doggerel that the captain used to sing:

Newfoundland of late's in a very bad state
All through the modus vivendi,
Caused by a lobster, sad to relate,
Killed by the modus vivendi.
The French they all say, "From our coast clear away":
The natives say "Who will defend me?"
The John Bull steps in with, "I'll settle this thing
By giving a modus vivendi."[13]

In fact, it would be that Greek chorus of women back in Englee and Conche who would haunt Faith's sleep, pouring out their story "with tears running down their faces." Her dreams were of "the weary tramp of women and children through ice and snow and bleak, stunted pinewoods in search of food." Months later, during the Christmas season, her thoughts return in one of her columns to the women of the outports and the sufferings they had endured the previous winter, their faces still etched in her mind against that bleak north shore landscape—"and the memory of those gaunt women-faces nearly breaks my heart."

Among Faith's papers that remain is a telegram from Louis P. Kribs that she kept and treasured all her life. It reads: "Everything all right. Your letters are splendid see P.E.I. by all means glad you are hom[e]ward bound." When she had first broached the idea of this summer trip, "Pica" Kribs had tilted his chair back and laughed at her vague notion of how she would get there. Five hundred and fifty miles later, after going by steamer to Quebec, by train to Halifax, and then making a two-day journey across a choppy ocean, she had proved herself worthy of his trust.

She did indeed visit P.E.I., "Canada's sea-garden," delighting in its unspoiled beauty and the informality that allowed her to cross the main street of Souris, without comment, in her bathing suit—all-enveloping as that garment would have been, complete with sleeves, an ample overskirt over bloomers and certainly no *décolletage*. But she was to save that column for later, and would devote more space to Newfoundland. There were other events to cover in Toronto in the fall of 1890.

VIII

Shrieking Sisters

. . . the day has passed when women were expected: to
keep quiet by the fire / And never say no when the world
says aye / To sit and darn and feed household sinners.

Faith Fenton, "Woman's Empire," 1889.

I pictured the face of the managing editor were I to go to
him with a request for such a column. Visions of woman
suffrage, communism, libel suits and general anarchy
would flit before him in swift succession.

*Faith Fenton, "Woman's Empire," 1891—in answer to
a letter asking for an unrestricted column for women.*

IN MAY 1891 ONE OF THE HOT TOPICS of sartorial taste in Toronto was
not women in trousers, but women in skirts—more specifically, the
appearance of two women in the choir at St. James Cathedral.[1] It was
not so much that they were in a traditionally male environment—
although undoubtedly that played a part in the furore—but that they
wore the same surplices as the male singers. One outraged church-goer
dashed off a letter of protest to *The Mail*, accusing the women of "masquerading in male attire."

That a woman wearing, not traditionally *her* skirts, but *his* skirts
should cause such a sensation gives twentieth-century readers some idea

of the tyranny of dress that restricted nineteenth-century women, however much fashion appeared to change. In her book, *In a Gilded Cage*, Marian Fowler provides the following description of a society woman getting dressed to go out:

> First she put on her "combinations," a one-piece garment of fine wool reaching to the knees; then her corset, steel boned and shaped and padded to produce the admired swanlike silhouette; lawn or silk camisole, short-sleeved and front-buttoned; lawn knickers, lace trimmed at the knee; silk stockings fastened with garters to the corset; full-circle petticoat; dress or skirt or blouse; if she was going out, huge flower- or feather-laden hat skewered to her hair with ten-inch steel pins; high buttoned boots for walking; buttoned gloves.[2]

The long trains and tightly swathed skirts of the 1870s in which women could barely sit down or climb stairs had gone—the British satirical magazine, *Punch*, got much cartoon mileage for its male readers out of the distress such fashion caused—only to be replaced by an updated version of the bustle, "the braided wire health bustle, warranted to be less heating to the spine than any others." Then there was the Langtry bustle, named after one of Prince Edward's favourites, Lillie Langtry, the Jersey Lily. This was an arrangement of metal bands, working on a pivot, that could be raised when sitting down and sprang back automatically when its unfortunate wearer struggled to her feet. By the beginning of the 1890s the bustle had disappeared, to be replaced by the S-shaped, hourglass figure produced by a corset that held the torso rigid, while at the same time throwing the bust forward and the hips backward.

The T. Eaton Company devoted much space to a wide array of corsets in its early catalogues. There was the aptly named "Erect-Form," the "La Grecque" ribbon corset with white, pink and blue ribbons prettily arranged over a cage of steel and whalebone seven inches high. There was the "La Vida," a new short Parisian model in diamond sateen, with flyaway lace frills on the shoulder straps, and the "Nemo," which claimed to be "self-reducing." There were even versions of these cages for nursing mothers that enabled the breasts to be freed for baby without having to unlace a hideously restricted waist. The illustrations for Ball's (health-preserving) corsets show a cupid peeking coyly out over a rigid beribboned rampart. Whatever twists and turns fashion demanded of it the corset remained, the quintessential symbol of Victorian hypocrisy: it enclosed a woman in bands of steel and whalebone, restricting her breathing, her movement and her internal organs, while at the same time emphasizing her bosom and her hips for male delectation.

Beneath those multitudinous layers of silk, lawn, wool, steel and whalebone that kept her decent, it is possible that the Victorian woman was not as unaware of her body as one might suppose. For some, the tight lacing brought about a sensual, even an orgasmic, awareness of their sexuality, "excitations" which they were forbidden to express or understand, let alone possess.[3]

In her column "Women in Church Vestments," Faith points out: "There is no suggestion of 'male attire' about the dress," and she suggests that the current practice of hiding women singers "in some sequestered nook behind the choristers" was much more compromising to Christian standards.

Over the next few years Faith Fenton would return frequently to the question of women's clothing and the movement for Dress Reform. "Rational Dress" had nothing to do with fashion and everything to do with freedom; it also had a great deal to do with the new interest among women in what was known as "physical culture." Many of the experts in the field visited Toronto, and Faith not only covered their lectures, but enrolled in their classes. Here is her description of the arrival of Laura Giddings of Boston in early 1892: "When Miss Laura Giddings of Boston was invited to Toronto . . . I enrolled myself among her pupils. . . . My attitude, indeed, was that of a sceptic rather than that of a believer . . . and now, halfway through that course, I confess myself materially benefited, much interested and unreservedly in favor of the art of physical culture. . . ."

Although not one for psycho-babble—what she called "psychological fogland"—Faith cannot resist pondering the link between the body and the mind, "the physical correspondences" she had been reading about in Emanuel Swedenborg's works that were causing a stir in the scientific and philosophical communities at the time. As usual she expresses it most effectively, not in the abstract, but in a scene between herself and an older woman:

> "She is one of those strong-minded American voting women, I suppose," said a dear old house-mother to me this week, when I spoke of Miss Giddings. "No," I answered, with a laughing thought of the graceful gentlewoman I had met. "No, indeed, she is not. You are thinking of women suffragists, perhaps."
>
> "Well, it's all the same, isn't it?" asked my friend, settling her cap-laces.

And of course, Faith's old friend was right. It was indeed all part of the same movement to break "the average Canadian woman" out of "the old conventionalities, the old-time proprieties and properness in which men have so carefully swaddled her." At this stage of her life it looks as if Faith herself does not see this, but possibly she is making the separation to reassure her conservative Canadian audience. The column is full of comfort-words: pretty, stylish, graceful, exquisite, cultured, womanly.

Earlier in the same year, Faith had attended a lecture on dress reform given by a Miss Jenness Miller. So explosive was the subject that the men in the audience had been asked to leave before Miss Miller modelled a daringly new garment that had evolved with the advent of women cyclists: the divided skirt. Faith comments wistfully: "It looked . . . so comfortable, such a splendid garment to take long steps in." As early as 1889, "Woman's Empire" readers had been informed: "I have worn nothing but health waists for the past two years, and now a corset seems to me the cruelest and hardest thing woman ever invented—if she did invent it."

Four years later, Faith's feelings about skirts were even more forcefully expressed, but by then it was not only the physical encumbrance she deplored. She described them as "a literal setback to us ever since we adopted them as the only and all-time costume of the sex. They have impeded our progress in every direction, by increasing, if not producing, our physical weakness, and emphasizing our sex." The double message of that costume was not lost on Faith. She then quoted her young sister—"La Soeur"—as exclaiming, "Just think—oh, just think—of the freedom that is coming; when every woman will be a girl, and every girl a child again. . . ."

The freedom that is coming: every girl a child—not male, or female, but simply a human being. These are opinions that still raise a few hackles in the twentieth century, and that faint but unmistakable celebration of androgyny must have seemed like anarchy and Armageddon rolled into one in the 1890s.

To a letter from "An Old Bachelor of Three-Score Years and More" who is concerned that his mother and sister may wear bloomers, Faith replies that the "'womanliness' of any costume is not inherent, but a matter of custom," and tells him that it is all very well saying woman is "lovely and noble and adorable and all the rest of it. But she has to fight rather a lonely and hard way in the world full often. . . ."

Certainly the lady journalist was doing just that, and would have found the way smoother without physical encumbrances. She who had climbed grain elevators and lighthouses in layers of skirts was quick to point out to experts and physicians who suggested there was a limit to how well or how fast women could run that they too might move somewhat differently if they "were embarrassed with the multitude of skirts that it is woman's lot to wear."

Toronto was fast becoming the centre of discussion of revolutionary ideas about women's lives. The decision of the Association for the Advancement of Women to accept an invitation to hold its annual conference in Toronto in October 1890 doubtless prepared the way for the parade of speakers that followed—speakers such as Laura Giddings and Jenness Miller—but the path had already been blazed in 1889 by Susan B. Anthony and reported by Faith Fenton.[4]

This time, when the congress assembled its speakers in the theatre of the Normal School and the Horticultural Pavilion the audience was not sparse, as it had been for Susan B. Anthony's first visit.[5] In spite of poor weather for two of the three days, both venues were packed, and this time the event was fully covered by Toronto newspapers, particularly *The Mail* and *The Globe*, rather than *The Empire*.

Faith devoted two columns to the congress, and as usual it was the people who interested her rather than the topics for discussion. The first column is quite brief and is headed by a cloyingly saccharine poem titled

"He Wanted to Buy a Kiss," written in an ersatz Scottish brogue that may have served as a red herring to editors and a reassurance to her readers. Faith's article is really just an outline of the history of the movement: an apologia sweetened with reassuring phrases: "It is not a suffrage association or prohibition society, it advocates no pet 'ism' . . . a platform that the most retiring can accept, and across which the men of the continent can stretch their hands to wish their supporters god-speed."

In her second column, headed by another sugar-coated set of verses called "Love's Eves," she assembles a cast of characters for "Woman's Empire" that range from the association's president, Julia Ward Howe, composer of "Battle Hymn of the Republic,"[6] to suffragist Mary Eastman from Massachusetts, who gives Faith one of her best quotes from the congress: "I have been asked to interest myself in [the] Humane society and dumb animals. But my work is among dumb women, to make them speak, to help them voice their needs and aspirations. There are too many dumb women in the world."

Faith also interviewed a handful of women writers—among them Alice Stone Blackwell, junior editor of the Boston *Woman's Journal*, the oldest woman's suffrage publication in the United States, and Kate Tannatt Woods, a novelist and magazine writer for *The Ladies' Home Journal*.

One can imagine how much pleasure it must have given Faith to share with these other far-from-dumb women their experiences of a life outside the normal patterns set by custom. As she said in her opening column: "To confer—to bear together; it is a wonderful way to lighten the load for each separate burden bearer who might otherwise droop in discouragement."

Although there is no evidence of Faith drooping in discouragement in the two columns devoted to the Women's Congress, there is certainly an uncharacteristic sense of restraint. For example, although personality is as always her primary interest, when she *does* mention topics on the congress agenda she chooses them carefully. "Crime and Its Punishment," "Hygiene of School Buildings" and "Common Sense in the Nursery" are some fairly innocuous titles that she singled out for inclusion.

Was she warned not to be inflammatory? Possibly. Or possibly she knew the editorial attitude to the congress—*The Empire* paid it scant attention—and was aware that these columns would be examined more closely than any others in her lace-collar ghetto. On this occasion, other newspapers and other columns give a truer picture than the one drawn by the usually outspoken columnist of "Woman's Empire."

Of the two leading Toronto newspapers that covered the congress, *The Globe* seemed particularly anxious to assure its readers that the event really had little to do with suffrage, "which finds no place among the objects of the association, which are 'To consider and present practical methods for securing to women higher intellectual, moral and physical conditions.'" The paper devoted a leader to the subject, assuring its readers that no one could object to these largely educational aims, failing apparently to sense any danger that an educated woman might well want to vote.

The Globe reported on the opening speeches of well-known male Torontonians who graced the occasion, among them Professor William Clark of Trinity University, and ex–Normal School principal, now inspector, Hughes.[7] Both firmly drew the distinction between the congress and the suffrage movement. Inspector Hughes in particular waxed eloquent on the subject, saying that he was "glad that the Visitors were not a Woman's Suffrage Association, so that they would run across the convictions of none of them"—meaning presumably the men who had lent their lustre to the occasion—ending with an oratorical flourish: "that he commended their work in trying to better their sister-women, and held that men should surely cooperate with them in uplifting the world."

It must have been a nasty moment for these male luminaries when, shortly after their addresses, Dr. Emily Stowe gave the "warm hand of greeting" from the Women's Enfranchisement Association to the congress, "rejoicing that there was no boundary line between the women who strive to help their sisters. They had seen men and ideas pass away, and would continue their united efforts 'until truth alone survives.'"

Even in her guarded coverage Faith hit upon the main threat to the male establishment of such affairs. Women were no longer isolated, no longer unaware of what each one thought, of the dreams and aspirations of other women. As the little lady with brown eyes had said when a "pitiful bit of straying humanity" was beaten to death: "If only I had known." Not only did she know, but her voice was heard. She was no longer dumb.

On the other hand, *The Mail*'s coverage gives some idea of how she could be made dumb by the censorship of selection. *The Mail* does not need to reassure its readership, because it simply omits Dr. Stowe's speech and concentrates on the much more general remarks of the president,

Julia Ward Howe, and gives extensive coverage to speeches on "Scientific Training for Mothers"—motherhood was usually safe ground—and "The Coloured Women of the South"—which was someone else's problem. It does however give some space to journalist Alice Stone Blackwell's "crisp and incisive sentences" about yet another attack by Goldwin Smith on women's suffrage, this time in the magazine *Forum*. Here, the motivation could be political rather than in the interests of fair play, since the only extracts given are inoffensive and vague, rather than crisp and incisive.

Yet, in fairness, both newspapers devoted what must have been for the era an inordinate amount of space to women's matters, certainly by comparison with the coverage given Susan B. Anthony's first Toronto visit. By the second day, when covering Mary Eastman's paper on "Woman and the State," *The Globe* was making such editorial comments as: "listening to so brilliant an exponent of women's disabilities, the men in the audience must have felt ashamed of their progenitors and not altogether comfortable with regard to themselves."

The erudition, passion and humour of these female pioneers making their way through the surrounding savages still springs fresh and vigorous from the close-packed print of a century ago. In a "scholarly as well as eloquent" presentation titled "Women in Ancient Egypt" Georgia Leonard equates the greatness of that civilization with the dominance of women in the society, and *The Globe* records the laughter that greeted her remark that husbands in ancient Egypt took the names of their wives.

Mary Eastman, speaking entirely without notes, used not only passion but humour to make her advocacy; reports *The Globe*:

> She was at one time a member of the board of a Public Library in the town where she lived, on which there were both women and men, and they worked harmoniously together . . . [until] a vote had to be taken on the question of whether a certain dog tax should go to the library or the Public School Board. The women, who had been strong enough to do the work, were either too weak or too stupid to perform the easy task of dropping a ballot paper into a box. (Laughter.) She saw a drunken Irish labourer being helped into the polling booth on that occasion, and she was afraid he voted against the library. (Laughter.)

On the third and last day of the congress, one of the more provocative papers was presented by Mrs. Ellen Mitchell, of Colorado, on the sensational playwright Henrik Ibsen.[8] Here was dangerous stuff—male egotism, the hypocrisy of society (even if the sexually transmitted disease in *Ghosts* is merely called "heredity"), wives walking out of their homes and slamming doors behind them. *The Mail* gives it nearly a full column of coverage, and it is one of the more challenging papers from the congress to which Faith does refer in her column, but only obliquely, and much later on.

Two years after the congress, she attended a lecture given by Professor Clark of Trinity College on Tennyson's poem "The Princess," in which Ida, a rebellious princess, seeks personal freedom before accepting the hand of the prince. Says Faith: "I was a little anxious to hear his opinion of the movement known in popular parlance as 'Women's Rights.' The Princess Ida being pre-eminently the leader in poetical literature. . . ." It would appear, however, that the learned professor of philosophy sat firmly on the ideological fence, speaking in a fatherly tone of "'that poor child—the 'Princess', and her struggles to go away and find herself, like Ibsen's Nora."[9]

Whatever Faith Fenton's true feelings and role in the woman's congress of 1890, they had gone underground. It is only in the light of future events that it becomes clear she was making connections, as she always did.

"Woman's Empire" spans the years 1890 and 1891 in Faith Fenton's usual manner: seasonal columns about Christmas and Lent, visits to what were then known as the insane and idiot asylums—although Faith chronicles much kindness and tenderness in those institutions—and the Toronto Homeopathic Hospital, the latest fads and crazes such as hypnotism and phrenology, a return to material gathered the previous summer in Newfoundland, the Magdalen Islands and Prince Edward Island (perhaps when Alice's school duties pressed hard upon Faith's shoulders) and various columns under the heading "Among Our Books." These were a regular feature of "Woman's Empire" and give a clear picture of

Faith's likes and dislikes—Kipling being one of the former. Faith loved stories about the Raj, "a place of cholera, heat and flirtations," and enjoyed Kipling's word-pictures—"the charm of Kipling's sketches are their sketchiness." Tolstoy was one of the latter; she loathed his gritty pessimism. Here is Faith on being handed *The Death of Ivan Ilich* by a landlady on her travels:

> "Here's a book that makes nice Sunday reading . . . it's sorter sad and mournful." . . . I picked up the book . . . and read on and on with much the same fascination that country folk of limited interests betray in details of sickness and death. Finally, when the dismal end was reached, I flung the book from me in utter disgust and ran out through the rain to where the waves rolled and retreated over the sand, leaving queer inert masses of jellyfish lying like great sponges upon the beach. . . . Tolstoi is credited with saying that he thinks it would be a good thing if every author would pigeon-hole his manuscripts, and publish nothing during his life. I wish he had lived up to his own belief. . . . *Anna Karenina* I read of my own accord. Ivan Ilitch [sic] was thrust upon me—and now I have done with Tolstoi, and absolutely refuse to read any more of his writings.[10]

But at the beginning of June 1891 there was another death that would affect Faith Fenton deeply and personally, and from which there was no escape. Shortly after his successful election campaign in March, Sir John A. Macdonald suffered a stroke, and died at the beginning of June. A stricken Faith dedicated three black-bordered columns to him under the heading: "Sir John A. Macdonald—One Woman's Tribute," and it reads not only like a eulogy to a lost, great leader, but like a letter from a woman mourning a dead love:

> Kindness! It is what we beg for always. A man says to a woman, "Be true." She looks up into his eyes and answering

entreats, "Be kind"—only that, and yet too often her petition is ignored or refused.

Call it magnetism, effectiveness, individuality—call it what you will, O men, as you endeavor to define the dear old chieftain's wonderful power of making and keeping friends. We who are women explain it in a simpler way when we say he was always kind. . . . We women give highest worship to heart and brain together; Heart alone wins us often; brain alone never.

Most interesting of all, it reveals a lot more about her visit to Rivière-du-Loup the previous summer. In the course of her tribute, Faith discloses that the letters of introduction that gave her access to top officials on her east-coast trip, including the governor of Newfoundland, Sir Terence O'Brien, were from the old chieftain himself and, moreover, that she paid a return visit to Rivière-du-Loup on her journey home: "I spent another little season in his company when my rambles were over, and my last personal remembrance is of a kindly hand clasp, and as we drove away the slender erect form of our premier standing upon the steps of his summer home to wave a light last farewell."

Only one of these letters has survived, dated July 9, 1890, written and signed by Sir John A., and it is to Sir William Whiteway, the Premier of Newfoundland, requesting his "kind countenance and council" for Miss Alice Freeman—"who as 'Faith Fenton' is well and favorably known on the Canadian press."[11]

Faith also mentions in her column a photograph of Sir John—a "cabinet portrait"—that was sent to her "over a year ago." Since the visit to Les Rochers took place less than a year earlier, it suggests that Faith had already met Sir John A. and, since she had not yet visited Ottawa, it must have been during one of his Toronto appearances. Faith loved to let her audience know about her powerful connections, but she had obviously learned when to keep silent about specifics. Keeping her public informed was quite a different matter from gratuitous name-dropping, and her reputation for discretion was to stand her in very good stead.

The photograph of "the thin, tossy hair, the kind eyes, the firm, powerful, humorous mouth—the whole countenance that no words can adequately describe, even as the original remains largely indescribable," stood on her desk, and she confided to her readers, "I have looked at it many times this week with eyes too full of tears to plainly discern the well-known features."

"Old Tomorrow," the strong centre of the Tory party, was gone. The newspaper he had been so instrumental in creating, and the empire built by Faith Fenton, were under siege. A new man stood in the wings, ready to lead the Grits back into power. In a beautifully detailed passage, Faith described the last time she saw her beloved hero: "The fur overcoat he loved to wear lay thrown across the back of the easy chair from which he had risen; a cluster of roses drooped near by, the light flashing through a glass water ewer sent scintillating sparkles across his face—a little pale and weary with fatigue, and his words dropped into stillness—the intense stillness of a vast audience."

In the early summer of 1891, Faith devoted some space to a discussion about "the matter written for feminine perusal." Her interest was apparently triggered by a discussion in *The New York Herald* "in which several bright women writers asserted that . . . the fads, follies and personal gossip [are] satisfactory neither to the women who write it, nor the women who read: but that editors, being as a rule of the opposite sex, are persuaded that only this class of matter is acceptable and refuse to publish any other."

It is quite possible that her appeal to her women readers—"You—mothers and daughters, I mean—who are on the farm and in the village. . . . And you, busy city woman"—was as a result of pressure from her own editors over the nature of "Woman's Empire," and that *The New York Herald* discussion served to distance and objectify her own appeal for support from her reading public.

There is evidence in the columns of the 1890s of disputes with her male superiors, and although Faith does not often identify the reasons, they are more likely to have been over editorial policy than the usual slings and arrows aimed at a working woman of the time. Those she could handle; an attempt to control her empire was far more threatening. The theatre critic of *The Empire*, Hector Charlesworth, writes of upheavals among the editorial staff in other departments after the death of Macdonald, caused by the internal dissension and stresses in the Conservative party, so it is unlikely that Faith Fenton was excepted. In October 1891 she records the following in one of her "Among Our Books" items:

> I was in a temper—there isn't any doubt about it, one of those tempers, you know, that begin with a stamp of the foot and end a very few minutes later with a lump in the throat and a quiver in the voice. I was wiser than to wait till the latter stage developed, because men always keep so provokingly cool and make a woman feel so impatient in her vexation even though they are the just cause of it. I rushed down the office stairs and out into the street, and by the time I had spent half an hour holding on to the strap of a crowded street car the world seemed generally blue and men particularly horrid.
>
> The "blueness" grew of more hopeful tint at the tea table, and afterward when I cut the cord that bound a parcel of new books it vanished altogether.

Books were her comfort, but we are not told what the office fight was about. However, a month later, under one of her regular "Here and There" headings, she records another exchange:

> Early in the season of last winter a chance newspaper notice informed me that Principal Grant had been asked to address the National Club at a certain date. . . . therefore I promptly petitioned that I might be present.[12]
>
> My particular editor is not advanced in his views concerning our sex. He doesn't believe that women should be in medicine or law, or on the platform or in politics—or anywhere except at home—and I shouldn't be surprised if sometimes he didn't want them even there. So his answer was prompt:

"Of course you can't go. There will be no ladies present. Why the chief charm of a club is that no women are admitted."

Whether this was Louis P. Kribs, Faith does not say, but the fact that Kribs was a kind-hearted man who was fond of his wife, and that the Kribs took in and cared for orphans, does not mean he necessarily approved of "the new woman." It was a given that women did not belong to organizations, although in 1888 the Imperial Federation League of Canada had admitted women, and Faith Fenton was one of their first female members.[13] In the case of the National Club, Faith discovered afterwards that they had invited a number of women and she could have attended.[14] She comments: "A broad outlook over national interests, an eloquent setting forth of national possibilities, lifts a woman from her narrowed stifling round of pettinesses and gives her a great deep in-breathing that makes her much more a patriot—and not less a woman."

A later column records an exchange between Faith and two editors that makes it quite clear what they would have preferred to find in "Woman's Empire":

> "A cooking school in June?" I queried, eyeing the courteous invitation somewhat distastefully. "Why not in June as well as any other month?" asked some one. . . . "I think a cooking school an excellent idea at any time," said editor number one. "It certainly should receive every encouragement; we are all agreed upon that," asserted editor number two emphatically.
>
> I puzzled for a few moments afterwards over their interest in anything so feminine. "Why, of course; they're men. That accounts for it," I said. To men a cooking school seems a much more desirable place for a woman than a lecture platform; and the better the men, or the more publicly they pose as apostles of equal rights, the more surely they prefer to see women in the cooking school.

The way through the jungle had become even more treacherous, for the old enemy was wearing a new disguise; prejudice was masquerading in permissive attire. For the "new woman" there was no "new man." Even educated men, such as Faith's own doctor, routinely handed out slights and slurs. When she was researching her article on the "modern madhouse," Faith asked her practitioner why what was then called "softening of the brain" was more prevalent among men, and his reply had been that "women didn't have enough brain to soften." A disillusioned Faith now believed that the truly enlightened man was a chimera; he simply did not exist.

However, Faith Fenton's growing interest in women's rights was not solely restricted to larger questions of politics and patriotism. There were other, more immediate problems for the ordinary woman. Take public conveniences, for instance:

> If the Local Council of Woman's Societies are in search of evils to be remedied, I should like to draw their attention to the need—the extreme need—there is for the establishment of sanitary conveniences for women in various parts of the city—especially down in the business centres. I speak from absolute knowledge, and because of the complaint of many a woman concerning this lack.
>
> Women who go down town for half a day's shopping . . . whether they have little children with them or not, are often put to great inconvenience, and frequently real distress. . . . I have known many a mother who has been forced to drag a weary little child all the way to the Union Depot [she is referring to Toronto's Union Station] or take him home by car. . . . This condition of affairs ought not to be; and it is time to say so.

It was also time to speak out about the harassment of women—with passion, anger, disgust:

King Street after dark—especially that small portion of it beteen Simcoe and Yonge—is not a pleasant place for a woman to walk alone. . . . After the theatre doors are opened, and the entertainments are begun, any woman found in that locality is subjected to little indignities of look or word that she resents hotly.

And they do not come from the toughs of York or Bay street, but from the so-called respectable citizen; the well-dressed man who steps out of office or hotel, with no higher motive than to ogle passing women. . . . They are middle-aged men generally. That is the worst of it . . . whom neither a look, nor a woman's quickening steps can put down—these vultures of men, who look and leer, who brush past the woman with underbreath comment as she waits uneasily for the delayed street car. Faugh! If they only knew how all women despised them. . . .

There is no doubt this is a reflection of Faith's own experiences as she walked about the city alone. Her own solitary occupation had made her aware of the dangers for the innocent abroad, or for the far-from-innocent and, a hundred years later, the picture is still familiar:

Two Toronto ladies much interested in philanthropic works have represented to me the desirability of having a properly credentialled woman officer . . . on duty at the Union depot, for the purpose of looking after girls and women who come as strangers to the city. . . . it is not unusual for girls who are runaways to arrive in Toronto and ask directions of the first person they meet on the platform. Mothers in search of daughters, women looking for work, wives seeking husbands, girls in misfortune, who know the world too well, and girls full of hope, who do not know the world at all. . . .

It would appear from some of her correspondence that male readers such as "Peter Parley"—like her editors—wished that Faith would spend more time on other topics: "of course men chafe; but their lives are larger, their work is not so monotonous or fretting. . . . This page is for women, Peter, that is why I write chiefly of them; but we will talk of men's discontent some day if you like—there is plenty of it. I know a few men who are right royal grumblers."

There was too much work to be done among her own sex, too many dumb women. Was it any surprise, Faith argued, if women lacked a sense of humour, as men said they did. If it were true, perhaps thus far the humour had been "too one-sided." How easy was it for a woman to laugh when a writer of the period felt the need to give detailed advice for the woman "who has wept until her eyelids and her nose are purple, her eyes bloodshot and her face swollen," and who "frequently makes matters worse by washing her face in cold water."

Faith passes on the advice to bathe her swollen face in rosewater so that "she will be prepared to face any company," but her final paragraph reads: "All of which is very nice to know, but nicer still would be the knowledge that a woman has no need to weep until her face is in such a condition."

Not all the women who read her column, however, were in her corner. After replying to a letter from "a devoted reader" in the section devoted to "Our Letter Bag," there comes this response to "B.A.":

> I rarely reply to letters written in so rude a tone. . . . Had your letter come from a man, I should simply have tossed it in the waste basket after reading the first few lines, but coming evidently from a woman, I grant her the courtesy she does not deserve. . . . The word Geneva, being substituted for Genoa, in Dr. Augusta Gullen's letter, was simply a compositor's error. I noticed it when in print; but as our readers average a fair degree of intelligence, I did not deem it needful to make explanation of so palpable a blunder in the next issue. I had forgotten there are exceptions. Do not write again unless you can change your tone.

But it would not be the likes of B.A. whom Faith would be thinking about on those occasions when she returned home from the office at four or five o'clock in the morning, standing on College Street "in the uncertain light of dawn" and watching as a paper boy whistled back at a robin in "that fine old tree that stands on College street, west of Spadina."

It would be women like the ones who wrote asking for details of the university extension lectures and who needed to be assured that "the fee for the course is very low, so that the girls and women whose pennies are hardly earned may take advantage of them." These were the women she cherished, and whom she would carry with her in spirit on her summer saunterings of 1891. For "the editor in all her wanderings" was off again on her first visit "under the Stars and Stripes."

The eleven columns Faith wrote for "Woman's Empire" with the collective title, "Under the Stars and Stripes," run from July 18 to October 10, 1891, and follow her travels to New York, Newport, Philadelphia, and Morristown, New Jersey. They offer a fascinating glimpse of turn-of-the-century American society through the eyes of a more than usually well-informed and independent Canadian woman who nevertheless had her own prejudices and preconceptions.

What they also offer is a glimpse of the influential people Faith Fenton had contacted to set up her trip, some of whom she had met out east the previous summer. She devotes the whole of an earlier column to one, a Dr. H. Storer, of Newport, who had been a leading physician in the United States, and was travelling with his French-Canadian wife in eastern Canada that summer. Quite clearly she also had access to any number of newspaper offices, since she could virtually choose which editors she wanted to see, and in another column she mentions in passing an unnamed American senator she had met on an earlier, unspecified, occasion.

The normally self-confident Faith shows an uncommon defensiveness in her opening column. It still continues to be a Canadian trait when dealing with "Uncle Sam's domain," but it is worth remembering that in the 1890s annexation was still being touted as a reality by the likes of Goldwin Smith. Moreover, many inhabitants of the Niagara

Peninsula, where the marks of war were not yet erased and where a young Alice Freeman had spent some time, had not got over viewing Americans as the enemy. Alice Freeman's own parents had spent some very unhappy months in New York State, and Faith Fenton treats some of her opening exchanges as if they were skirmishes in a battle, instead of with the open-mindedness that is her more familiar trademark.

First, though, came the experience of travelling in a sleeper-car with strangers around her, some of them male. Unmarried Faith describes the shock of opening the curtains of her berth and finding a pair of stockinged feet topped by grey trousers descending from the berth above: "I shut my eyes and curled into the far corner of my berth during the minute that the owner thereof sprang lightly down. . . ."

In her first recorded conversation Faith was informed by a New Yorker that she would find the pace of America surprising: "You're rather slow in Canada . . . one word in our country means as much as a whole sentence in yours." She got back at him when the train passed a sign saying "Look out for the locomotive" by telling him, ". . . our sign posts just say 'Danger.' We haven't time for a whole sentence, and we say 'Engine.' It's shorter than 'Locomotive.'" After which verbal nose-thumbing the New Yorker, not surprisingly, left for the smoking-car and Faith gleefully tells her readers, "I quietly scored one for Canada."

She hated the American silver dollars—"great, ugly, heavy things"— and even got in a crack at the "flapping" eagle and the motto, "In God we trust"—"as if our American friends ever trusted anything or anybody except themselves."

But she enjoyed "the mellowed loveliness" of the landscape beyond the train window, and although she had problems with her luggage when she changed trains, she thought the policemen in New York wonderful: "It made me feel rather important to have a long line of drays held in check by an uplifted finger while one small woman passed over." Her first night "in Yankeedom" was spent in "a pretty suburban town filled with summer homes, revolutionary memories and Washington relics," and then she was off to explore New York City.

Faith's unnamed escort could not show her Broadway and Fifth Avenue without informing her that Canada had nothing like it, and Faith observes, "The Americans speak of Canada benevolently, as though it were a town or small and rather insignificant city." Being Faith, she gave back as good as she got—meekly, as she describes it, which her escort found rather confusing: "'No . . . we have lawns and boulevards and shade trees. But, of course, you couldn't afford that in New York.' He was not quite sure which way I meant it, and changed the subject."

As time passed Faith grew accustomed to the brashness of her hosts. Her defensiveness and hostility largely disappeared and were replaced by her usual response to the foibles of others: humour and a gentle sarcasm. She brought her readers the sights, sounds and smells of that torrid summer city: the street vendors, the "misfit stores" specializing in secondhand clothing, the abundance of inexpensive flowers sold on the street corners, the shop-girls, the beggars—"There is one man who stands on Sixth avenue, and his face haunts me for hours after I have passed . . . so woefully thin, with such sharp bones and shrunken flesh and faded blue eyes. . . ."

Then there was Tiffany's. Faith, who never really cared for "old china and stones, fossils and bric-a-brac," spent two hours wandering in "this palace beautiful." Dazzled by displays of diamonds, gold, incredible opals, overwhelmed by Tiffany's collection of rare bronzes and marbles, she declared: "Shopping in New York is a delight—a fascination. Like a jolly little water drop you roll recklessly along in the great human river, swept on by the strong, vital current, whirled in and out and about through the roar and rush, until you find yourself stranded in some quiet shallow, with empty purse and plethora of parcels, breathless and excited, yet quite ready for another plunge."

Like the rapids at the Sault, the energy and vitality of that extraordinary city had caught Faith up and were carrying her along. Defensiveness and inferiority complex forgotten, she opened herself up to the experience. Only the heat and humidity gave her problems, and she decided to take herself to Coney Island: "I hadn't the faintest idea of how to get there; but that did not make any difference. It is impossible to get lost in New York if you speak any known language. And I knew that immediately I stepped upon the street it would appear as though the city were full of officials whose sole business it was to direct people to Coney Island."

The bands, the bathing pavilions, roller-rinks, candy stalls, concert halls—Faith gave her readers a taste of them all, and herself a taste of her first hot dog: "The fragrant odor of sausages greeted me, and I stopped to watch the celerity with which the vendor clapped the hot sausage between the long white roll. . . . He did a good trade and the sausage rolls were very nice—I tried one."

For a woman who enjoyed crossing the main road at Souris, Prince Edward Island, in her bathing costume, she seems surprisingly disconcerted by the bathers on Coney Island, but chiefly because the women bathers had a sublime disregard for their appearance:

> They were stretched all along the white sand . . . fat men and fatter women, clad in heavy, ugly, shapeless suits that dripped and streamed about them. The women wore inverted cone-shaped baskets—called hats—that were supposed to protect their heads.
>
> I sat upon the pier and watched them, wondering if I had ever seen women look quite so shapeless or so ugly. They were so very fat or so very thin; the bathing dresses flopped away down over their ankles, the hats flopped over their ears, at every step the fat ones shook, at every step the lean ones shuddered.
>
> But they ran out to meet the incoming waves; they screamed and shouted, coming in occasionally to sit in the sand, dig for clams, dine off cheese and lager beer.

Although Faith's Victorian upbringing with her brigadier-general mother and the oh-so-correct Margaret Reikie initially gives her problems when she encounters such uninhibited physical displays—particularly from women—the vitality of the scene has once again won her over.

Faith's reaction to Wall Street and the New York Stock Exchange is much the same, as she watched the inmates "grouping and ungrouping, shouting, gesticulating, sometimes jumping, tearing up bits of paper to add to the falling snow-shower." The uproar and exuberance are at first stupefying: "Dr. Buchan allowed me one day to accompany him through the maddest ward of the Toronto Asylum. . . . I saw very little difference. By and by I began to see into the confusion a little."

Faith ends her New York columns with a description of her last night there in a hot bedroom on Sixth Avenue close to the elevated railway, the "El." This passage makes it clear that the editor in all her wanderings had visited the underworld of New York's Other Half that day:

I had wakened suddenly and could not sleep again, so I rose and sat down by the window, longing for a breath of sweet, pure air. . . . I put my head down on the sill and watched the passing trains, counting the few passengers, and noting the grotesque shadows that flickered in the roadway below the mass of upreared trestle work.

The electric light lit the street up and down, revealing every passer-by . . . solitary spectres coming out of the darkness and vanishing again into the darkness. Then came the roll of a gleaming-eyed ambulance, a group of young men, a policeman pacing steadily, a woman clasping a little child and muttering indistinctly.

I held my watch in the gleam of the light and its hands pointed to 2.

I thought of the slums, through whose depths I had wandered in the afternoon hours—those terrible slums filled with festered tenements, violent odors and squalid women and children. I remembered the riotous wealth of the uptown marble mansions. And in the heart of the heated night, while the fevered city pulse flowed sluggishly, I realized how all-mighty and all-pitiful—aye, and all-enduring also—must be the God of New York.

Contrasts always fascinated Faith, and there were few greater than the contrast between Coney Island and Newport, the wealthy playground of New York's "Four Hundred."[15] Presumably one of her hosts was Dr. Storer, but she also stayed with a Quaker family from Philadelphia who had a summer home in Newport. It is very possible she made the acquaintance of one of the family members during the women's congress in Toronto; not surprisingly, many of the women in the forefront of the women's movement, such as Susan B. Anthony, came from Quaker families.

Faith does not always reveal her contacts, and sometimes it is only months later a reader discovers that she was doing other things with other people—often with an eye to advancing her career, or getting her work published elsewhere. During this first American trip it is safe to say that there was a great deal more going on behind the scenes than is immediately obvious from her "Under the Stars and Stripes" columns.

There was contrast even within Newport itself. There was the holiday life of her Quaker hosts in their old family home, with its low ceilings, small window-panes and heavy front door with its unusual brass knocker, mealtimes gathered around the long plain wooden table, where the conversation moved from "bright, breezy talk . . . the pretty 'thee' and 'thou' in the family speech" to Canadian politics and annexation. There were expeditions "on the darkling waters of Narrangesett [sic] bay, where our oars lit with the gleaming phosphorescence of jelly fish. . . . Then came an hour on the broad piazza, when the daughter of the house sang softly to her guitar, dropping after a while into our own national anthem."

And, of course, there were the Belmonts, the Astors, the Vanderbilts, the Paran-Stevens, who lived in the "cottages" of Newport—the marble mansions of the Four Hundred. There is no evidence that Faith had access to any of them, nor is it likely, but they gave her a chance to do something at which she excelled—to observe, and to observe them observing each other:

> It amused me much to see how watchful each is of the other. Seeing without seeming to see, these matrons and maids know exactly who is present, what gowns are displayed, and which are most becoming. They know, too, where the masculine interest centres, and exercise certain little manoeuvres for controlling the same. . . . They have a wonderful self-possession, these New York society maids. They have the shibboleths of their world at their finger tips. . . .

And here is Faith on the way the Four Hundred shook hands:

> I have watched it with much amusement at the Casino. It is not at all cordial or expressive; it is very stiff and dab-by.

You hold your hand out, palm up, and on a level with your
elbow. The gentleman brings his up to the same level, palm
down. He places his fingers above yours, thumb below, and
gives your hand one little downward jerk, absurdly suggestive of a pump-handle.

Or the way a gentleman lifted his hat, which "must be lifted quite from
the back; not at the front."

There were veils, veils everywhere, of every kind, worn both morning and afternoon: "pretty lacey affairs that look like bits of sea foam.
White net, dotted with large, soft white dots; also white net, dotted with
black and deeply bordered; black, dotted with black, and occasionally a
mass of soft tulle."

Did those veils remind Faith of a grieving Alice Freeman twenty years
earlier, swamped by black mourning veils at Margaret Reikie's funeral,
vowing she would never, ever, wear a veil herself? If they did, how she
must have marvelled at what had happened to Alice in those intervening
years, since she had become Faith Fenton of "Woman's Empire."

Faith's visit to Philadelphia undoubtedly came about through the
good services of her Quaker friends, and she used it to make contact
with some American editors, in particular the editor of *The Ledger*,
which she chose largely because it looked "solid and respectable and
Conservative and reliable." In this case, she met not only the editor, but
also the millionaire owner of the paper, George W. Childs, with whom
she got on famously. However, there was another encounter with an
American editor of a Morristown newspaper, *The Stars and Stripes*, that
did not go so well.

Since this was Faith's first meeting with an editor in the United
States, she was extremely nervous, and apparently quite thrown by the
gentleman's way of dressing: "I am not accustomed to editors in broad-
cloth—we do not have them in Canada—and the shock sent my eyes
down to the floor."

Why broadcloth was so outrageous she does not explain, but in
Canada, which tended to follow Britain in matters of dress, men's clothing changed very little in the 1880s and 1890s and it was still *de rigueur*
to wear a frock-coat or a morning coat in town. Tweeds or serge would

be kept for the privacy of one's home—as, presumably, would broad-cloth. So conservative were men's attitudes to fashion that, in 1893, it caused a sensation in London when a member of the aristocracy wore trousers with turn-ups in the House of Commons.

The ensuing conversation has patriotic Faith on the defensive once again:

> "I see from the New York papers that your government is having some bad scandals," [the editor] remarked presently. "As, well, over here we believe Sir John was a good deal of a corruptionist."
>
> "Yes," I answered. "He was very much admired by the Americans."

It was a cheap shot, but it was enough to render the editor of *The Stars and Stripes* satisfactorily speechless.

Both in Philadelphia and Morristown, Faith saw something of another American "Other Half"—the black population. Apart from occasional editorial comment on problems with the black population in the South, there were virtually no accounts of this nature in Canadian newspapers, and certainly none by a woman. There are two specific references, and both give a somewhat rose-tinted picture of nineteenth-century black reality:

> But I fear me I have wearied my readers with comparisons—and yet I have not told you that Philadelphia holds over a million people, and of these about 100,000 are colored. There is a section of the city almost given over to them. I got into it by chance on the first day of my arrival and experienced a novel sensation. They are well housed, and many of them are well-educated. They have their own schools and churches; and make, generally, good citizens. . . . One prominent citizen told me they make desirable citizens—another informed me that they were undesirable— "bumptious," I think he said. But the general opinion is that

they are infinitely better than the Italians and Russian Jews
that are flooding the eastern states and settling in large
numbers in Philadelphia and elsewhere.

"A section of the city almost given over to them" is, of course, a
euphemism for "ghetto," but it is unlikely that Faith saw it that way. She
appears to see nothing wrong with blacks being held as a race apart, and
she records the hostile attitude towards Italians and Russian Jews without expressing her own views. She had used the same approach in her
own country when speaking of the Native population.

In Morristown, New Jersey, Faith and her companion attended "a colored folks service." She was clearly exhilarated by the experience, and a
little thrown by the uninhibited exuberance—much as she was by that of
the women bathers on Coney Island—but not enough to stop her taking
her usual copious notes in shorthand:

> The preacher was a direct importation from Carolina. . . .
> He had a voice [that was] clear, vibrant, melodious and
> powerful beyond anything I have ever heard. How he
> hurled out the bell-like tones, that despite their volume
> never jarred because of their perfect roundness! . . . In a
> few minutes I was listening half-magnetized:
>
> "Run, fo' de thunder is rollin'; run fo' de lightnin' is
> blazin' de word 'damnation' in red streaks on de clouds;
> run fo' de wind is sighin' an' screamin'; run to de Rock dat
> will keep off de downpour for de vials of wrath—run—
> run—run—An' may yo' all be saved, is de praar ob yo'
> humble servant, Peter Slimkins."

During the ensuing scene in which the congregation was exhorted to
give generously to God's humble servant, Faith was overcome by a nervous fit of the giggles, but she too put something in the collection plate.
It would have been hard to resist the preacher's eloquent appeal.

Whatever Faith Fenton's prejudices may have been, and she appears to have been less rigid than a lot of other Victorians, there is not the least doubt that she enjoyed the "colored folks service" far more than another service she attended with a woman friend in the same town in an "old Scotch church. Clap-boarded, square-towered, uncompromising, it stands as it has stood for over 100 years, a veritable 'kirk.'"

The text chosen was: "The woman, she gave me of the tree, and I did eat." While outside the window the katydids shrilled on and on, "the preacher, solemn and severe, rambled on about the woman's sin—her greater guilt—her just punishment; while he fearlessly plunged into the theological quagmire of 'original sin,' and generously gave Eve two-thirds of the blame, two of Eve's daughters sat listening to the shrill, never-ceasing assent from thousands of tiny chirpers: 'Katy did it; she did, she did.'"

Contrasts again: on her last day in New York before she returned home, she and her young woman friend from Morristown arrived at Park Place on the "elevated" to find themselves in the middle of a disaster: a five-storey jerry-built tenement had collapsed two days earlier, killing eighty people, and the salvage crews were still digging through the wreckage, looking for bodies. A few minutes later and they were on "brilliant, beautiful Broadway," and it seemed to Faith a million miles away from the horror of Park Place. Soon, however, they too had forgotten that "vision of down-town suffering in a whirl of up-town delights."

Like many another New York visitor, Faith spent her last few hours in Yankeedom "in and out at Macey's and Brummel's, Pond's and Huyler's, sometimes buying, always admiring, and wishing ever for the Midas touch that would turn our pennies into gold."

It would have been no hardship for Faith to include items on fashion and decoration in "Woman's Empire." She loved clothes, and her favourite colour for winter was "a warm rich crimson." The studio photographs she had taken around 1890 show that she had a real sense of style, choosing clothes with deep colours and dramatic lines. Her favourite stone was the opal, and she deeply regretted it was not her birth-stone, so that she could wear it without risking misfortune. Her detailed descriptions of stage costume go beyond journalistic accuracy. Here is her account of the costumes for the opera *Carmen*:

The Carmen dresses were very artistic, that worn in the first act—a crimson skirt with white bodice—being perhaps the most effective. In the second act a dainty dress of robin's egg blue satin, with panels of canary colour, the whole exquisitely hand-painted with what seemed a wild rose vine, made Carmen a gypsy most fair to view . . . and in the fourth act a robe of heliotrope satin shimmered beneath a network of gold spangles.

Little wonder she felt the need to apologize for "trespassing on Touchstone's domain"! Quite apart from her feelings about the opera—she found Carmen less admirable than Marguerite in *Faust*—she obviously had taken pleasure in its beauty. As Faith expressed it: "Women love the beautiful things of life so dearly . . . the poetry of life is not only congenial but necessary to them, without which their womanhood becomes a hard and repellent thing."

In spite of her misgivings and her very Canadian trepidation, Uncle Sam's dominion had won Faith over. Out of the carriage window she whispered an overwhelmed and dazed goodbye: "'Good-bye you fascinating, beautiful, awful New York,' I murmured; 'you enchanting, terrible city good-bye.'" She concludes the series on a rather self-consciously patriotic note that stylistically echoes her title: "And with the morning sunshine I awakened gladly once more, under the Union Jack."

After Coney Island and Broadway, the Casino at Newport and rowing on the phosphorescent waters of Narragansett Bay, after being shown the gilded cup and saucer of the Emperor of Brazil from among the treasures of a newspaper tycoon, shrinking back that fall into buttoned-down Miss Alice Freeman, Junior Book Classes teacher at Ryerson School, must have been very difficult indeed.

IX

Head of the Lady Journalists

I smiled a little at first at your enthusiasm, and, then, at
a second reading, I grew grave. To know that one's
words are so implicitly relied upon, that one's thought
about life is so simply accepted, should make the woman
who writes very careful. Do not idealize me. I am only a
woman and a desperately human one.

> Faith Fenton, "Woman's Empire," 1893—*in answer to
> an admiring letter.*

ON THE LAST DAY OF THE OLD YEAR, Faith sat at her desk writing the first
"Woman's Empire" column for 1892. Outside her window an east wind
shook the street-lamp, sending fantastic shadows across the roadway
beneath a starless, cloud-covered winter sky. She was just back from a
pilgrimage to Cataraqui, and her visit to the grave of Sir John A.
Macdonald was the subject of her final column for 1891.

In Kingston she had been the guest of George Monro Grant, principal of Queen's College, who, as a young man, had preached to such
well-connected church-goers of St. Andrew's in Ottawa as Sir Charles
and Lady Tupper, but how she came to meet him and to be his guest she
does not say. It was Principal Grant who introduced her to her guide on
the trip, the Reverend Dr. Williamson, Macdonald's brother-in-law, who
also taught at the university.

On their journey to the cemetery, Dr. Williamson had told Faith
"many things of Sir John himself, incidents of his early life, traits of

character known only to those who stood closest," but unfortunately she chose not to share such intimate details with her readers. However, "Woman's Empire" readers learned that Macdonald's father was "a good violinist for a dance," and that his mother was original and humorous—traits inherited by her celebrated son.

As in her tribute, Faith's feelings are on full display, but the overwhelming emotion here is disbelief that he is gone. Yet though she says she feels his spirit is still alive somehow, somewhere, there is a sense of her putting the past behind her: "I gathered a few green blades of grass, laid my face for one brief instant upon the cool, moist earth, and came away. . . ."

The memories of that charming man with the magnetic personality, whom she may have first glimpsed as little Alice Freeman in Bowmanville, would never leave her, and the private Faith Fenton would be a Conservative all her life. But although the reins of power were still in the hands of the Tories, led by Sir John Thompson, the lady journalist was about to make powerful allies whose political preferences lay elsewhere—even though they were not supposed to have any political preferences whatsoever. Whether it was fortuitous or whether it was calculated, the apparent shift in Faith's allegiance would leave her perfectly placed when the succession of Tory premiers after Macdonald gave way to the Liberals, and to Sir Wilfrid Laurier, in 1896.

By 1892 "Woman's Empire" occupied from three to five columns in *The Empire*, and the name "Faith Fenton" was often incorporated into the headline for that issue: Faith Fenton Talks of Theosophy; Faith Fenton Talks of Mr. Barrie's Latest Book; Faith Fenton Visits a Day Nursery. There were still battles for space with her editor, but now she sometimes won and left him "growling on the field." There were several subheadings that her readers must have looked out for each week: "Among Our Books"; "Here and There"; "Odds and Ends." One of these, "As You Like It," would later develop into a separate column of its own written by Faith Fenton.

Among these columns, readers would often find Faith's response to their enquiries, their opinions and their speculations about her. Some of these readers were obviously regular correspondents, and some of them were men. One of the men, "L'Alsacienne," may have thought to conceal his sex by using the feminine French ending. He didn't fool Faith, who firmly inserted the word "sir" in her replies to his letters. There is a faintly flirtatious buzz about some of this correspondence—not in Faith's language so much as in the nature and "tone" of the questions to which she responded.

"L'Alsacienne" didn't fool Faith, but some of Faith's readers wondered if she was fooling them. Could this strong, independent journalist who travelled all over and who spoke her mind *really* be a woman? Sara Jeannette Duncan had assumed the identity of a man, but here was a new twist: was this a man posing as a woman? In one of her "Odds and Ends" columns Faith quoted this comment from a correspondent: "'If I had the slightest doubt concerning your sex, it would all have flown when I read that you were allowed to remain in the lecture hall, after the gentlemen had retired, to learn the mysteries of the divided skirt.'"

After a wry introduction to this piece of speculation, Faith continues in a serious vein: "If I had been born a man, I should have chosen to be a diplomat, an ambassador, one sent out to represent Canada. . . . But I suppose even the divided skirt will not make women eligible for embassies." It has taken a hundred years, but women have now begun to move into those posts—with or without divided skirts. And Faith Fenton's diplomatic gifts would have a chance to flower in the 1890s.

Success brought piles of correspondence, gifts of all kinds: flowers—once, even, a garter!—and books, many, of course, from authors who hoped Faith Fenton would give them a nod of approval in her "Among Our Books" section. It would appear that some of the editors were in a double bind over their female colleague's popularity—they needed her readership to boost circulation, but resented her success:

"Take this thing off my desk; it has been staring at me for the past week or more," said the editor.

"My mail shouldn't come to you," I said reproachfully.

"Well, this got here somehow. Open it," he commanded.

I cut the binding string and opened the booklet full of pretty etchings, and read the few words of kindly inscription from an Empire reader; then pointed to the date.

"See that you acknowledge that next week. You should have done so long ago," was the peremptory response to my pointing.

It's a way the editor has, when he's in the wrong, to take

the bull by the horns and make you feel as if you were the guilty party.

It says not a little about the significance of "Woman's Empire" to the newspaper's circulation that by now Faith was unafraid to share such conflicts in her professional life with her readers. Later in the same year, in a column entitled "Women As Readers," Faith observes of the paper of choice in a household: "Who cons [studies] that paper most if not the women of the household. And who is it decides what paper shall come into the home . . . but these same quick, out-reaching women intelligences? . . . Most journals have come to recognize that the paper that gets into a house . . . must be one that will in some department win the favor of women."

In April 1892—presumably during Alice Freeman's Easter break—Faith Fenton made her first trip to Ottawa. There is no doubt she could have visited Ottawa before she did, and one can only suppose she did it now because she had made the right connections during her visits to Rivière-du-Loup, the East Coast, and, finally, during the Kingston trip three months earlier.

As a mere lady journalist with a column for women, she would not have needed to assemble such a stellar cast of contacts, but Faith never saw herself simply as a purveyor of chit-chat and society gossip. The three Ottawa columns under the heading "About Canada's Capital" give very little clue to her private meetings with political figures and very little interesting information about them. They describe the city and the Houses of Parliament, and list some of the members Faith knows already by appearance: "Mr. Laurier, Sir Richard Cartwright, Mr. Mulock in the Opposition: and on the Government side Sir John Thompson, Mr. Foster, Sir Adolphe Caron, Mr. Carling, Mr. Weldon, Mr. Tupper and Mr. Chapleau."[1]

Apart from a tour of the parliamentary library that was her "chiefest delight in Ottawa," the columns reflect Faith's cynicism about the dedication of members of Parliament—a cynicism that goes back to Stella—and her interest in good-looking men: "I . . . look across at the press gallery, endeavouring to find a handsome man among the busy staff. Failing in this I turn my attention to the floor again. . . . Mr. Laurier is the handsomest man on the one side, Dr. Weldon on the other, so I decide, although both sides boast of some superb specimens of French-Canadian manhood—great dark-eyed, broad-shouldered men who might pose as painters' models."

The tone is so light, so flippant and traditionally "female," that one might wonder what Faith was doing in Ottawa and, given the nature of the trip, whether she had made, or indeed needed, any significant contacts for this type of journalism. After all, she didn't even sit in the Press Gallery like a journalist; she was in the Ladies Gallery with the other females. Again, it is only in later columns that she shows her hand, and one realizes that much of what happened during her trip was kept from her readers—and from the editors of *The Empire*. And there is also the fact that she stayed in the Russell House while she was in Ottawa.

The Russell House was, in Faith's words, "really an adjunct of the buildings on the hill. Here it is, in the airy rotunda, that the members gather after an exciting day in the Commons to discuss the situation; here it is that quiet little caucuses knot themselves about the corridors outheroding Herod in dark designs. . . ."

The Russell House hotel, at the corner of Sparks and Elgin streets, was indeed much more than a mere hotel, and some major newspapers maintained offices there. It was where many MPs stayed when the House was in session. Wilfrid Laurier was one, and Faith saw him in the dining-room:

> Not far away sits Mr. Laurier with his pretty dark-eyed wife. . . . There is altogether something very attractive about the Opposition leader—something in his face and bearing that is very winning to a woman . . . always I say: "I wish he were on our side. I'm sure he's quite nice enough to be a Conservative," which is the very highest compliment I can pay to this honorable and clever gentleman.[2]

Other eminent parliamentarians Faith recognized across the dining-room were Sir Peter Mitchell, one of the Fathers of Confederation, and William Mulock, the postmaster general.[3] She does some name-dropping and then shares with her readers a laugh at her own expense:

> "Waiter," I say, "who is that very clever-looking young gentleman who has just entered?" "That's a drummer, miss." I finish my fruit and venture another enquiry. "Do you notice that elderly man, rather care-worn, walking up the aisle? Do you know who he is?" "That's a waiter, miss," responds my servitor gravely, and then I cease my search for geniuses of state.

Although Faith Fenton's salary from *The Empire* may well have increased by 1892, it is extremely unlikely that she paid for her stay at the Russell House, but it seems doubtful that her editors at *The Empire* would voluntarily have paid her way. They may have been *told* to pay because of her influence, or an unnamed sponsor may have funded the trip. Faith's usual pattern was to stay in the establishments specially run for women travelling on their own—in fact, her column for January 23, 1892, is called "Women Wayfarers" and is devoted to giving her readers information on "two New York Institutions that are of special interest to women, particularly those who travel occasionally and in an independent way." By 1892 not only was Faith saying to other women, "Look at what I'm doing," she was now pointing out that they could do what she was doing, and showing them how to be "utterly alone, utterly unknown, and altogether jolly." But the Russell House stay most likely reflects the company she was keeping. Faith Fenton was out of her usual league and into another.

For her summer saunterings of 1892, Faith returned again to the islands of Georgian Bay and to the Sault, taking with her one of her younger sisters.

Identified only as "the little sister," this was probably seventeen-year-old Grace, who shared some of her adventurous big sister's expeditions. Among all those brothers and sisters there were three to whom she was particularly close—Grace, Florence (at this time twenty-one years old), and Fred, whose home she shared for many years, and with whose wife she seems to have had a warm relationship.

This time around Faith watched from the bank as the First Officer on their steamer, the *City of Midland*, accompanied Grace who, "half afraid and wholly entreating," wanted to shoot the rapids, just as her big sister had done. And this time, when it was her sister out there, Faith "stood with anxious eyes" as "the tiny canoe shot out into the middle of the stream, and tossed down through the white foam."

Faith has no difficulty finding new material for her readers, and returns again to "the Indians we see here and there skirting the shores in their tiny canoes." In 1892 she is a little more outspoken in her feelings: "I am always pitiful for a vanishing race; and though the Indian of today may hold little resemblance to the fierce vindictive braves of a century ago, yet the same blood is theirs, the same restless instinct; and in our advancing civilization we have forgotten oftentimes to be just or merciful."

There was a considerable vogue for travel articles in the nineteenth century since, for most people, armchair travel was all they could afford and the whole process was difficult and time-consuming. Faith attended lectures in Toronto given by explorers in darkest Africa, such as Stanley, and lady travellers to the Far East, like Mrs. Mountford. On this trip she directly counsels women to follow in her footsteps, and see their own country:

> I have told you of the six days' trip and the three days' trip, but there is yet even a one day's journey possible. . . . I do not recommend what I have not tried, friends. I give always the best of my knowledge and experience to the gentle women whose kind eyes search weekly the columns of the Woman's Empire; and to the weak ones and the busy ones—ay, and the poor ones too, for these trips are wonderfully low-priced. . . .

Here are the comfort-words again, "gentle," "kind," to encourage women to break out of a familiar rut—so reassuring for a well-bred woman to know it is not just "all right," to exclaim, "How brown one grows and how hungry!"

But Faith Fenton was about to urge her English-Canadian readers to break out of an even deeper rut. Here she was treading on treacherous ground, and she knew it; you couldn't live in the Toronto of the 1890s and not know it. She would be challenging the deeply entrenched prejudices of race and religion brought from an old world and made more bitter by a war fought on the Plains of Abraham, and Riel's hanging in Regina. Faith was to spend the month of August 1892 in Quebec and to devote eight columns to *la belle province*.

Faith's Quebec columns have no umbrella heading, apart from "Summer Saunterings," which may have been a deliberate choice. Perhaps if she had given them such a title as "Under the Fleur-de-Lis," many Ontarians would not have read them. As usual, each column is headed by a poem that has nothing to do with the topic and is usually taken from another publication, generally American. And, as usual, Faith builds up her pictures through observation of people rather than description of place, although there are more scenic details in these articles. However, this time she obviously felt the need to make a very clear statement of her own position:

> We, who are of English Ontario, do not know our country unless we have visited this French province and formed some conception of the race and creed that make its existing conditions and needs so different from our own.
>
> I am convinced that the lack of sympathy between the provinces is chiefly due to lack of knowledge. . . . I, who am essentially English, find many a prejudice vanishing as I travel in this French Canada, while day by day my indifference for these, my countrymen, is developing into real, kindly regard.

> I am not afraid to tell English Canadians what is true; that
> the bitterness and prejudice between the races and creeds is
> largely of our own making, and that it is our bigotry and our
> selfishness that forms the chiefest barrier to unity.

Issuing such a statement in *The Empire* took about as much courage
as running the rapids at the Sault, for not only was Faith Fenton telling her
readers to open their minds, she was telling them theirs was the greater
prejudice. However, having made such a forceful declaration, she does not
continue to preach at her public, but allows her articles to speak for her.

Faith Fenton's travels in Quebec took her, first to Quebec City, and
then by rail on the Ontario and Lake St. John Railway two hundred
miles north into the Laurentians, to Lac St. Jean—she calls it "Lake St.
John"—and the tiny settlement of Roberval. She had originally hoped to
go on to Anticosti, but it would have meant a journey by steamer to
Labrador and then taking her chances on a schooner or hiring one, and
"the possibility of having to charter a whole schooner for one small
woman dismayed even the Woman's Empire. . . ."

Quebec City enchanted her. She took her readers with her in *calèches*
as she drove around that ancient, walled city, let them see the old stone
houses and the steep flights of steps up the hills to the great citadel, let
them hear with her the sound of French around them in that city of bells:
"There is such a tolling and jangling and crying out of bells. . . .
Sometimes a solemn, deep-throated monotone, sometimes duos and trios
of sharper clanging, but most often a clamorous outpouring that fills the
old city and overflows down the blue St. Lawrence, to break in faint
melody upon the banks of Isle d'Orleans."

She took them into the great Quebec fur stores, with their floors covered with "huge glossy bears and tigers, whose heads lift themselves with
glaring eyes and fierce fangs about our feet. . . . The proprietor being a
Frenchman it followed that his entire staff were the perfection of courtesy, and we were permitted at will . . . to array ourselves in the prettiest
garments, and standing before long mirrors, to behold ourselves for once
glorified into beautiful women."

She took "Woman's Empire" readers to the market with her to buy
armfuls of sweet peas and let them hear her trying out her French with

ever-increasing confidence. At first she was defeated by what she called the "patois":

> My English queries were invariably met by a shrug and the inevitable "Sappo." "Whatever does that mean?" I enquired of a citizen soon after my arrival.
>
> "It is really 'Je ne sais pas' condensed into patois," was the answer.

But then there came the gratifying moment when she asked the way of a young lad "in the very best text-book French" and got the reply, "I don't speak French." Although she added that she didn't know whether to feel complimented or the reverse, she was clearly delighted.

Much of Faith's word-picture of Quebec City was done from memory, because she confided that her notebook had been sadly neglected. She shares one of her brief entries with her readers: "Describe Quebec (if possible)—narrow streets (must not be called lanes), caleches, patois (take care of spelling), markets (women sitting on ground), Lower Town (indescribable)." She added, "My note book and pencil lie idle while I wander through this picturesque old Canada . . . permitting the spirit of the place to enthrall me and sway me as it will."

There is only one political allusion in the Quebec columns, and that is to the Quebec Liberal leader, Honoré Mercier, who had been the voice of his people's anguish over the Riel affair and leader of the attack on Macdonald's vision of the Dominion of Canada. It was Mercier who, in 1888, had pushed through provincial Parliament the bill compensating the Jesuits for the confiscation of their estates that had created much of the anti-Quebec feeling in Ontario. On her visit to the Parliament Buildings, Faith asked her companion why there wasn't a portrait of Mercier among the official oil-paintings:

> My companion gives an expressive shrug. "It is taken down," he said. "It is in the cellar."
>
> Poor Mr. Mercier. How very sorry I am for him. Looking

about in this luxurious Senate chamber, with the splendid portraits of statesmen lining the walls, and remembering that portrait degraded to cellar depths, I realize the greatness of his fall. I wish they had not taken his portrait down, still more that it had not been necessary to do so. To fall from so great a height is a shock sufficient to kill any man.[4]

The tone is only lightly sardonic, but Faith Fenton displays here more than just a touch of animosity towards the man who had led the Opposition against her beloved chieftain. Although she found many of her prejudices vanishing on her travels, her political views remain, for the most part, unchanged. However, the comments on Mercier are the only exception to the affection and delight with which the Quebec columns are written: "Oh you dear old Quebec. . . . My pen flies fast over the paper, but it cannot keep pace with my longing to tell you of my wanderings. . . . there may be Torontos anywhere, my friends, but there can be only one Quebec." Quite a statement from a woman who constantly sang the praises of her own "pretty young city."

Quebec was enchanting, but the wild Laurentians through which the train passed on her journey to Lac St. Jean were more than that. They were enthralling, overpowering—everything that a romantic nineteenth-century woman could ask for. Faith gives her readers some gloriously gothic description as the train took her 1,600 feet above the St. Lawrence through wild mountain peaks and alongside deep gorges before dropping down again into the tiny settlement of Roberval. Here one is reminded of Sir Walter Scott rather than Dickens:

We are climbing up into the very heart of the Laurentides [Laurentians]—those blue-misted peaks that stand as sombre outguards of Quebec . . . beside a swift flowing river . . . and, frowning down upon it, so close that the yellow water is darkened by the gloom, are numberless precipitous pine-covered peaks, whose solemn magnificence equals, even surpasses, that Thunder Cape that overlooks Superior's stormy waters. How sombrely beautiful it is! I look up at the dark heights as one after another they appear and disappear. . . .

With a gothic novel, *Doom of the Mamelons*, as her reading material on the journey, Faith peoples the Laurentians with "brave men and lovely, barbaric women—a kingly race of primeval days; a mighty race mayhap—for so myth whispers—whose monuments are these sombre secret-holding mountains, whose requiem is sung by this rushing white-foamed river." Here the writing is less like Walter Scott and more like Rider Haggard.

Contrasts again when she reached Roberval, a tiny settlement in the middle of that magnificent wilderness, with a luxury hotel large enough for three hundred guests, furnished in light oak and bird's-eye maple, with fine carpets on the floors, "telegraphic connection" with the outside world, electric light, and an Italian orchestra among the potted plants in the dining-room. Faith stood in her travelling dress at her window that first day and marvelled: "I am 200 miles north of Quebec. I have come through mountain masses and primeval woods, and out there beyond the uplands there are vast forests, while great rivers, as yet unnavigated, pour their waters into the lake that sparkles beneath my vision." Then she adds: "I say it to myself many times, and then smile again at the luxury that enterprise has brought to this verge of civilization. . . . tonight I am north of the Laurentides that guard the Ancient City, away on the very confines of civilization, and beyond this tiny settlement of Roberval, even all about it, is the unexplained, the mysterious, the unknown."

Of course, being Faith, she wanted to experience that unexplained, mysterious, unknown world on the edge of civilization. She did not restrict her visit to the delights of the interior-sprung mattresses and the electric light of the Roberval Hotel, but went on one of the camping trips organized by the hotel and guided by the Montagnais—one of the migratory hunting bands belonging to the Algonquian language group of Native peoples—from a nearby reserve.

Faith's portrait of the Montagnais catches both their romantic appearance and their harsh reality. It was the evils of civilization that corrupted them and made them miserable, in her eyes. To her they were the epitome of philosopher Jean-Jacques Rousseau's noble savage, who was still much beloved by nineteenth-century romantics. When she sees them on the trail she exclaims, "It was a marvel to me how swiftly and noiselessly they made their way through the woods, their easy pace carrying them with their loads quickly to vanishing distances, while we struggled after to find them afloat and placidly waiting our arrival." When she visited the reserve she found "canvas tents, very small and very dirty . . . bundles and babies and general confusion," and this time her exclamation is one of shock: "Dear heart! It is wonderful how meanly human beings can live and yet retain their humanity." She concluded: "Our Ontario Indians have become so distressingly civilized that they have quite lost the charm of romance. The Montaignais [sic] are yet *au naturel*, although they are not likely long to remain so, now that the railway skirts their mystic lake, bringing curious tourists within a few miles of their primitive camps."

Of the forty-mile expedition itself, Faith observed:

It is the real thing. It means guides and canoes and a supply of unspoilable provisions and an emergency chest. It means durable costumes, sunburn and mosquitoes, portages and rough scrambles and occasional bears. . . . Oh, the charm of it. Could words ever depict the blueness of the sky, the greenness of the trees, the swirl of the waters, the aroma of the pine, the swift flashing of our canoe, the grave guides' faces breaking into sober smiles at my laughter and delight. Oh the lovely aloneness of it all—so far away from men and women and bricks and newspapers.

I do not know how far we went. I did not care. Miles, I suppose; for miles are only minutes in rapids, you know. I should like to have gone all the rest of the way—clear to Chicoutimi. . . .

Back again in Quebec City, she devoted two articles largely to showing her readers something of the province's religious life—a daring-enough subject in a Conservative Ontario newspaper. She told her audience: "This

Grey Lady of the North . . . is a lady of fasts and feasts, of incense and of prayer. All day long the church doors swing open, all day long the incense burns and the lights glow. Every hour sees kneeling devotees at the altars, every hour beholds beads counted and offerings made."

One of the two columns describes a visit Faith made with a friend from Halifax to the shrine of Ste. Anne de Beaupré, thirty miles outside the city, on the Montmorency and Charlevoix Railway. She makes no judgmental statements about the blind faith of the supplicants, no comments about superstition, but her answer, "It is supposed," to her friend's question "Were they all cured?," posed when they pass "two high pillars built of crutches," speaks for her. Deeply moved by the hopelessness of those who came, and shaken by the suffering she saw—the bandaged eyes, the twisted and shaking limbs, the pews filled with crutches she describes for her readers the statue of Ste. Anne: "Loaded with . . . rings, bracelets, watches, pins . . . weighted with jewels slipped from the arms and fingers of her devotees . . . humbler offerings . . . spectacles from those who beg for or have received better eyesight, pipes and pouches from those who have given up smoking . . . sealed letters that lie like a drift of snow in the nooks of the pedestal." And she concludes: "Here, if anywhere, is the strong faith that moves mountains. . . . What matters it I say, so long as the strong faith is present and the cure is accomplished."

Armed with a letter of introduction to one of the Ursuline nuns, seventy-six-year-old Mother St. Croix, and accompanied by her French-Canadian hostess, Faith visited the Ursuline Convent in Quebec City, and gave "Woman's Empire" readers a lighthearted glimpse of life inside the convent walls.[5] They arrived on a feast day and, to Faith's amazement, the nuns were dancing:

> Snatches of music—of orchestra and women's voices in singing, floated from an adjoining room, whose door opened beyond the lattice work.
>
> "It must be a feast day," said my companion. "That is not sacred music."
>
> It was very pretty to hear the voices rising so high and sweet in melody, then breaking in snatches of soft laughter and speech.

> Across the court and through the open windows we saw black-robed figures flitting back and forth. Presently the movements took rhythm and step, the black robes fluttered, the spotless white bandeaux gleamed. Two figures . . . drifted in light galoppe past the windows, another pair, and yet another.

Such pieces must have been as much of a revelation to her Ontario readers, who would have formed their own opinions of convent life in an environment hostile to Roman Catholicism, to French language and culture and, for that matter, to the very province of Quebec.

Faith's conclusion to the Quebec series was a column on immigration—more specifically, an account of her visit to the Louise Embankment in the Lower City, timed for five o'clock in the morning, when a Dominion Line steamer was unloading steerage passengers. Obviously this visit had been set up in advance, since the information was brought by messenger from the immigration agent to the house where Faith was staying.

Faith details the physical set-up of the immigrant sheds, and the people who work there:

> The sheds are . . . really fine stone buildings, well fitted up . . . a post-office, a broker's office, a store and a restaurant. Above are the matron's private apartments and a number of simply furnished bedrooms . . . windows looking out on the rippling river, white walls, fresh white bed linen, blue coverlets, white toilet sets—I should rather like to sleep in one of them on a warm summer night.

But most of the piece is not so charming. Faith describes the groups of immigrants and gives the reader a verbatim account of the immigration officer's remarks:

> "The immigrants landing this morning are chiefly Swedes. . . .
> There are a few English and some Russian Jews also. We con-
> sider the Swedes and Norwegians the best class of immi-
> grants."
> . . . The fair skins, blue eyes, straight noses and bright
> looks of the Swedes contrasted favorably with the unkempt
> appearance of the solitary swarthy knot of Russian Jews
> who huddled together waiting for the ferry to take them to
> Levis for Grand Trunk shipment.

The anti-Semitism just below the surface of her observations would
have sat comfortably with Faith's readers. Canada was not a tolerant
country in the late nineteenth century, and the increasing arrival of
European immigrants only served to intensify the feelings of English
Canadians. Perhaps the only surprise is the fact that the English
appeared to be considered inferior to Scandinavians, but the officer
probably meant Irish. There were also twelve young English girls,
orphans perhaps, from a "Colonial Home," who had spent three months
there "to learn about life in Canada" and who would be found permanent places as servants.

The Swedish immigrants, who were on their way west to the
prairies, provided Faith with a pretty vignette:

> Presently one ruddy fellow picked up an old-fashioned
> accordion and began to play a waltz. There was a shuffle
> of heavy boots, a swaying of bodies, and then a young cou-
> ple were on the floor; another pair and another. They
> danced well, despite the heavy boots and corduroy suits of
> the men, and the ulsters and scarves of the girls. Some
> English girls looked on sympathetically and soon they too
> were dancing, while the accordion drew out its sweet
> melodies and the men's boots beat time.

The conclusion to the scene touches again on racial issues. In response to her observation that "human nature is the same everywhere," the officer remarked, "You would not say so if you were an immigration agent. . . . It is decidedly of higher grade in the Swede than in the Russian Jew, we think." Faith Fenton, who had an opinion on most things, had no comment of her own. She would encounter Russian-Jewish immigrants again, but the next time there would be a faint murmur of protest against the endemic anti-Semitism of her society.

With Miss Alice Freeman back in school again, "Woman's Empire" resumed its normal pattern for the remainder of 1892. Among the cheerful, bright columns on books and theatre visits are interspersed, as usual, Faith Fenton's pleas for public support for many of the charitable institutions of Toronto. In November she took her readers to the Children's Shelter run by the Children's Aid Society and showed them the small sufferers in an uncaring society:

> "These," [said Mrs. Embury] putting a hand on two small heads, "are a brother and sister of two and four years, children of drunken parents. Only last night a woman brought a two-months-old baby of the same family to me, saying that the mother had gone away, and there was no one to look after it. Of course I could not take it, at that age. The woman threatened to leave it on the doorstep, but finally went away. I do not know what she did with the baby."
>
> Only last night! I remembered the wind, the rain and the cold—and the cry of the forsaken baby seemed to ring even now down the dull street.

The conclusion is powerful, and there is more than an echo of Faith's admired Elizabeth Barrett Browning: "There is a great cry of the children going up in the land, a pitiful, bewildered cry of suffering and neglect—a cry that the laughter of happy childhood cannot drown. Let us answer it with what comfort and relief we may."

In December she went in disguise to a city dispensary for the poor, making a follow-up visit as herself. By now Faith Fenton was concerned that the various agencies in the city might be able to identify her, and put on a special show for her benefit. Her opinion of the city dispensary was positive, even though she felt the premises and the overcrowding left much to be desired—and even though the doctor there told her that, if she had two or three children to look after and less time to think of herself, "your pain would largely disappear."

Faith Fenton's Christmas column for 1892 also reflected her star status. There were letters for her readers, from Lady Agnes Macdonald, Emma Albani, and the actress Julia Marlowe, the originals of which are still among Faith's papers. There was also an apology from Lady Aberdeen, whose husband was about to become the governor general, written by her personal secretary, Teresa Wilson, for not being able to do the same herself, because of ill health. Faith says, "Because of her interest in Canada and Canadian women, her knowledge of us, and her prompt kindliness towards us, we do not look upon her as a stranger, but as a friend. . . ." In the next few months these would turn out to be prophetic words.

X

The White City

To what shall I liken it—this fair White City . . . ? A res-
urrected Pompeii, a modern Athens, a pleasure palace of
the Pharaohs? Yes, it is all these; but it is even more. . . .
I think of that quaint old vision of Mirzah and his happy
isles of the blest. And then my thought flits further to
that other White City, with its wondrous gates and shining street, whose people shall not be pilgrims as are
these I see, but who, having once entered, shall go out
no more.[1]

Faith Fenton, "Woman's Empire," 1893.

OVER THE YEARS FAITH FENTON AND ALICE FREEMAN had established a
pattern of life—a *modus vivendi*—that both could work with. Faith
Fenton's lifestyle occasionally made Alice Freeman late for work, and
latenesses were noted in the school records. By 1892 there were more
of them—usually about one a month—and only one other woman
teacher at Ryerson was regularly late, as Alice was. In 1891 and
1892, Alice Freeman's salary was $636, but in 1893 it drops to $597,
and the reason is that, for the first time, the careers of Alice and
Faith collided.

In May 1893, the World's Exposition was held in Chicago, and Faith
Fenton was there. She had obviously taken unpaid leave to attend, and it
would be interesting to know what reason Alice Freeman had given. She
was docked approximately three weeks' salary, and she seems to have

been in Chicago for just over two weeks. She is unlikely to have told the school authorities what Faith Fenton told "Woman's Empire" readers:

> This week at least I must devote to an account of that great World's Congress of Representative Women. . . . I think it due to our own Canadian women . . . that they should have as full an account as possible of this conference. The time for ridiculing such gatherings has gone by. Women have grown wiser, men more tolerant and generous. So that we know, and all fair-minded and progressive men acknowledge that a woman's conference is not a place of scandal and gossip; not a vantage ground for the promulgation of unfeminine views, not a stage from which unwomanly women can harangue men, but an assemblage for . . . wise, thoughtful discussion.

As in her Quebec columns, Faith felt the need to make a declaration, and the language she uses is business-like and undecorated. But in the twelve columns she devotes to the World's Fair, from the end of May to the beginning of August, Faith's prose is as embellished, as euphoric, as full of comfort-words as anything she had ever written. She is a woman who has had a vision, and her language is that of someone who has had a profound mystical experience. All this ecstasy for an exposition, however grand—why?

Her colleague "Pica" Kribs, who also attended the exhibition, did not have the same reaction. In a grumpy interview in *The Empire* on June 5, he admits that the exhibition is "indescribably grand," but goes on to find fault with almost everything, including the fact that it is in Chicago, which he characterizes as "the dirtiest city in America [with] the poorest hotel accommodation," and castigates "the grasping character of its people." He found many of the exhibits not entirely completed, although he gives high praise to the Canadian exhibit. Certainly he found much to admire, but the overall tone is far from eulogistic.

From her opening paragraph, where an exhausted Faith refused to go "Moody and Sankeyward" on Sunday with "a little lady in a brown cloak 'from off in Colorado,'" the impression is of someone dazzled and overwhelmed by her surroundings.[2] Alice was in Wonderland. What bliss to play hookey for the first time, to be in Chicago when she should have been Alice at Ryerson School! What heaven to be among women who dared to think and feel, and act in ways that women had never dared to do before:

> From my place at the press table I scanned the great build-ing. . . . Such a sea of upturned faces—such a wonderful gathering of women—thoughtful women, clever women, representative women, each one of whom had achieved some good work in her own land . . . journalists, educa-tionalists, business women, philanthropists, society women, physicians, lawyers, ministers, bankers. As the chairwoman Mrs. Sewall said, there was only one department of the world's work unrepresented, and although every civilized country had been scoured to discover one, there were no women engineers to be found.[3]

In fact, the main purpose of Faith Fenton's visit was to cover the meeting of the International Council of Women, which had been arranged to coincide with the World's Fair, and she was on the platform as a representative of the press for the advisory council, with her double identity made public for the first time: "Miss Alice Fenton Freeman (Faith Fenton)." Canada had sent delegates to the conference, and two of them, Mrs. Willoughby Cummings and Mrs. Mary Macdonnell, would be elected provisional vice-president and secretary of what would become the National Council of Women of Canada.[4] They would spear-head an umbrella organization that would combine women's groups of every conceivable kind—many with opposing views—to work towards change in every aspect of women's lives, and one of the prime propagan-dists of that new organization would be Faith Fenton.

With her customary sensitivity to what made her female contempo-raries fearful of change of any kind—that it was not so much the new ideas in themselves, but that those new ideas would make them somehow not female, "unfeminine," and therefore not appealing to men—Faith wrote a brilliant series of columns that contain far more about the social aspects of the fair, its sights, sounds, fashions, colours, than about the speeches from the platform.

Faith did not tell her women readers that they too *should* be like this, feel like this, or want to change that. Instead, she described people and evoked scenes in such a colourful and irresistibly fascinating way that those women must have been, like her little Halton correspondent five years earlier, "green with envy." She gave them specific advice on how they could make the trip if they wanted, where they could stay, and what it would cost. This time she also shared with them how light she travelled—a major accomplishment for a clothes-encumbered woman of the period—although modesty prevents mention of her unmentionables, her underwear: ". . . my luggage will consist of my favorite hand valise only. . . . Dress, consisting of black skirt and soft blouse waist; black coat; black straw hat; coat, with plenty of pockets; skirt, with a delightfully deep pocket also; rain cloak, rubbers and umbrella. That's the Woman's Empire, as a Chicago policeman will probably inventory her when her funds are all gone. . . ."

And as before, these columns that challenged a nineteenth-century woman's received views on appropriate behaviour are loaded with comfort-words. Faith describes the "novel and pretty sight" in the Palmer House Hotel: "There were women all about the luxurious and spacious rooms—women in pretty dinner dresses of dark silk, or in neat travelling gowns brightened for evening with soft lace and flowers—women gathered in knots, or walking with linked arms up and down the soft carpets . . . the sound of gentle speech in every accent, or merry laughter and kind words in the warm perfumed atmosphere."[5]

The Canadian contingent to the congress seems unthreatening:

> Someone touched me lightly on the shoulder, and I turned to find myself amid a group of Canadian women. . . . I was decidedly proud of them; they were all so prettily gowned—so womanly in appearance, yet bright and clever in converse. There was Mrs. S.A. Curzon, pale, delicate, yet ardent in spirit. . . . There was Mrs. John Harvie, graceful and calm as usual; Mrs. Mary McDonnell [sic], motherly

> and smiling . . . and pretty Miss Gibbs. . . . As I noted their
> pretty becoming gowns and gentle ways, I was woman
> enough to feel somewhat proud of my compatriots.

No shrieking sisters these, she is saying to the woman in Toronto, or Barrie or Niagara; see how gentle, calm, motherly—even pale and delicate—a woman activist can be. The atmosphere is perfumed, not poisonous. Here is Faith at her most subversive: "The day of the strong-minded frump has passed, and the day of the clever, deep, broad-thinking, daintily-gowned woman has arrived." If you do not fear the daintily gowned revolutionary, you are far less likely to fear her clever ideas.

Some of her euphoria may also be a reflection of how desperate she had felt nine years earlier, when she had read the columns of that other schoolteacher-turned-columnist, Sara Jeannette Duncan, at the New Orleans World's Fair and known that there was no escape for Alice Freeman from teaching. This time she was in the White City when she should have been at Ryerson, walking through the pavilions and listening to the myriad languages around her, watching Senegalese, Japanese, Swedish and Syrian, admiring the fine African faces, the fountains: "Beautiful Diana shone out like a golden dream beneath the powerful rays that flooded her superb figure. Rainbow sprays sparkled upward from the electric fountain. It was Venice glorified. It was a world of flame not in fierce burnings, but in pretty sparkling radiance—and we were drifting idly, merrily, in the heart of it."

But there was another reason for Faith's euphoria that had little to do with idle drift and everything to do with purpose and power. There was one distinguished visitor to the Chicago Fair that May 1893 who would have a real impact on Canada and a profound effect on the course of Faith Fenton's life. One of the keynote speakers of the conference was Ishbel, Countess of Aberdeen, who learned while she was in Chicago that her husband had been appointed governor general of Canada. At the end of the conference she accepted an invitation to serve as the first president of the newly formed National Council of Women of Canada (NCWC), which embraced many of the causes and organizations to which she was so passionately committed. It was the first in a series of overt political moves that the governor general's wife would make over the next five years.[6]

The evidence for the relationship between the governor general's wife and the lady journalist is contained in seven letters, one two-page telegram, two signed photographs and a small card—all that is left from what was clearly a fairly extensive correspondence between the years 1896 and 1909. Nowhere else does it exist. It cannot be found in "Woman's Empire" (though Faith does mention Lady Aberdeen), or in any of the Aberdeen diaries or papers. Only three issues remain in archival collections of the nineteen issues of the *Canadian Home Journal*, edited by Faith between 1895 and 1897, which was the principal propaganda machine of the fledgling NCWC between October 1895 and April 1897, as arranged in private correspondence between Faith Fenton and Ishbel Aberdeen during those years.

It is possible that Ishbel Aberdeen's private secretary, Theresa Wilson, was also part of this hidden relationship, but none of her letters to Faith has survived. However, it was she who wrote on Lady Aberdeen's behalf at Christmas 1892, and it was Theresa Wilson who handled a great deal of the work connected with the NCWC. Ishbel Aberdeen's itinerary of official duties was staggering, and the governor general's lady was not supposed to be involved in anything that smacked of politics or partisan behaviour.

For Ishbel Maria Marjoribanks Gordon, Countess of Aberdeen, that second condition was quite impossible. She married John Campbell Gordon, seventh Earl of Aberdeen in 1877, and before the end of the honeymoon she had purchased from slave dealers on the Nile, set free, and then adopted four small Sudanese boys. By 1880 she had persuaded her husband to cross the floor of the House of Lords and become a Liberal, as she and her family were. At the beginning of the 1880s she was president of various groups in Scotland lobbying for the admittance of women to universities. When her husband was made lieutenant-governor of Ireland in 1886, she won the affection and admiration of Dubliners by devoting herself to finding work for the unemployed, markets overseas for their goods, and food for the hungry.

During her years as First Lady of the Dominion of Canada, Ishbel Aberdeen gave new meaning to the phrase "the power behind the throne." She was into everything—including Parliament, where she took the unprecedented step of seating herself front and centre alongside the Speaker, and not up in the gallery—involved above all in any movement or organization that affected the freedom and well-being of women and children. In spite of warnings from the colonial secretary and British prime minister William Gladstone himself, she found it impossible to separate her beliefs from her honorary position. For Ishbel Aberdeen, politics did indeed signify its root meaning, "of the people," and she could never draw a line between the small "l" liberal and the capital "L" Liberal. All she could do was try to hide her involvement when it seemed absolutely necessary to do so.

Ishbel first visited Canada in 1890, and stayed with her four children for a while in Hamilton, Ontario, in a house found for them by Senator William Eli Sanford, who was later to play an important role in Faith Fenton's life—a role that would have been unknown, were it not for a reference in one of Ishbel's letters to Faith.[7] However, they do not seem to have met at this point, and although they would conceal their relationship later on, there would have been no need to hide a meeting in Hamilton. The Tory *Hamilton Spectator*'s views on the Aberdeens later became apoplectic, its editorials characterizing Lord Aberdeen as an "amiable and mediocre person . . . controlled by his ambitious wife." It was a view held by many and not only by *The Hamilton Spectator*.

Faith records in her column of May 20, 1893, the first meeting with Ishbel in Chicago:

> . . . as the great audience dispersed Lady Aberdeen honored me with a few pleasant words as I tendered to her in the name of Canadian women most cordial welcome to Canada's queenship.
>
> "It is fitting that the Woman's Empire should be the first to extend to you the welcome of Canadian women, Lady Aberdeen," I said. "I can assure you it is a welcome given from the heart."
>
> The countess' sweet English face lit with a gracious smile. "Indeed I am glad to come. Indeed we are very glad to come to you," she answered. "You may tell the Canadian women that; but I must not say any more to you, because Mr. Gladstone has told us not to."
>
> I laughed with perfect understanding. . . . The countess believes, as you know, that women should be an active

force in politics, and her reasons for this belief were most
persuasively advanced.

You will perceive that I have lost my heart to this fair
British woman, who is so soon to reign at Rideau Hall. . . .

Faith Fenton's family have always maintained that there was a
friendship between the two women. Faith told them it was so, and the
letters from Lady Aberdeen suggest a relationship similar to one Faith
described in a column two weeks before meeting Ishbel Aberdeen in
Chicago:

Can real friendship exist between women? . . . It can and
does, friend. But you must remember that the friendship
that exists between women is often a very quiet and hidden
sentiment. It does not show itself as does the friendship
between men. The latter may be seen in the office, on the
street, at the store, in many public expeditions. . . . The
friendship that springs up between man and man is usually
born of outward circumstance; that between woman and
woman is born of inward perception.

Though it is highly unlikely that the two women were intimate
friends—Ishbel was unmistakably of the aristocracy—it was undoubtedly a relationship born of both outward circumstance and inward perception. Both women scorned precedent. Ishbel Aberdeen was considered scandalously familiar with her servants, and Faith was interested in
people of all classes. And they shared a devotion to the cause of women's
freedom.

If ever their conversations became personal, it would have stood
Faith in very good stead that she had never been associated with her
storekeeper father, and was always much more interested in talking
about her literary and artistic antecedents in Britain. It is possible that
Ishbel Aberdeen never knew about Alice Freeman, and if she read

"Woman's Empire"—as she probably did—she might never have guessed that her accomplice was a schoolteacher.

Faith rarely spoke about her education, but when she did, she made it sound somewhat more elevated than it was. She selected such events as the frequent visits of Lord Dufferin to her school when he was in Toronto, giving the impression that she was in a private school and not the publicly funded Model and Normal Schools.[8] This was not just to mislead her public, but almost certainly because both Alice, the daughter of a tradesman, and Faith, of the Colchester Fentons, would have enjoyed the opportunity to enhance their position in a class-conscious society. And how valuable those years of training with Margaret Reikie in etiquette and elocution must have been when it came to conversing with a countess!

Separated by class they may have been, but they had a great deal in common. They were the same age. Neither of them was beautiful, or even pretty, in the nineteenth-century sense. Ishbel was tall, big-boned, with smallish features on a broad face; Faith was small, with strong features in a tiny face. Both believed passionately in finding new roles for women to play, but neither used inflammatory vocabulary—in fact, Ishbel also used comfort-words, particularly anything to do with motherhood and, like Faith, hers were effective because they came from the heart. Both had attractive speaking voices. Both had objects of admiration in common, such as the journalist W.T. Stead—"Enthusiast, socialist, mystic . . . clever, brilliant, earnest," Faith called him—a personal friend of Ishbel Aberdeen's, from whose influential British magazine, *Review of Reviews*, Faith often quoted.[9]

Above all, both were brilliant at getting what they wanted by working behind the scenes. For all of Ishbel's obvious manipulation of her husband and her known involvement in matters of state, the correspondence with Faith Fenton suggests that there was even more going on than met the public eye. By now, Faith would have acquired a reputation for discretion with those in high places, and at some point Ishbel Aberdeen decided she could trust her and use her.

Ishbel's undercover use of women journalists to advance her beliefs was not confined to Faith Fenton. In 1896—about the same time as the first extant letter to Faith—she used an Ottawa-based *Globe* reporter, Emily McCausland Cummings, as a go-between, carrying letters between herself and Wilfrid Laurier when Sir Mackenzie Bowell's Tory government was tottering to extinction. In this case, she recorded her use of Mrs. Cummings in her diary, stating that the reporter could come and go without suspicion, since they often communicated on NCWC business.[10]

As Faith was not in Ottawa, much of the business had to be carried on by letter, and it is possible she destroyed any correspondence from Theresa Wilson. But for all her discretion, Faith could not bring herself to destroy all Ishbel's letters, knowing that it was only by those handwritten letters from Ishbel Aberdeen that she would ever be able to prove in later years how high she had climbed. The daughter of a Barrie storekeeper, reared by the class-conscious Margaret Reikie, would treasure those letters in the distinctive handwriting of Canada's first lady.

It is unclear if the correspondence started in 1893 on a regular basis, either with Lady Aberdeen herself or through Theresa Wilson. The 1893 interview in "Woman's Empire," however, suggests that more was said than Faith chose to divulge.

Lady Aberdeen's comment that she cannot say anything more than that she is happy to be in Canada, "because Mr. Gladstone has told us not to," is an obvious joke at the British prime minister's expense.[11] Faith reminds readers that Lady Aberdeen believes women should be an active force in politics and had "persuasively advanced" her views on the subject. And, although one might expect Faith Fenton, of the Colchester Fentons, to fawn, be it ever so slightly, on "this fair British woman who is soon to reign at Rideau Hall," there is something about the phrase "I have lost my heart" that suggests an immediate rapport between the two women.

Why, if Ishbel recorded her use of Emily Cummings in her diaries, did she not mention Faith Fenton? Surely the carrying of letters between the governor general's lady and the Liberal leader just before an election was even less prudent than a relationship based on advancing the fortunes of the National Council of Women? It was undoubtedly to protect Faith that Ishbel Aberdeen never mentioned they were hand-in-glove. Every Tory newspaper in the country suspected—with good reason—that Ishbel Aberdeen was advancing the cause of the Liberals, and repeatedly attacked both her and Lord Aberdeen on those grounds. Emily Cummings worked for the Liberal *Globe*; Faith Fenton wrote for the Tory-funded *Empire*. In her relationship with Ishbel, Faith crossed party lines; disclosure would have wiped out years of careful networking at a time when you chose a political party for life.

By 1893, with Macdonald gone and the Conservative party floundering, it must certainly have occurred to Faith that she should be looking to make contacts on the other side—and here she was, joining forces with the noblest Liberal of them all, the She who reigned supreme over the capital city of Ottawa. No wonder the tone of her White City columns was euphoric: "The White City letters in the Woman's Empire are ended, friends, for I have no desire to weary you. . . . I must be content if I have given you even the dimmest conception of what it is almost impossible to conceive—the wonderful beauty of the World's Fair of 1893."

With the summer over, it was back to school at Ryerson. Faith's depression that fall is easy to understand. She had watched the face of Julia Ward Howe as hundreds of women sang her "Battle Hymn of the Republic"; she had been with Susan B. Anthony at what Anthony herself described as "the crowning moment of my life." She had thrilled to Buffalo Bill's Wild West Show and to the music of Sousa's band.[12] In a private interview with Isabella Beecher Hooker, the suffragist sister of Harriet Beecher Stowe, author of *Uncle Tom's Cabin*, she had been given a photograph of the old family homestead signed by both women that she would treasure all her life, and that would survive the disappearance of so many of her belongings.[13]

Now it was back to the shrunken, repressed world of Alice. In a column of reveries on the White City, her mood of introspection plunges her into sentimentality and turns her sadness into bathos: "Ah me; how it hurts—hurts like the pressure upon some old wound—to know how soon rough hands will ravage and despoil those fair, gleaming palaces. We women who have seen its wonderful beauty, shrink from the thought with a very real pain."

Faith records the fire that destroyed much of the exhibition after her visit, but this is not the root of her distress. The language is so rarified that it is difficult to be sure what is the real suffering the writer is experiencing: the pain of being Miss Alice Freeman again, or the greater agony of dreams closer than ever to fulfilment, but not yet reality: "The White City has given . . . such wonderful delights that we cannot tell of them, but wrap the happy secrets away, as a lover does his lady's words of tenderness, to con over, to treasure and recall in long after days."

Those happy secrets of which she could not tell may well have been Faith's private conversations with Ishbel Aberdeen and others about her future. The summer saunterings of 1893 and the return to Ryerson School for the school year of 1893–94 were the last repeat of a now familiar pattern for "Woman's Empire." As Miss Freeman faced the Junior Book Classes once more, she hugged to herself a wonderful delight indeed—that Faith would have to be Alice for only a little while longer: "Yet we shall see it again. For sometimes its towers and palaces shall shine from the red heart of the winter fireplace; its white pillars shall gleam between the trees of the summer woods . . . the White City of our dreams."

XI

An Unheard-of Thing

That a woman should criticize the law and the prophets,
with a view to acceptance or rejection of the same, was a
quarter of a century ago, an unheard-of thing.

The average Canadian woman is very conservative. It
is a hard thing for her to loosen the old conventionalities, the old-time proprieties and properness in which
men have so carefully swaddled her.

Faith Fenton, "Woman's Empire," 1895.

THAT DECEMBER 1893, THE RED HEART of the winter fireplace recalled for
the lady journalist a mountain road on the Gaspé coast where an old her-
mit-woman had built herself a cabin, carrying the lumber, plank by plank,
from the nearby villages and then filling her tiny home with her few precious possessions. How would she spend Christmas, as the wind from that
icy sea pierced her woman-made cabin under the shadow of the mountain?

Out west, Prairie Lily and Wildflower would be making the
Christmas pudding, filling the stockings and struggling to hold back the
tears of homesickness as they looked out across the great snow-covered
wastes—how did they keep Christmas, remembering the life left behind?

Throwing aside, as always, the "cheap cloak" of pessimism, Faith
Fenton begged for compassion and kindness from her readers—"How,"
she asked them, "can we be cruel in a world that has graves in it?"

And Faith Fenton's Christmas that year? "I am to eat my Christmas
dinner in New York, probably in a big hotel or restaurant, and all alone.

Even as you read this I shall be treading the streets of Gotham, a very insignificant atom in the great mass of humanity that will bustle and push and throng as only New Yorkers can on Christmas Eve."

Insignificant atom maybe, but it is very unlikely that Faith Fenton trod the streets of Gotham that Christmas of 1893 on a whim—not that there is the faintest suggestion of an ulterior motive anywhere in her three columns from the United States. The only companion mentioned is an unnamed nurse who worked at a Church of England hospital, St. Luke's, on the corner of Fifth Avenue, and Fifty-fourth Street. However, Faith does not appear to have stayed with her, but in a women's hotel close to Fifth Avenue endowed by a member of the Vanderbilt family. She uses her visit to the hospital for the bulk of her New York column, and says that she managed to get to the theatre, although she missed seeing Henry Irving and Ellen Terry. She then went on to Boston.

School records show that Alice Freeman took a certified leave of absence for five days in January 1894 and, given the events of the next few months in Faith Fenton's life, that Christmas visit was probably about finding markets for her writing, renewing old contacts and making new ones. The highlight of her visit was without a doubt her trip to Boston and her interview with Oliver Wendell Holmes.[1]

Essayist, poet, novelist, professor of anatomy at Dartmouth Medical College, with a degree in medicine from Harvard, Oliver Wendell Holmes was one of the pre-eminent literary and public personalities of his era. Being granted an interview with him more than demonstrated that the interviewer herself had clout. In this case, Faith may well have got access to this grand old man in the final year of his life through Ishbel Aberdeen, for during the course of the interview she tells her readers that Lord and Lady Aberdeen and their daughter had recently called on him. Faith was a great admirer of Wendell Holmes's writings, but it is interesting to speculate whether there was more to this interview than a great name to drop into "Woman's Empire" and a chance to meet a writer she admired—when the interview was over and he took her hand, Faith had "touched her lips to the hand that touched her own," and Wendell Holmes had returned the gesture—for while she was in Boston she stayed in some style in "a costly villa" with "the best of Boston folk" in "the richest suburb on the continent." Faith, it would seem, was now moving in exalted circles, and could not resist boasting about it to her readers—a rather different perspective from the wry comments on Newport society she made two years earlier.

She also paid a visit to the publishing house of Houghton Mifflin and Company—Wendell Holmes's publisher—and had a meeting with Harry Houghton himself. This was followed by a trip to the Riverside Press in Cambridge, where she watched copies of *The Atlantic Monthly* rolling off the presses, and was presented with a beautifully illustrated book of verse signed by Houghton—another treasured possession that has survived. It is doubtful that Faith Fenton was merely on a sightseeing tour at Christmas, and much more likely that she was prospecting for new markets for her work in the United States.

Back in Toronto, Faith Fenton was off with *The Empire*'s police reporter—"tall, strong, fine-looking"—to spend the night at the Central Police Station on Court Street. Disappointingly enough it was a quiet night, with two men, a forger and a drunkard, and one woman in "a large iron walled cage. . . . [When] she saw me, she caught my cloak between the bars. . . . Had I come to take her out? She had a sick husband—a baby. It was only because she was married that she drank . . . her voice followed us. . . ."

After a look through the pictures in the Rogues Gallery and a chance to stroke the horses that pulled the patrol wagon, and after carefully mentioning the names of all the officers she met, Faith Fenton puts in a plea "to Architect Lennox to make all speed with the big new Courthouse in the square."[2] Then she moves on to fashion for the Ottawa season.

The column concludes with lengthy coverage of Lady Aberdeen's book *Through Canada with a Kodak*—"Hart and Riddell have it in stock"[3]—followed by the magazine put out by the Onward and Upward Organisation started by Lady Aberdeen for her staff and tenantry in Britain, and *Wee Willie Winkie*, a "little folks" magazine edited by Ishbel's daughter, Lady Marjorie Gordon, "with her mother's aid." Since at least two of those items were on Faith's desk, it is not too far-fetched to suppose that a letter asking for some endorsement from "Woman's Empire," accompanied them—or perhaps that endorsement had already been arranged.

A week later, and Faith was back again at ten o'clock with the police reporter at Central Police Station for "a night tramp" with Detective Black to the Jarvis Street Mission, a night lodging-house for men, and then on to Wilton Street, where the Salvation Army ran a hostel. Faith had nothing but praise for "these busy soldiers." Over the years of

"Woman's Empire" she had seen what they did for "the needs of the submerged tenth," the people of the streets.

The final January column for 1894 concludes with an interview with the lady violinist Miss Nora Clench, who was in town. There are some social notes on the Toronto Cricket Club Ball, describing "the zenith of the evening" as the arrival of the Lieutenant-Governor and Mrs. Kirkpatrick (Isabel Kirkpatrick could not abide Ishbel Aberdeen and helped spread ludicrous stories about the Aberdeens playing hide-and-seek with their servants through various stately halls). There is a rave review of *Beautiful Joe*, by Margaret Marshall Saunders—the author's reply to what was obviously a personal letter of congratulation is still among Faith's papers.[4] The columns appear normal but Faith, in fact, made a momentous decision. In the minutes of the Toronto school board for February 1894 there are two items about Alice: one records a letter received from Miss A. Freeman, teacher in Ryerson School, tendering her resignation. The second reads: "#12. Management Report #3. Toronto, February 22nd, 1894. To the Toronto School Board: At the meeting of the above named committee held this day . . . it was decided to recommend as follows: 1) That the resignation of Miss A. Freeman, teacher in Ryerson School, be accepted." After nineteen years, the multiple life as Stella and Alice and Faith was finally over.

What did she feel? Relief, certainly. She was thirty-seven, and must by now have been feeling the wear and tear of the long hours, the lack of sleep, and even the subterfuge. No more keeping her rebellious thoughts to herself. Faith Fenton had never criticized Alice's fellow-teachers, saving her barbs and her criticisms for those in authority in the school system, particularly the school trustees, above all when they fought to keep women from being appointed to the same position, or to appropriate school funding for their own incomes at the expense of teachers.

She had stepped uncharacteristically out of line in a January 1894 column by supporting a Model School teacher, Kate Hagarty, whom she said she had known for ten years or more, and who had been dismissed after being overlooked for promotion in what seems to have been a political move within the system. Faith knew that she was soon to be free, and could afford to risk speaking out for a teacher she admired.

Later, Faith, free of Alice, would comment on the fate of women over forty and of married women in the teaching system:

So the cause of married women has prevailed; and the common sense majority of the School board has prevented the minority from making a laughing stock of the whole. Had the mediaeval resolution before the Board on Friday evening carried, the next step would have been to compel all women over forty to resign, as already I believe no woman beyond that age is engaged by the Board.

Oh, they are deep, sirs, deep—Messrs. Fitzgerald, Douglas and confreres. Being young and handsome themselves, they want to reign and rule over a garden of girl bachelors.

Faith had barely escaped the fate of those women. But she would also have felt some regret for losing the one element that had kept her going all those years: the children. In the stories Faith Fenton told of schoolchildren, she never admitted they were her own charges, yet her delight in their energy and their humour shines through. Even in difficult situations she was able to see the bright—or the funny—side. She told her readers the story of Jim, a slow and difficult nine-year-old in a class of five-year-olds, and what happened when he was sent home with a note to his mother: "The answer came promptly. It was brief and to the point. 'Dear Miss, You may just be glad you haven't got his father—that's all.'"

Still among her papers are the longhand and typed copies of a list of answers given by a group of ten- to twelve-year-old boys to a hygiene test, which she used in one of her columns:

Q.—How may the stomach be injured?

A.—By the food going into the wrong pipe. . . . Don't swallow a pin or some money. Don't get it stepped on. . . . By a shot from a gun if you are in the way. . . . By swallowing a hot potato whole. . . . You may injure your stomach if a fellow jumps on it.

Q.—How may the teeth be preserved?

A.—. . . Use Van Buskirk's fragrant zozodont. . . . You must not drink hot tea and cold water together, because the hot tea expands the teeth and the cold water brings them together again, and then they crack.

If she managed to derive such pleasure from the slow and the non-academic members of her classes, what delight she must have taken in the bright and intelligent children, those sensitive to the poems, stories and plays she shared with them. Faith loved the little ones, and they adored her. But life had given her a chance to do what she had set her heart on doing so long ago, when she sat with kindred spirit Margaret Reikie in the octagon parsonage and discovered the joy of being a writer.

By the end of 1893 it was common knowledge that Faith was Alice. It seems scarcely credible that at least some of her colleagues would not have known by now about the *alter ego* of the Junior Book Classes teacher. Toronto was a small city, and Faith was by now one of its better-known personalities. Even in an age without Social Insurance Cards, or income-tax forms to complete, and only the print media to worry about, her dual identity must have been difficult enough to keep secret. Over the last two years of her double life, Faith had made powerful political friends, and it is more than likely that those connections protected her from the wrath of the Toronto school board. But Alice was not driven out of the classroom by the discovery of Faith; it was a choice she was able to make herself.

Why February? After nineteen years, had dedicated and responsible Miss Freeman finally not been able to hold on until the end of the school year, abandoning her little charges before Easter? It looks from the records as if Faith left in February, but returned briefly in March—perhaps to fill in until another teacher was found. There are four certified days off in March, she was late twice, and the letter from Marshall Saunders of the same date talks about Faith having been ill. What the financial arrangements were one can only guess, but certainly *The Empire* must have been paying a great deal more to the writer of their popular women's page for her to resign from her other career.

As usual, most of the evidence is indirect: there was her unexpected visit to New York and Boston only a month earlier and the arrival of

Ishbel Aberdeen's publications on her desk in January 1894. Faith had covered the founding meeting of the National Council of Women of Canada that was held in the Toronto Horticultural Pavilion on October 27, 1893, and attended by about two thousand women.

The NCWC embraced established church groups, temperance groups, women's suffrage organizations, cultural groups—in fact, any organization at all that concerned women. There was no single aim, no single ideology, and certainly its sole intention was not to pursue universal suffrage: rather, its purpose was the betterment of every aspect of women's lives.

Faith's coverage is sketchy, lightly humorous in tone, an attempt to make a distinction between women's suffrage and the aims of the NCWC: "Canadian men scent suffrage or prohibition at every woman's meeting. . . . To speak upon a platform, they say, argues a certain degree of strongmindedness; a strongminded woman always goes in for suffrage, therefore the gathering of last Friday was a suffrage meeting— Q.E.D. [*Quod est demonstrandum*: point proven], as we used to say at school."

From later events it seems almost certain that Faith had private meetings with Ishbel Aberdeen, who was elected president of the council, and that she was deeply involved—not that anyone could have guessed from her own brief account of an event that Faith herself said was "fully reported, even to the extent of two or three columns, in the Toronto daily press." Lady Aberdeen was "noble and motherly," and when she spoke her words were "gentle, womanly." Everything was pretty, and perfumed, and feminine: "Daylight waned and soft shadows fell. The warm atmosphere dimmed, and the ragged blossoms [of chrysanthemums] sent forth drowsy fragrance. I peered from behind my sheltering palm. These were Canadian women, and this was Canada's chiefest lady. It was a gracious and pretty sight."

There is more lotus-eater than liberated lady about those two thousand women in their autumn bonnets pictured by the intrepid lady journalist concealed in the palmy undergrowth. She was going to have to advance with stealth if she wanted to free Canadian women from their conservative swaddling-clothes.

Faith continues to lay a falsely feminine trail by concluding the column with a reminder of Toronto's annual chrysanthemum show, suitably traditional fare for a woman's page—thus distracting any husband glancing over his wife's shoulder from the potentially explosive combination of "the suffragist, the prohibitionist, the worker in philanthropy, the theosophist, the devoted King's Daughter, the deaconness, the woman on the stage and the woman in the home" that the NCWC represented.[5]

Beneath the scented surface, much more was going on. The first private talks between Ishbel and Faith probably took place at this meeting, with Ishbel inviting Faith to attend the Quebec Winter Carnival in February 1894, and then to visit her in Ottawa in April before covering the first general meeting of the NCWC. No correspondence has survived from this period, but there is evidence in an 1897 letter that Ishbel Aberdeen tried to arrange Faith's attendance at such meetings. Fate in the formidable shape of Lady Aberdeen had helped Alice to leave the teaching profession.

Quebec in carnival was a winter wonderland—"five feet of snow, a cloudy grey sky, a revel of fun"—but this time a city of dreams fulfilled. Seven years earlier, another woman reporter, Sara Jeannette Duncan, had covered the same scene. Faith kept for ever her elegant press pass of broad moiré ribbon with the picture of the citadel, pressed between the pages of the book Harry Houghton had given her.

No wonder her column opened with "Hurrah for Quebec, hurrah!" Her descriptions of the parades, the masquerade ball, the ice carvings and the Fort de Glâce resonate with vitality and joy. She gave pride of place to her description of the Château Frontenac near "Citadel-crowned cape Diamond . . . sweeping with its far vision the broad range of river, mountain and sky."[6] Faith Fenton, like anyone who was anyone, was staying—up under the eaves maybe, but under the same roof as the Astors, fed by the same chef (formerly, she told her readers, of the Devonshire Club in London):

> Looking out as I wrote the few last lines, I saw a Levis
> ferry making its slow way through the floating ice floes
> across the river, and throwing down my pencil I scrambled

hastily into my furs, sped down the hill—down, down
down—to the ferry, and boarded a waiting boat.
Presently we were under way, crashing the boat's nose
against the loose, white masses, splitting them into a
hundred pieces. . . . It is growing cold and dark. . . . There
are the lights of the chateau springing out from a hundred
windows. . . . soon the light of one little dormer room is
added to the many that shine down upon the ice floes
from chateau Frontenac.

Faith was now a full-time journalist, and Quebec City in carnival
was a city of contacts. She spent some time at Spencer Grange, which
was on the same estate as the home of Quebec's lieutenant-governor,
with the Quebec historian James MacPherson Le Moine, who wrote in
both French and English.[7] One of his letters to her, which he sent along
with one of his books, *Picturesque Quebec*, to the Château Frontenac
requesting the pleasure of meeting "the sympathetic delineator of
Canadian Homes and Canadian scenery," is still among her papers.

Interestingly, representatives of the major newspapers, including the
American press, were in Quebec—probably because members of New
York's Four Hundred were also attending the carnival. Faith paid particular attention to Julian Ralph of *The New York Sun*, who was also a
well-known magazine writer: "It is delightful to sit beside him at a table
d'hote, and listen while he sparkles out all sorts of bright table talk.
While, to plunge with him through the drifts, to walk or rather slide
about Quebec streets, to look on this dear old city through his artist's
eyes—that is even greater pleasure."

Faith was making a determined effort to place her material in other
newspapers and magazines, and she sold an article on the Quebec carnival
to *The Canadian Magazine*.[8] She was undoubtedly hoping to go into syn-
dication in the United States, like Pica Kribs. A series of five letters dating
from May 23, 1894, to May 10, 1895, from Cyrus Adams, who was
appointed editor with *The New York Sun* in 1894, suggests that Faith got
herself an introduction to him from Julian Ralph while in Quebec.

The first letter acknowledges receipt of two manuscripts from
Faith—Adams likes them, but is not sure they will appeal, and gives the

usual warnings: "Bushels of essays and stories are sent to the Sun, not one in a hundred has any chance whatever." He adds, however, that she has a chance of success "if you have lots of newspaper instinct, a keen scent, so to speak, for what is newsy and interesting. . . ."

Off went another manuscript, a column written in 1893 called "Should Woman Obey Man. Back came the reply—Adams liked it and thought their women readers would like it, but the powers that were didn't. Again he gave advice, four pages of it:

There is a man in a small town of this state who has actually . . . not a particle of literary gift except that he knows
how to say what he wants to without waste of words. But
he has an uncommon faculty for finding at a cattle show or
a woman's sewing circle a hundred and one things that we
don't care a snap for, something that most anybody would
read with more or less interest. The Sun prints about all he
sends, and many of his topics are under twenty lines long.

He warns her, "Don't imagine we are after mere cut and dried news. We get lots of it."

A month later came this reply: "Your article went to the printers an hour after it was received. That is the sort of thing the *Sun* likes." The sort of thing the *Sun* liked was a rather pedestrian article on some new eye-tests for children in Toronto, adapted from an *Empire* column of 1889, that appeared in the *Sun*'s Sunday supplement without a byline. In July, Adams told Faith that her last three articles were excellent, and that as he was off to Britain, she should in future address her work to the managing editor.

As Adams did not mention the subjects of the articles, one can only guess which are Faith's, but one on the dying art of letter-writing bears some of her distinctive traits. The word "dainty" appears in the sub-heading, and she uses two other favourite techniques of personification: she calls the principal character "Dame Critic," and she objectifies oth-ers by a kind of group classification—"The tall girl, the short girl, the bright and the stupid girl." The article is longer than her first, at the top of the page, and the heading is in a much larger typeface. Letter-writing would certainly be a topic dear to her heart, since she wrote and received hundreds of letters.

Adams' final letter, written almost a year later, suggests that Faith had problems getting paid, because he asks her to send him all her clippings with dates, "so a check may be sent you for the amount of space." In this case, there is a record of what Faith was paid: "The Sun pays $1 for anything with a head, if the item is five lines long. Under that 50 cents." At those rates it would have taken a lot of freelancing to make up for her teacher's salary, meagre as it was.

There was certainly a Quebec meeting with Lady Aberdeen, in her "private parlor" at the Château Frontenac, because this time Faith shares it with her readers—or some of it. The atmosphere was informal, and it was interrupted by Ishbel's youngest child, ten-year-old Archie, who was impatient for a much-anticipated children's carnival to begin:

> As we talked, there was a gentle tap at the door, and a fair little face with darkling eyes peeped in.
> "Mother," said the soft little voice, "mother"—
> "Go away, dear," answered Lady Aberdeen gently.
> "But mother, is it time to go?" persisted the soft voice.
> "Go away, Archie; go and lie down, dear," Lady Aberdeen repeated.
> "But mother, what stockings shall I wear?"

This particular member of the aristocracy obviously did not allow nursemaids or protocol to separate her from her children, and the two women are clearly very comfortable together. It was probably during this meeting that they discussed Faith's attendance at the first annual meeting of the NCWC in Ottawa.

Even in such exalted company, Faith did not forget her letter-bag: "It is always . . . the finishing touch of our page." She took her correspondence with her and attached her replies to the end of her Quebec-carnival columns, answering her readers "as I would like to chat across their tea-tables." There was decorating advice to a husband and wife who both read her columns, advice of the heart to "William N.," that probably came as a shock: "Your girl friend probably thinks of you as a very conceited young man—as I do." There was practical advice to one of the many would-be writers who sent her their work, finishing with her personal credo: "Remember also that you can only write to the depth of your soul's life." And there was a lengthy response to a clergyman who accused her of "gush": "What do you know about it, or about women? . . . Go back to your sermon. . . . Do not speak of the little children, of the field lilies, the erring woman, the loving John, the sea shore, the evening light. . . . prune your sentences for fear a suspicion of 'gush' may enter in. How soundly your congregation will sleep tomorrow."

From time to time Faith Fenton had a habit of distancing herself stylistically from her material, by calling herself "the woman." It is usually a clue to events that were of particular significance to her, and, though to the modern reader there is something affected about it, it was common, in all kinds of writing at the time, to objectify oneself in that manner. The individual writer, or character, took on a universal and symbolic status in the perceptions of a Victorian audience reared on a literature loaded with archetypes and exemplars, such as Christian in *Pilgrim's Progress*. Charles Dickens created powerful individual characters, but he too made use of the same technique: "This boy is Ignorance. This girl is Want. . . ."

What was almost certainly a visit of great professional importance to Faith begins on an informal note and keeps that tone for the six columns of her Ottawa visit in April 1894. The subheadings of her first column give the flavour: "Canadian Homes," "As You Like It," "Social Snap Shots," "The National Council." The real meat of the matter is tucked away at the end. Pride of place is given to her meeting with Ishbel Aberdeen in her private suite of rooms at Rideau Hall, and her readers are treated to a detailed description of them.

One can hardly call it an interview, since the content of their conversation is far less detailed than the setting of the scene, but it is certainly worth noting that Ishbel showed Faith her family photo album, "with sketches of Haddo House in Aberdeenshire, of the London house, and gay snap shots of bits of home life."[9]

The rest of Faith's visit that day was in the company of Theresa Wilson, Lady Aberdeen's private secretary. Though Faith suggested the bulk of the conversation was about the Aberdeen children, in fact it was probably about the affairs of the National Council of Women. Theresa Wilson was not the children's governess, and the lunch the two women had together "in the great gloomy dining-room" was undoubtedly a business luncheon.

The subterfuge was necessary not only to beguile her conservative readers into broadening their horizons, but to keep her private agenda secret from her bosses. The story that has survived in Faith's family is that *The Empire* sent her to Ottawa, probably having decided to give their women readers the kind of social column about Canada's capital city that was then popular.

Certainly the Ottawa columns bear this out. Social events dominate: Rideau Hall was constantly aglow; the Russell House drawing-rooms held by the wives of the Conservative members were a-ripple with alluring *valses*; Lady Aberdeen was gowned in black velvet and looking somewhat tired after continuous sessions of the National Council during the day; none of the Cabinet ministers and their wives entertained more extensively than did the Honourable J.C. Patterson and his wife, who gave many gay little informal receptions—and so on. However, as Faith reminded her readers, "the social factor is not one to be ignored in politics, for it is stronger than men or even women are aware."

As Faith well knew, it was impossible in Ottawa to divide the two, and many of her observations at social occasions or her apparently light-hearted comments on government and political events reveal the subtle and not-so-subtle intertwining of the social and the political. After the Macdonald years, the Conservative government was struggling to find a new direction under Sir John Thompson, who once acknowledged he could not have an opinion on aspects of Canadian history about which he knew nothing. (Such misplaced frankness from a political leader would not be the factor that ended his political career. In her Ottawa columns Faith commented on the fact that Sir John had put on weight so that he shook when he laughed; in England six months later, he would suddenly drop dead, almost in the presence of Queen Victoria.) She noticed how the compact nature of the capital city facilitated social contacts among government wives:

> In their endeavour to fulfill their social obligations, the best known sessional ladies are really much harder worked than

are their husbands in the house. . . . Calling is not an affair of distance in Ottawa . . . officials and ex-officials are constantly bobbing against each other on the main thoroughfares . . . one can make a dozen calls in Ottawa in the time it takes to make two in Toronto or Montreal. The city is small, and the residences of the society people are nearly all within a few minutes walk of each other. . . . Madam's social debt . . . looks a trifle less formidable in view of this fact.

She also noticed how many of the men forgot to bow to Lady Aberdeen after they had bowed to the governor general, "and hurriedly moved on," although she does not suggest that it was deliberate. As she observed, after some caustic comments on a prolonged Budget debate, "I am dipping into matters political, and the editor said I mustn't."

But Faith Fenton could not resist attending Parliament, where she looked down from the Public Gallery and caught the sergeant-at-arms "deep in a love story behind his desk." She described Wilfrid Laurier and John Thompson thus: "The Opposition Leader resembles a rather handsome colley [sic]—very sagacious, faithful and loyal—while the Premier suggests a cute skye terrier, agile, good-humoured and alert." Even when driven to distraction by the procrastination during an all-night debate in the Commons—"I'll never, ever, be able to do anything for Canada that way"—she couldn't resist returning to a favourite theme:

Won't it be fun when women have the franchise? And what many avenues of enjoyment the possession of the same will open to the sex. A thousand dollars per year, railway passes, the range of a large and delightful library; broad corridors, smoking and reading rooms—poker rooms too, mayhap; and the lazy luxury of the Commons chamber, with the opportunity for unlimited dozing. No wonder the men are loth to share their parliamentary privileges.

> And if in the delightful future of women [sic] franchise
> the sterner sex are crowded out from the Commons, they
> can always seek refuge in the Senate chamber. No woman
> will clamor for admission at its green doors; she will never
> arrive at the necessary age.

Faith's respect for parliamentary procedure had been shaken when she was Stella, and nothing she saw in Ottawa changed her opinion that most politicians were like "a lot of schoolboys playing marbles." But, at this stage of her career, that did not stop her cultivating them, and her visit to the Government Experimental Farm, for instance, was probably at the behest of some parliamentarian who wanted coverage in Ontario to impress his constituents. And, despite taking pot-shots at the Senate, she devoted three full columns to it that are a direct contradiction to her tongue-in-cheek comments quoted above:

> A useless chamber? Nay, not so. But one needs to pass
> from the turbulent, democratic and oftentimes angry air of
> the Commons in order to fully appreciate the uses of this
> calm patrician place. Here is dispassion; here is fair judge-
> ment and experience; here are men honourable and full of
> years, who in the late afternoon hours of their lives are able
> to sympathize with the passion and energy of the morning,
> yet to see and legislate beyond it.

Gush, but with a purpose. Later events would show that Faith had cultivated certain members of the Upper House for her own purposes. First, Stella, and, then, Faith Fenton of "Woman's Empire," had learned how to play the game. She reported her attendance at the NCWC sessions almost in passing—but she reported Ishbel Aberdeen's speech to open the assembly almost in full:

We are somewhat accustomed to women's meetings and women's organizations in Toronto, so that the holding of them does not create any atmospheric disturbance. But it seems to be a new thing in Ottawa . . . for verily the National Council meetings of last week charged the Ottawa air with the dynamite of the New Crusade. . . . The discussions at the Council sessions floated out into the street, climbed the pulpits, crept into the dinner parties and dances, even stole past the stalwart doorkeepers and policeman in the Commons chamber.

Between the potted palms, the tables decorated with roses, carnations and smilax, the lustrous tinted silks with harmonizing blossoms, the glittering assemblages and brilliant salons, "the skilful conduct of which is woman's highest social art," the "dynamite of the New Crusade" was being planted by the New Woman—women like Faith Fenton and her colleagues in the profession of journalism, knowingly aided and abetted by women like Lady Aberdeen and Theresa Wilson, and assisted, often unwittingly, by the government officials, parliamentarians and senators that they cultivated.

Ottawa men may not have been "accustomed to advanced women," they may have "veiled their laughing scorn courteously," but that scorn nevertheless remained "sufficiently perceptible." It was those concealed weapons of flattery, the workings behind the scenes, that would help take the New Woman into the broad corridors of power, the avenues of enjoyment and "the lazy luxury" of parliamentary privilege that men were so loth to share with them.

On her return to Toronto, Faith carried in her luggage a prettily bound volume of *Through Canada with a Kodak*, with the following inscription on the flyleaf: "To 'Faith Fenton' with kind regards from the author—Ishbel Aberdeen. May 1894." Perhaps she had taken her copy to Ottawa to be inscribed by Ishbel; perhaps Ishbel gave it to her. Unlike other, similar gifts, this, surely the most prestigious of all, is not mentioned in her columns.

Sir John A. Macdonald's government had been primarily concerned with the building of a nation; now, that new nation was beginning to examine its relationship with the rest of the world. In 1894 the readers of "Woman's Empire" are taken into the very highest reaches of Canadian high society, and the first occasion is the Colonial Conference, held in Ottawa in June and early July.

The conference was, as it sounds, a meeting of officials and ministers of self-governing colonies to reinforce the ties of Empire, and to establish the roles of those colonies in what historian Donald Creighton has called "three chief aspects of imperial relations—commercial, political, military."[10] The 1894 conference had been preceded by a similar event held in 1887, and would be followed by another held in connection with Victoria's Jubilee in 1897.

The word "Special" is at the head of Faith's column and she was again staying at the Russell House, escorted by someone she identified only as "the man of knowledge." Her personal invitation to the at-home held by Lady Thompson, Lady Tupper and other wives of high government officials has survived, and suggests that she had arrived—as does the fact that "the gentlemen of the press—called in familiar parlance 'the boys'—courteously gave her the sesame [admittance] to their gallery."[11]

This may have been when she first met Wilfrid Laurier, whom she admired in spite of his politics: as Faith so rightly said, "I like Mr. Laurier—every woman does." She also could have met the Conservative prime minister himself, Sir John Thompson, on this trip. Two months later Faith Fenton was at Sans Souci, on Lake Rosseau in the Muskokas, spending time with "the Senator, the Cabinet Minister, the pretty young mother and four Great Dane dogs."[12]

The senator was William Eli Sanford, the wealthy Hamilton businessman who had found a house for the Aberdeens during their Hamilton stay the previous year; the Cabinet minister was the Honourable Mackenzie Bowell, at that time Minister of Trade and Commerce; the pretty young mother was Senator Sanford's second wife, Harriet—a far more important contact than might have appeared from Faith's articles. Harriet Vaux was an active member of the NCWC and eventually would travel to many countries, including France, Italy, Romania and India, to help set up national councils.

Three hundred yards from Sans Souci was an island called Lorelei, where Sir John Thompson and his family were on vacation. Senator and Mrs. Sanford would be with Sir John on his fateful trip to England four months later, and Lady Thompson was on close terms with Lady Aberdeen. Never were "the social factor" and politics more intricately intertwined than on Lake Rosseau that summer of 1894.

From Faith Fenton's columns it is evident that the atmosphere was relaxed—"lazy luxury," indeed. Everyone was quite easy with this journalist in their midst: Lady Thompson took her early morning dip; Sir John talked baby talk to Connie, the eighteen-month-old daughter of the Sanfords; at breakfast and dinner on the patio, the senator and the minister tried to outdo each other with incredible fish stories; everyone had their pictures taken by Senator Sanford at Lorelei—"a merry half hour posing in every possible and impossible way. . . . Once we were snapshotted in the middle of a hearty laugh." Everyone got on the scales at Port Carling and weighed themselves—Sir John weighed in at over two hundred pounds. And they all went cruising on *The Naiad*, Senator Sanford's yacht, to be greeted wherever they went "by remarkable salutations . . . the pretty dipping of the flag . . . ringing bells, startling torpedos, unique camping songs and other novelties in between." Whatever the chronology might have been, whatever the warp and woof of Faith's networking, those columns written during "the fair summer days in Muskoka" suggest that she already knew and was known pretty well by her exalted hosts.

Faith's clerical critic would have found gush galore: the baby Connie had the biggest of blue eyes, Senator Sanford was a prince of entertainers—even the Great Danes couldn't resist him—no one could troll more rollicking ditties than Mackenzie Bowell, and hostesses didn't come more winsome than Mrs. Sanford. Faith calls on Canada to "thank God for the happy homes that gird the private lives of her most exalted officials."

As the Chinese lanterns swung in the light night breeze beneath the stars, as the great cedar logs on the bonfire glowed in the darkness and the camp-fire melodies echoed into the Muskoka night Faith Fenton, no longer little castaway Alice Freeman, basked in the knowledge she was finally welcomed into the circle of warmth and cheer—and influence.

From the moment Faith lost her other identity, she lost a vital part of herself. It was Alice Freeman who had been her connection to the world of her women readers, even though they had known her only as Faith

Fenton. It was Alice, not Faith, who rode on the streetcars and watched the worn, anxious faces of the women searching for the fare in their purses, Alice who saw through the tram window the old men bent double beneath the heavy sandwich-boards on their frail backs. It was Alice's contacts with "the great multitude of women whose lives are a fret and a chafing" that gave Faith Fenton some of her best columns, Alice who endured the arrogance and condescension of her male colleagues in the teaching profession, and who understood the plight of the working woman.

In March 1888, Faith Fenton had written a column for "Woman's Empire" that she called "The Domestic Question":

> The question of domestic service is becoming a very serious one with us . . . [because of] the difficulty of securing and retaining competent servants in consequence of the Canadian working girl's preference for factory life.
>
> We must bear in mind that the lines that mark the several grades of English society are not so clearly defined in Canada, in its present shape of development, and that it is possible for any young person to rise from the lowest estate into what we term the best society by the acquisition of wealth and the exercise of tact.
>
> . . . The working girls among us share largely in this ambition. Rightly or wrongly they have come to feel that a certain stigma is attached to the term "servant" that would militate against their social success should the turn of Fortune's wheel bring them prosperity.
>
> . . . A foolish and false view, we say, but who is responsible for its general adoption? Not the working girls most assuredly, for they unwillingly accept the dictum of society in this matter.
>
> . . . Now, while the feeling exists . . . what is the use of prating about the dignity of service and the nobility of labour? . . . Are we, who stand higher in the social scale, very much broader in our views, I wonder?[13]

Working-girl Alice had worked hard, Fortune's wheel had turned, and she had obtained entrée into the best society. The Canadian class system might not have been as clearly defined as "the several grades of English society," but Alice Freeman was the product of a transplanted section of that class-conscious world. She knew only too well the stigma attached to her family background in trade, and that to have worked as a teacher—indeed, to have worked at all as a woman—made her little better than a servant in the eyes of "the best society." So conscious was she of that "dictum of society," she concealed her background from her benefactor, Ishbel Aberdeen, champion of women's causes. It is ironic that an important element in this transformation was her friendship with Ishbel Aberdeen, but from the moment the two women meet, Faith's writing takes on an anxious-to-please, sycophantic tone—a positive fountain of gush. When Alice was still working for a living, Faith Fenton spent half her life as a journalist and reporter in Alice's shoes. When Alice retired from teaching, Faith Fenton cast her away and lost her independent voice. It is sad, but not so surprising, that Faith Fenton of the Colchester Fentons was seduced by the siren-song of the upper classes.

Faith was now performing quite a balancing act, juggling the approbation of her readers; the Conservative party, to which she had given her allegiance; and the secret relationship with Liberal-leaning Ishbel Aberdeen, who should have had no political views at all. Even when her fame and her influence were approaching their apogee during that glorious year of 1894, Faith had not yet forgotten it was her relationship with those readers—with Wildflower, Prairie Lily, Narcissus, Elfin of Bowmanville, Bent Face, and even L'Alsacienne—that had got her there. Her answers to their letters were still the finishing touch of "Woman's Empire," as rich in humour and humanity as anything she wrote.

Then, as in 1890, the unexpected happened. One of Faith's most prestigious contacts, the prime minister, died suddenly while in Britain, and her column of December 17, "As We Knew Him," shared with her readers personal recollections of that Muskoka summer she had spent with him: "It came like a revelation to those who passed beyond mere outer acquaintanceship when they discovered how thoughtful and tender he was—especially for those who were weak or in trouble." Sir John was gone, but the man Lord Aberdeen called on to take over the mantle of leadership was none other than the rollicking, ditty-trolling minister of that summer, Mackenzie Bowell.

Faith's fireside thoughts on the passing of the old year are surprisingly sombre for someone whose career appeared to be soaring. Not only did she now have "Edited by Faith Fenton" at the top of "Woman's Empire," and an attractive illustration, but she had another column during the week, called "As You Like It." However, there were constant rumblings in the office that trouble lay ahead for *The Empire*. The Conservative party had been in a state of disarray since the death of Sir John A. Macdonald, and the death of his successor had only made matters worse. David Creighton was finding it impossible to run the newspaper and to please all the fighting factions at the same time. One of Faith's subtitles at the turn of the year was "Facing the Future"; obviously she was finding it difficult to face 1895 without facing up to "Truth with a capital T" and "every nastiness and bitterness under the sun."

The year 1895 opened with a fire at the offices of *The Globe*, and the temporary housing of that Liberal organ, surprisingly, on the premises of the Tory *Empire*. Faith's column on the subject, "A Press Millenium [sic]," is one of her finest pieces of satirical writing, opening with the suggestion that the occasion offered "the materials for a first-class comic opera," particularly as there was a municipal election in Toronto the day after the fire, with *The Globe* backing one mayoralty candidate, and *The Empire* another:

> . . . the foremen of both papers worked at adjoining desks . . . endeavouring to avoid the possible contretemps of having a Globe diatribe against protection appear in the Empire columns, or an Empire comment on Mayor Fleming's nothingness serenely bobbing up in The Globe. . . . The fun was fast . . . when state secrets came over the wires intended for The Empire and fell by chance into the hands of the Philistines; when the said Philistines realized that only a thin partition separated

their inner sanctum from the enemy host . . . when the
staunchest of Reformers shook The Empire woman long
by the hand, patted her shoulder and asked her sympa-
thetically how she felt and was the shock very great; and
upon the assurance that it was, went away under the
impression that he had properly condoned [sic] with The
Globe woman. . . . Upstairs in the composing room . . .
the foremen with their assistants . . . [are] endeavoring to
prevent the mixing of copy, making such occasional
queries as the whereabouts of The Globe's 'Pink Pills ad,'
or 'that Empire Indigestion cut.'

Less than a month later, the presses of *The Empire* were stilled for
ever. That cheerful singer of ditties, Prime Minister Mackenzie Bowell,
killed it off with no provision for anyone but David Creighton, and in
the merger with the former Tory newspaper, *The Mail*, it was the staff of
The Empire who lost their jobs. A year to the month after Alice had
resigned from teaching, Faith found herself without steady employment.

Some said later it was a cabal of ministers who did the deed without
Mackenzie Bowell's knowledge—even claiming it was a factor in the
Tory defeat the following year. Whatever the truth, the first edition of
The Mail and Empire appeared without preamble on February 7, 1895.

Twenty years later, one of Faith's contemporaries, Kit Coleman,
would call "Woman's Empire" "one of the brightest, tenderest, most
sympathetic pages ever written by any woman." Wildflower, Prairie Lily,
Narcissus, Bent Face and hundreds of other women lost their heart
friend of the past seven years, the editor of "Woman's Empire," when
Faith Fenton lost her job.

The only reader's letter that remains from that period in Faith's life,
however, is from a physician who had written a year earlier on behalf of
himself and his wife, praising "Woman's Empire." They had been guess-
ing who Faith really was, because in her reply in "Our Letter Bag" she
concluded by saying "it is not the name you have heard but only—Faith
Fenton." She had also referred to editorial troubles, telling him that she
would hand his letter to the editor, "to counterbalance some of the
scolding letters he sometimes receives about me."

Dr. R.R. Hopkins wrote to Faith again on the demise of *The Empire*, and his letter summed up the emotions of hundreds of men and women at the loss of Faith Fenton:

> To Madame or Mdslle Faith Fenton:
> I am constrained to write to you again & say how much we are regretting your writings so much enjoyed formerly . . . pointed—liberal—yet truly Canadian in all respects. . . . [We] trusted your descriptions far more than any others we read on the same subjects. Indeed I am sure the women of Canada have largely to thank you if they have got in any way any idea of the importance of this Canada of ours . . . it is a debt not easily repaid. I have known my wife—when prevented by "the cares of the world" from keeping "up to date" with "Faith Fenton" save up that part of "The Empire" for weeks. . . . Poor little woman. Her bewailings are great at the loss of Faith Fenton. . . . If we do not hear from you again we should let you know that you have done us both good. . . .

There were no summer saunterings in 1895; Faith had new schemes under way, trying to place her writing wherever she could get accepted. Because of the disappearance of Faith Fenton from the journalistic history of her country, much of her freelance work has yet to be uncovered, but she sold her series on Ottawa and the Senate to other newspapers, such as *The Union Advocate* in New Brunswick and *The Ottawa Citizen*, and she started a newsletter in *The Galt Reporter* in Galt, Ontario, and *The Evening News*, in Toronto. By October the women of Canada would find their long-lost friend again in-between the covers of a brand-new women's magazine as this country's first woman editor. The first issue was called *The Home Journal*, but from then on it was known as the *Canadian Home Journal*.[14]

The Home Journal came out in October 1895, and in her opening editorial, "Just You And I," Faith resumed her suspended conversation with her readers: "We were speaking, when we were interrupted. . . ."

The publishers of the *Journal* were a group of Toronto and London businessmen who incorporated themselves in July 1895 as "The Home Journal Publishing Company of Ontario (Limited)" with a capital stock of three thousand dollars. They clearly saw it as a golden opportunity to reach the rich advertising market of Canadian women. The principal shareholders, such as the Ellis brothers, who were jewellers, took out whole pages to advertise their wares. It is not surprising that they would have tried to secure the talents of the only proven woman journalist who came with a ready-made audience of readers and who was out of work at the time.

The publishing company's offices were at 3 King Street East, but the journal was produced at Manning Arcade, on King Street West. Faith had been shown over the offices of *The Home Journal* in Philadelphia three years previously, and it looks as if the *Canadian Home Journal* operated along the same lines, but on a much smaller scale. The subscription rate was a dollar a year, and a single copy sold for ten cents; the first edition carried a plea for young ladies "who desire to increase their pocket money" to sell the magazine, informing them: "we allow a generous commission whether you secure one subscriber or a thousand."

Most of the department heads worked at home and brought their articles in to the office. There was a printing department, whose presses threw out the double sheets that were sent on to a folding room, where they were assembled and sent on to the mailing room. There was a tiny office for the editor, and a room where all the mail that came in was read and sorted. Possibly Faith did that herself. She almost certainly wrote most of the magazine copy under various pen-names—"Portia," for instance, wrote about "Stageland." Doubtless it was Faith who asked for "Canadian" to be added to the title.

From her first editorial, Faith made clear her aims for this new magazine: "it is our intention to make the HOME JOURNAL just what its name implies—not a ladies' home journal, but a Canadian home journal, whose pages will contain interesting reading for all members of the household. . . . our outlook has widened so much during the past decade . . . we are getting ready to vote, you perceive."

To those who knew Faith Fenton and her views, this would not have been such a surprise, but it was a revolutionary approach for a magazine of the time aimed chiefly at the women's market. The magazine would, of course, have articles on fashion, but they would be original and based on Toronto and Montreal. There would be a regular ladies' sporting page; a musical and arts page; a children's section; articles on personalities in the worlds of theatre, writing, politics. And in the middle of the editorial is this statement: "Beginning with the October number, the HOME JOURNAL purposes to devote as many pages as is necessary to monthly reports of women's organisations throughout Canada. . . . we confidently expect to show, within a few months, a monthly record of womanly activity that will prove a revelation. . . ."

At last Faith had found a space she could truly call her own without having to fight with a male editor. In her years in the newspaper business, she had seen how women were denied access not only to most professions and organizations, but to one another's views. In the first issue, that particular space was given over to a mixture of reports on organizations such as the WCTU and the Young Women's Christian Guild, under the heading "Women At Work." Faith, however, had bigger plans.

In the November issue of the *Journal*, the first article in the series, "Wives of Our High Officials," is devoted to Ishbel Aberdeen, and it is Faith at her most sycophantic—"How am I to describe her, Canada's Chiefest Lady, whose smiling, tender, motherly face . . ." and so on, for one large, long, fulsome page. In the December issue, Faith quotes from letters received from the high and the mighty, just as she did in "Woman's Empire," complete with copies of the signatures. The shortest extract is from Lord Aberdeen's letter, and simply says: "I should like to add that we are much pleased with the CANADIAN HOME JOURNAL and wish it all success."

The original letter is still among Faith's papers—over two longhand pages, topped by the word "Private." Lord Aberdeen thanks Faith for sending the November number of the *Canadian Home Journal*, says he cannot help writing to tell her how delighted he is with Faith's article on the Countess of Aberdeen, and adds that it cannot fail "to be helpful"—presumably with Ishbel Aberdeen's image problem. The postcript wishes the *Journal* success and ends with this apparently casual remark: "It occurs to me that you may possibly be interested in the enclosed account of a meeting of the National Council of Women which was held here on

Ishbel Aberdeen, photographed for the Victorian Era Ball in Toronto, December 1897, held to commemorate Queen Victoria's Diamond Jubilee.

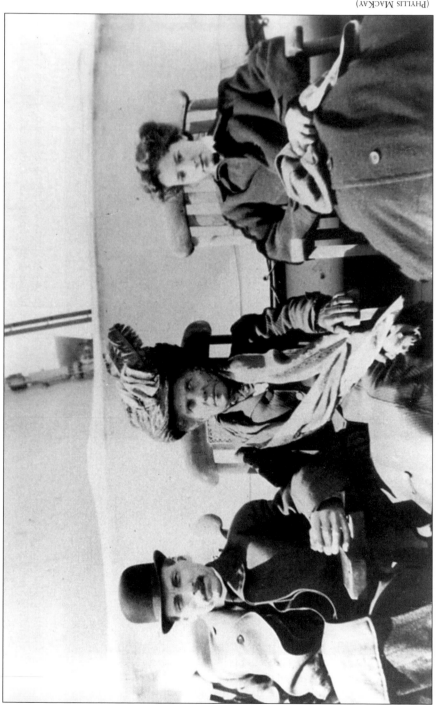

John, Faith and Olive on a steam-ship trip, probably taken around 1912–1914. Faith is wearing a veil. The body-language of the three is interesting and does, to use a phrase of Faith's, "admit of certain inferences."

Thursday evening." The "here" was Government House, British Columbia, where the Aberdeens were staying on their western tour.

The idea of Canada's governor general spontaneously putting pen to paper to thank a lady journalist in this way is revealing; Lord Aberdeen clearly supported his wife's views on women, even going so far as to offer Government House as a venue. But however genuine his support, it is surprising he would have written such a letter in the first place. It suggests that not only the governor general's wife, but the governor general himself, was becoming involved in the affairs of the nation.

By June the NCWC had accepted a permanent space in the *Canadian Home Journal* that was to be "under the direct personal supervision and control of Her Excellency, the President." By July, the section devoted to monthly reports of women's groups was under the heading of the umbrella organization that encompassed most of them, the NCWC, with a photograph of Ishbel Aberdeen set like a cameo in the middle, and a facsimile of her signature at the end.

In the centre of the closely packed print is the statement that Faith Fenton, "on behalf of the proprietors of the *Canadian Home Journal*," had offered the two pages to the organization, that the arrangement had been agreed upon for a year, and that it could be terminated at a month's notice. Ishbel gives the impression that she has accepted editorship until someone else could be found. The section concludes with a clarion-call to order from the first lady in the land to her followers: "We hope that the members of the National Council—and we must remember that this includes *all* members of local Councils and affiliated societies throughout the country—will support this new venture by taking the CANADIAN HOME JOURNAL."

A loftier endorsement Faith could not have wished for. From then on, the centre section was devoted to NCWC reports edited by Ishbel Aberdeen, and occasionally stretched to three pages. Arrangements were made to send all returned, unsold copies of the *Journal* to various local groups for distribution to the thousands of women members of the association for their consideration and, of course, to persuade them to subscribe. By January 1897, Faith revealed she had made even more extravagant offers: "To our offer to share with the local Councils the profits of the JOURNAL, we have received, in many cases, very encouraging replies; and we are looking forward to the time, in the near future, when every one of the hundred thousand members in affiliation with the

National Council will be a subscriber, and the success of the Council and the JOURNAL bound up with each other. We are doing all we can with this end in view."

A hundred thousand subscribers—what more could any magazine want? It must have seemed to Faith that nothing could go wrong. The magazine was growing; there was plenty of advertising, and some had to be turned away for lack of space. The problems of distribution—getting the *Journal* out in time and in good condition across nineteenth-century Canada—would largely be answered by this special relationship with the NCWC.

And what about the rest of the magazine, the other thirty pages or so around the First Lady's pages? They stuck to the approved formula of the time—short stories, fashion articles, travel pieces, book reviews, a children's corner—with the possible exception of the sports page. Faith was able to get hold of some distinguished contributors—writers such as Horatio Gilbert Parker, one of Canada's leading novelists, whom she already knew from her "Woman's Empire" days. A signed copy of *Pierre and His People: Tales of the Far North* is still among her possessions.[15]

In fact, those old ties from her newspaper days gave her the bulk of her articles. The magazine must have been published under considerable time pressure, and Faith occasionally revamped earlier work, but there is some interesting new material, including an interview with ninety-four-year-old Catharine Parr Traill, whom Faith visited in her Lakefield home in December 1895.[16] The author sent Faith a copy of *Pearls and Pebbles, Or the Notes of an Old Naturalist*, published in 1894 when she was ninety-two, a charming thank-you letter and this little poem based on the old schoolchildren's doggerel:

> Catharine Parr Traill is my name
> England was my nation
> Lakefield is my dwelling place
> And Faith Fenton my admiration.

As in "Woman's Empire" days there is a letter-bag, but it is quite brief, and the bulk of the enquiries were obviously about household rather than personal or political matters. Many of the women reading the magazine still had the traditional female preoccupations, and it is worth noting that the incentive of a book for those getting three new subscribers was changed to a gift of cutlery. There is virtually no mention of "The Other Half," that submerged tenth of the population. But occasionally there is a flash of the old Faith:

> Professor Goldwin Smith, whose antipathy to advanced women is well known, must have found himself in an uneasy position as guest at the Cornell Alumnae luncheon in New York on Feb 28th. Dr. Schurman and Professor Goldwin Smith were the only male guests present. . . . Nay; worse still; Dr. Schurman was unkind enough to leave early . . . and the Professor was left absolutely alone, a solitary man, amid numerable clever and degreed women—physicians, lawyers, politicians . . . yet he made a pleasant speech. . . . Perhaps it is only Canadian women who are to be kept in due domesticity.

Three of Ishbel's letters from this period have survived. The first, dated August 14, 1896, is from New Brunswick, and explains that she has waited until the last minute to receive material for "my two pages," but has had to put together what she can and hopes it is enough. There are even instructions about the size of print to be used for one section. She then gives Faith her itinerary for the next few days, adding, "Please wire me before 2 p.m. on Monday if you need more copy." The postscript suggests on what a comfortable and equal footing these two women were with each other: "Pray forgive these terrible smudges. I let the paper slip with this fatal result. And it is so late that I will not re-write the note."

The second letter is a day later, from Ottawa, so presumably Faith had wired her. It enclosed an account of a council meeting at Regina, and again has specific editorial instructions, suggesting how Faith could cut it down. She also requests a proof copy of her "notes" to be sent to Ottawa—"Indeed I should always be glad to have a proof, even if there were only time to wire a correction. But I would ask you never to *wait* for my corrections or to make any delay." It finishes with a request that, being from Ishbel, reads more like an order: "I should be glad to have 100 copies of the 'Hints for forming new Local Councils' struck off in leaflet form." As always, it opens "Dear Miss Fenton" (with the "ss" in the old script "f") and closes: "Yours very sincerely, Ishbel Aberdeen."

The third letter, dated May 14, 1897, is from Government House, Ottawa. It is typed, not longhand, and has Ishbel's signature at the end:

> I was very sorry to receive your letter of May 11th, and to find that your hopes had not been realised.
>
> It must be a considerable trial to you to find all the work which you have devoted to the Canadian Home Journal for the last year frustrated, but I trust that the new woman's paper which you have in view may become a reality before long.
>
> In the meantime, may I trouble you to direct that the copies which I receive monthly of the Canadian Home Journal need not be continued.

Somewhere around the beginning of 1897 a bombshell had fallen. Who can doubt Faith Fenton cried herself to sleep that terrible night when her editorship of the *Canadian Home Journal* was terminated. The last issue edited by Faith Fenton came out in April 1897, but the magazine was to continue on without her, and without Ishbel Aberdeen.

The end had come suddenly and apparently without warning, because Faith edited the April issue and wrote to Ishbel on May 11. The most likely explanation is, of course, that the proprietors saw their property turning into a propaganda machine for the NCWC and Ishbel Aberdeen, and had told Faith to terminate the arrangement. Faith would never have chosen the proprietors over the governor general's wife—the tradesmen over the lady.

The only discernible new factor around that time was the influx of new capital from the Stewart Publishing Company, which joined the proprietors of the *Canadian Home Journal*. Sturgeon Stewart was another Simcoe boy, who, among other things, had published a Liberal newspaper in Richmond Hill. Although he was Liberal, like the Aberdeens, possibly this time Faith's old Tory Simcoe County roots tripped her up.

Ishbel Aberdeen had as well many opponents in the various women's organizations, and they may have objected to having to submit all their material to be vetted, edited and approved by Ishbel herself. Head of the list would certainly have been Isabel Kirkpatrick, wife of the lieutenant-governor of Ontario, who had what Ishbel herself called "a violent antipathy" to her Ottawa superior. Ishbel was not only anathema to the Toronto society led by Lady Kirkpatrick, but was disliked by "the great army of the Temperance people," and the Toronto medical profession, headed by Dr. Charles O'Reilly—"organised in virulent bitterness and complete ignorance" against the Victorian Order of Nurses (VON), which Ishbel was promoting. Many women wanted to hear what Faith Fenton had to say, not the voice of Ishbel Aberdeen.

Faith Fenton's prime contact, who had probably been her downfall, would be gone from the country in another year. Faith had just turned forty. She was single. She was out of work. What was there to do? Where was there to go? Only Faith would have come to a decision as outlandish as the one she made. She hitched up her skirts and went to the Klondike.

XII

A Woman's Birthright

When beauty in women ceases to be the chief magnet to
men . . . then only shall women cease to place beauty
first and above all of their desires.

To most women life is simply one long "waiting."
Even in these modern times we cannot go out to seek
"our own" in friendship and loves, especially in that one
greatest love that is present in every woman's thought as
she reads the[se] lines. It must come to us or we miss it
for ever.

Faith Fenton, "Woman's Empire," 1893.

WHY DID FAITH MAKE THE EXTRAORDINARY DECISION that she made—to
leave all that was familiar and secure in middle age, to abandon a network
built up over nearly twenty years that surely could have been mended?

In her letter of regret, Ishbel had mentioned Faith's plans for a new
magazine, but obviously those hopes came to nothing. Whether Faith
was unable to raise the capital, or whether she set her sights on the
Klondike and abandoned the idea, can only be guessed at. If there was
one thing that year and a half running the *Canadian Home Journal*
would have taught Faith, it was that if chief editors packed their bags
and went off gallivanting around the country, problems arose. Even Alice
Freeman had had more opportunities for travel.

By the time she was let go by the *Canadian Home Journal*, Faith
would already have known of Ishbel Aberdeen's plans to form a group

of travelling "district" nurses to look after the sick and suffering in Canada's isolated communities. The original proposal had been made through the NCWC and recorded in the *Canadian Home Journal*, and by 1897 Ishbel Aberdeen was attempting to obtain funding and fighting opposition from the medical profession and from nurses themselves for the proposed Victorian Order of Nurses (VON), named to commemorate Victoria's Diamond Jubilee in 1897.[1] Sometime towards the end of 1897, when the tent cities began to go up around Rabbit Creek in the Yukon, and Rabbit Creek became Bonanza, Ishbel came up with a brilliant publicity stunt for her much-maligned VON: they would take their skills to that most isolated community of all. And at some time in 1897 Faith Fenton took the greatest gamble of her life; she went to those high-placed contacts of hers and called in her markers.

The year 1896 had been one of glittering success for Faith. She had absented herself from Toronto in February to cover the great Historical Ball organized by the Aberdeens in Ottawa and held in the Senate Chambers. In her diary Ishbel said that the idea was to take everyone's mind off politics, "and the everlasting discussion of hockey and winter sports varied with Ottawa society scandal." By all accounts the event was a huge success.

In the March issue of the *Canadian Home Journal*, Faith gave her account of the ball, describing for her readers the various tableaux depicting significant periods and immigrant groups in Canadian history. What she chose not to tell them was that she had been no mere onlooker, but had herself been in one of those historical groups—namely, the United Empire Loyalists—and that she had portrayed a Mennonite, Sister Martha Quincey. Given the elaborate nature of many of the costumes, the simple Mennonite outfit was a sound choice for a journalist of modest means—and who better than Alice Freeman, who had lived in a Mennonite community, to play the role?

That ninth historical group was organized and headed by one of Ottawa's leading families, the Scotts, whose roots in Canada went back to the creation of Ottawa as capital city. The Honourable Richard Scott was made secretary of state in 1896 and was one of the most influential ministers in Wilfrid Laurier's government when the Liberals swept to power that year. There were representatives of other leading families in the group—the Ritchies and the Desbarats—and one very interesting member of the Scott family, Agnes Scott.[2]

Agnes Scott has been revealed only in the last decade, by Sandra Gwyn, as the society journalist who wrote for *Saturday Night* as "Amaryllis," and as "The Marchioness" for *The Ottawa Free Press* from 1897 for the following five years.[3] Could it have been the contact with Faith Fenton that inspired the niece of the Cabinet minister? Certainly their concerns were similar: both enjoyed being part of high society, while at the same time laughing at its foibles, both had a social con- science, and supported the National Council of Women.

In her "Entre Nous" column in the *Ottawa Free Press* in 1898 "The Marchioness" says of Faith: "Faith Fenton, one of the leading journalists of Canada, is in town. . . . we may look for some interesting articles on that august body [the Senate] from her brilliant pen. The Senators, how- ever, need never fear. Faith Fenton's pen, though brilliant, is never unkind."

Treasured from that wonderful period when Faith was not just an observer, but a participant in the rituals and celebrations of the high and mighty, are a handful of invitations: at-homes with the Aberdeens, Sir Mackenzie Bowell, Mrs. George Foster (Faith probably met George Foster when he was Minister of Fisheries in Sir John A.'s government; he wrote a congratulatory letter to her about the *Canadian Home Journal* in 1895). Her invitation to the Historical Ball has survived, as has her programme, complete with tiny pencil and coloured pictures of the Senate buildings on the front, and the explorers Cartier, Ericsson and Cabot on the back.

There is a pencilled star against the fourth tableau and dance, "BOURREE . . . the Early Settlers in Acadia," which was Mrs. Dickey's party, so presumably Faith had something to do with this section of the entertainment, or planned to give it special coverage. Arthur Dickey was Minister of Justice in Mackenzie Bowell's Cabinet and would soon play a role in his leader's resignation.

Mrs. Potter Palmer, the leader of Chicago society, was there, of whom Faith had observed on that ecstatic White City sojourn "how beautiful middle-age may be made by a beautiful and wealthy woman." Also in attendance was the great Canadian diva Emma Albani, and Faith could thank her personally for the letters and best wishes that Albani had sent to Faith's readers over the years. Faith Fenton probably knew and had met as many of the glamorous, the government leaders and their wives, as anybody in Ottawa that fabulous February 1896.

In May 1896, Faith attended the annual meeting of the NCWC in Montreal, and she spoke at one of the sessions. It was another chance to meet with old acquaintances, one of whom was E. Pauline Johnson, the poet and performer who called herself "The Mohawk Princess," and whose letter of appreciation—"to a fellow craftsman—or rather woman?"—for a glowing review in "Woman's Empire" is still among Faith's papers.[4]

The Montreal meeting was the last Faith was to attend. In Ishbel's letter of regret she says how sorry she is that Faith is unlikely to be at the 1897 annual meeting in Halifax—"[but] hope that your attendance there may yet be arranged." Records for that meeting do not mention the name of Faith Fenton. The party, it seemed, was over.

This time she was afraid. When *The Empire* folded in March 1895, there had been only six months before the *Canadian Home Journal* began publication, so presumably plans were under way soon after the merger with *The Mail*. But the lady journalist had now exposed herself as a feminist before the word was invented. To cap it all, she had made enemies by allying herself with a woman who was, by her own account, hated in Toronto.

Loss of power meant not only loss of face, but loss of income. At this point in her life Faith was living on what savings she had and spending her waking hours and sleepless nights wondering how she was going to manage. She could not turn to her siblings because they were far from wealthy and, although she was a regular columnist for *The Evening News* from April to September 1897 and also wrote for *The Mail and Empire* and *The Mail-Express*, it would have been a hand-to-mouth existence.

She would never have gone to her parents. There is some tangible proof that her mother was proud of her renegade daughter, because she presented Faith with a leather-bound book of the issues of the *Canadian Home Journal* she had edited with the simple and unvarnished inscription: "Alice from Mother." But having chosen her independence, Faith could never return to the small world of her parents.

Then, in the late summer of that bleak year of 1897, Faith had a stroke of luck. She obtained an interview with eighty-two-year-old Janet

Carlyle Hanning, the sister of the great philosopher and historian Thomas Carlyle, "The Sage of Chelsea," who lived in Toronto, and the ensuing article was published in *The Mail and Empire* on October 2. It was more of a visit than an interview with the old lady, who was by then in her second childhood, and on that occasion, Mrs. Hanning's daughter, Jane Carlyle Laing, agreed to give Faith access to all of her uncle's letters to his sister, to copy and make use of as she wished. Faith had struck paydirt.

To understand what a journalistic coup this was, one must understand the significance of Thomas Carlyle to his age. Getting access to his correspondence was somewhat comparable to being given exclusive rights to hitherto unpublished private letters from Voltaire or Freud—or even Shakespeare. The Sage of Chelsea was almost as popular as the Bard of Avon, particularly in the United States, and to justify such a claim one need only quote the figure Faith was paid. The literary agents and magazine publishers the S.S. McClure Company of London and New York, paid two hundred dollars for exclusive American rights to a series of articles on the correspondence, to be published in the magazine *The Critic*.[5] The buying power of that fee today would be around eight to ten thousand dollars—a little different from "a $1 for anything with a head"!

Day after day Faith sat in the offices of the Toronto General Trusts Company, copying every letter out longhand, making notes as to how useful or interesting each letter would be for her purpose, even noting where the signature of the great man was missing or appeared to be cut off.

The potential for making money on the project was so great that she had involved publisher Herbert Johnson of the Massey Press in Toronto—who coincidentally was married to her sister Lily—and an attorney with a confusingly similar name, Hubert Johnson, who witnessed the permissions she needed to gain access to the letters. Presumably the Massey Press was hoping to publish Faith's articles in Canada—the *Massey Magazine* carried an article by Faith, "On Canada's Capital," in their June issue.

When she got home at night, Faith organized and typed out her pencilled notes, and wrote her articles, which were sent to the McClure Company. Back came the two hundred dollars. *The Critic* trumpeted their upcoming, exclusive series on hitherto unknown letters of the great Carlyle, to be published in 1898.

Then trouble struck in the shape of one Reverend George Franklin of Ripley, Ontario, a relative by marriage of Carlyle's. He wrote to the

McClure Press, threatening legal action if they went ahead and published Faith's articles on the letters, which, he said, had been copied "by stealth." He himself had obtained access to the letters and had set up a deal with—of all people—the Houghton Mifflin publishing company, who sent legal documents to the McClure Company to prove "the heirs had legally assigned to them all rights." There was no Harry Houghton for Faith to appeal to; he had died the previous year. At this point the McClure Company got cold feet and tried to withdraw—not only that, the company's treasurer, John S. Phillips, asked for their money back: "It seems to me, on the whole, best that we should return the manuscripts to you and that you return the $200. to us. We have all got into this affair, and I don't see any other way out of it honorably for all concerned."

Herbert Johnson wrote angrily to the McClure Company, defending Faith and attacking the Reverend Franklin, suggesting he had jumped on the bandwagon when he realized the financial potential of the correspondence. In fact, it was his wife, who, as one of the heirs, had given written permission to Faith. There was a furious exchange of letters, with accusations, evidence and affidavits volleying between Phillips and Johnson.

Hubert Johnson fired off a demand for copy of the permission given by Mrs. Franklin to be printed in *The Critic*, "according it the same prominence that the letter of Mr. Franklin received," and challenging the reverend gentleman's motives for "vilifying the character of a lady, who would be the last to use the means ascribed to her, and who stands in the highest ranks of Canadian journalists."

Looking back a hundred years with the help of the evidence that has survived, it does indeed seem as if the Reverend Franklin jumped into the publishing fray when Faith's interest awoke him to the market for the Carlyle letters. However, it also seems probable that the heirs did not realize that giving Faith permission to copy the letters might infringe upon their own rights, and their chances of making money. The two women, Jane Carlyle Laing and Mrs. Franklin, were unworldly "housemothers," and may have thought Faith Fenton was only going to write an article for *The Mail and Empire*. Nowhere did those permissions enforce any conditions or control over the material and, in legal matters, *qui tacit consentire*. Technically, Faith had done nothing wrong.

An outraged Reverend Franklin wrote:

> It is quite likely, I understand, that when the "copyist" of
> this correspondence returns to civilization, certain New York
> publishers will give the party "a bad quarter of an hour" or
> longer. . . . I very much regret that Miss Fenton has so far
> forgotten herself (whatever may be her standing as a literary
> woman) as to sell these copies . . . to a literary agency in
> New York and then start for the Klondyke. It looks bad.

Look bad it certainly did, for the Reverend Franklin and the
McClure Company's two hundred dollars. In September 1898 Herbert
Johnson wrote to the McClure Company reproving them for not publishing Faith's articles, but saying that there was not much he could do
"until Miss Fenton's return from the Klondike, which we trust will be
shortly." It was going to be a long, long wait.[6]

Faith now had her bankroll, but she needed more than that. She
needed a publisher and a sponsor. She probably lined up her sponsors
first, and then took her proposition to *The Globe* for a series of articles to be written en route to the Klondike while accompanying the
four nurses chosen from the newly formed VON. Family records suggest that *The Globe* approached her, but Lady Aberdeen's letter about
the Klondike trip says that it was Faith who decided to offer her material to them. The five women were not setting out on the adventure
alone, but were accompanying an army unit that had been created to
protect Canada's ill-defined frontier with the United States in that
region—the Yukon Field Force, under the command of Lieutenant-
Colonel T.D.B. Evans, a veteran officer of the Royal Canadian
Dragoons.

Apart from Ishbel Aberdeen, Faith's only known sponsor for the
trip was her old friend Senator Sanford. Given his wife's association
with the NCWC, it is more than likely Faith had them both in her corner. A letter sent by Ishbel to Faith in April 1898 names Senator
Sanford as the supplier of her travel outfit, which the Sanford
Manufacturing Company was also supplying to the VON nurses, and to
the military contingent. He may have done more, and certainly Ishbel
did more. Not only did she back Faith to the committee of the VON,
but she also sent off letters to British newspapers, among them *The*

Dundee Advertiser and *The Westminster Budget,* offering them Faith's Klondike columns.[7]

Ishbel Aberdeen was not the only distinguished correspondent on Faith's behalf to Britain's fourth estate. The premier himself, Sir Wilfrid Laurier, recently knighted by Queen Victoria, wrote to Alfred Harmsworth of *The Mail*:

> The Canadian Government will send in a few days a small military force to the Yukon. Miss Faith Fenton . . . will accompany them as correspondent for some newspapers. Miss Fenton has had a long experience in journalism and she is a facile and forcible writer. We expect that she will contribute no small share in making that section of our country known. . . . I am happy to bear testimony to her ability for such a task.[8]

She had her publisher. She had her kit: two suits in dark green mackinaw cloth, with a skirt that came to the knee (the VON wore blue, with a longer skirt) and was designed to be worn with bloomers; a lighter summer-weight suit; a Norfolk-style blouse with plenty of pockets; a long overcoat of brown duck (a kind of heavy cotton); a long racoon coat, which would be presented to her and the nurses by the Hudson's Bay Company in Vancouver; and a sleeping bag.

There were only a few wrinkles to be ironed out, according to that letter of April 6, 1898, from Ishbel Aberdeen. One was the question of rations, and Ishbel had applied to the government for Faith to be supplied in the same manner as the troops and the VON, with government money. The other was the health and strength of Faith herself:

> And now may I ask you to be good enough to forward to me a certificate as to your health and strength, signed by some well-known Physician in Toronto? We have had to require this from the nurses. . . . I know that you will understand that this is a matter of business and will not mind.

Perhaps I ought to tell you frankly that there are some of our Committee who are a little nervous about your undertaking.—They think that you do not look strong, and are afraid of their responsibility.

The physician's report must have been favourable, because the following announcement was given a prominent place in *The Globe* on April 16, 1896:

Arrangements have been made with "Faith Fenton," who, in the capacity of special correspondent, will accompany the Victorian Nurses to the Klondike for the supply of special correspondence. The Globe has secured the exclusive right of publishing these letters in Canada. Leaving Ottawa in the course of a few days, the ladies will proceed to Vancouver. There they will join the troops under Lieut.-Col. Evans. Thence to Glenora, and over the mountain passes to the head waters of the Yukon is the course mapped out, and it is by no means an easy or unadventurous journey for women to essay.

Faith's life had been by no means an easy or unadventurous journey to that point in 1898, but the difficulties she would encounter over the next six months would test her endurance in ways she could not have imagined. How could she know if the hours of walking, the miles of rowing, the countless climbs up the city's ravines were enough to prepare her physically for what lay ahead? She had fought fiercely to make the journey; she would not have allowed herself to think of failure. Faith was not just running away from lawsuits or lost jobs, or lost dreams. She was setting out on a quest to find what had not come to her, and what she now yearned for more than fame, or fortune—or even being "Faith Fenton."

In October 1893, Faith Fenton wrote a column for "Woman's Empire" titled "The Marriage Question." In it she wondered how any man could imagine that any woman would not think "marriage to be the noblest career for women," and stated she had yet to meet an independent woman, "no matter how successful in her chosen profession, who would not instantly lay it down at love's behest, who would not deem happy matronhood a career far above the most successful career of solitary independence."

That Faith is speaking about herself at this time in her life, there can be little doubt. The point she makes in the article is that it is ridiculous to believe that, for women, "marriage is one among the occupations or professions open to them to be adopted or turned from as they prefer." She concludes: "Women do not take up outside occupations in preference to marriage . . . but rather because marriage—the right and happy marriage—may not be; or marriage, having been, has proved neither right nor happy."

Faith is not championing the blind acceptance of marriage as the ideal; she is doing something more revolutionary than that. She is suggesting that only a good marriage is ideal, that an occupation is "preferable to a marriage of convenience," and that a woman should only leave her independent state "to become the wife of the man she loved."

During the years since her childhood in Bowmanville with her own parents and with the Reikies, Faith had been able to look closely at another marriage. For most of her "Woman's Empire" years, when she was holding down two jobs and two identities, she had lived with her brother Fred, whom she called her "best friend," and his wife, Elizabeth. Jack, the "Boy Blue" of her columns, is her nephew and their son, called "Frederick" after his father. So close is the relationship described in her columns that many thought she was a married woman—"Mdme or Mdselle Fenton"—and on one occasion she calls Jack "my six-year-old." She talks of him climbing into bed with her and singing to her, of sharing his secrets with her, of reading to him. Readers sent him hugs and kisses. It was Elizabeth who helped Faith dress for her excursion in disguise to the House of Industry, Fred who took her to the station at the start of many a trip.

Faith herself had become more than a best friend to her sisters. She had become their shining example, their mentor and, in many ways, their mother. Her sister Gracie was another familiar figure in her columns, and Edith was trying to be a journalist. The Toronto Street Directory of 1899 shows Edith calling herself "Edith Fenton." Edith and Florence were to follow in their sister's footsteps in more than a metaphorical sense in the near future. By the age of forty, Faith had become a matriarch without a marriage.

For all the success, the admiration, the emulation, Faith Fenton was haunted by the sense that what she was doing was only second-best. Anna Jameson, who also shot the rapids at the Sault, maintained that three-quarters of the women writers she knew suffered from a sense of being "placed in a painful or false position." If you worked, you were not a woman—even if you were married. How much more painful and false, then, to be an unmarried woman writer. Faith comments:

"You are not a suffragist; you are too womanly for that," said one [man] to me recently in commendatory tone.

The speaker was well aware that I valued his good opinion; and after that how could I confess that away down in my heart I do believe in woman suffrage, and so stand confessed in his eyes—unwomanly.

Now she stood confessed in the eyes of the world "unwomanly." She was forty and she had never had confidence in her appearance. Her writing is full of references to her looks—directly and by implication. She had thought of herself as a homely child; she talked of having "few bodily graces," of glancing into a hand mirror in a store and putting it down hastily, "because it reflects so truly—so truly." She told one of her correspondents, Aline H., that it is too bad she had missed seeing her— "but it isn't a serious loss; I'm really afraid you would have been disappointed." She was chided by her readers for a column headed, "Our Birthright of Beauty," in which she stated that she and a group of women friends had agreed that "we had no desire to be clever; and that we wished for beauty above every other possession." It is a particularly poignant statement from clever Alice Freeman, who had striven all her forty years to excel.

Faith's misgivings about her own looks never stopped her complimenting the beauty of other women in her columns, whether they were actresses, activists or just women she saw in the course of her career. At a theatre matinée she took time to admire the woman sitting directly in front of her: "As she turns her profile towards me, I note her lovely face, and for the remainder of the afternoon she has a larger share of my admiration than the celebrated beauty upon the stage."

She also commented frequently in her columns on handsome and good-looking men—from the *Empire* police reporter to members of Parliament. She particularly admired the dark eyes and dark hair of many of the French-Canadian politicians, and joked about Sir Wilfrid Laurier's attractiveness, regretting that he was not a Conservative.

She certainly had more contacts with men than most single women of her era—she talks of being escorted home by various males, including Divinity students from Knox College, and different members of *The Empire* staff.[9] She spent days in the company of Julian Ralph of *The New York Sun* in Quebec City. She spent hours alone in the book-lined studies of Professor Clark of Trinity College and Professor Grant of Queen's University in Kingston, talking with them as very few women of her era were able to talk to distinguished and intelligent men; their charming letters to her are still among her papers. Professor Grant addresses her as "my dear friend." But most of these men were already taken.

If she had admirers she kept that fact hidden from her readers. Yet surely someone, sometime, somewhere along the way, tried to be more than a friend to independent, passionate Alice, with her direct stare and her beautiful voice. The problem for Alice Freeman would have been that it was a rare man indeed who would have agreed to live with two women, particularly the woman called Faith Fenton.

Now, however, she was half-sick of shadows and looking for "a guiding hand to clasp—a warm, human hand," a companion with "the kindly nature, the loving heart, the strong yet gentle human-ness" of the two university professors she admired. In her early thirties she had written that "a woman's bitterest moment, I think—especially if she be a woman unloved and therefore lonely—is when she turns from her mirror realizing for the first time that the fair flush of youth has vanished."

Had she left it too late? And where would she find him? The stock of husbands for a forty-year-old was virtually non-existent, and Faith was not one to settle for second-best. As she said to "Adele," who wrote to her in 1894 about the scarcity of men: "The Minister of Trade and Commerce says that wives are badly needed out in the North-West. . . . If twenty or thirty nice young women, who were not afraid to work, desired to go out into great grain country I am sure he would find a way of sending them; and it would be nice to have a choice of husbands, wouldn't it?"

Fate had put her in a position where she had nothing to lose by taking her own advice, and fate brought Faith the interview that may well have decided her on an incredible journey.

William Ogilvie was an unlikely cupid. In 1896 he had been appointed Dominion Minister of the Interior to survey and establish the boundary line between Alaska and Canada, and he was in the Yukon as the Canadian government surveyor when the first gold was found at Bonanza and Eldorado. He had already won fame by his explorations on the Mackenzie and Yukon rivers, and had been elected a Fellow of the Royal Geographical Society for his work. Faith managed to get an interview with him when he visited Toronto in 1897.[10]

As might be expected, most of the interview was about the sort of women who were going to the Yukon—were they all adventuresses? No, Ogilvie assured her, not all of them. With the Klondike boom, many brave wives had gone with their husbands, and also "a few, respectable, sturdy, single women, attracted by the prospect of work and high wages."

Faith asked him how such women stood the rigours of the journey— well, she was assured—and whether a single, respectable woman would be able to live her life without molestation. Ogilvie assured her that the law was "wholesomely observed," and that the miners' moral code would make them prompt to protect any woman who "wished to earn her living by honest work."

How then, Faith asked, did such women earn their living? Ogilvie told her that they took in washing, did cooking and sewing—such services were in high demand—and added that eastern women should remember that these essential occupations were not looked down upon as they were in Toronto. However, he advised women thinking of going to the Klondike to wait a year until communications were better and new towns established.

"What about the prospects of marriage for women out there?" she asked him. Ogilvie replied, "Very good . . . the loneliness is great and the incentive to marriage strong." Possibly it was this answer that mattered most of all.

In August 1897, William Ogilvie was off again to the Yukon with a party of thirty, including a young doctor called John Nelson Elliott Brown. Brown turned up at Union Station in Toronto with a hundred and fifty pounds of equipment in three canvas bags, and a typewriter. Ogilvie promptly made him his secretary.[11]

Faith did not possess, as so many women did, "the terrible power of waiting." Waiting for something to happen had never been her way—if her prince was not going to come to her, then she would go out and look for him. In April 1897 she set out to find him. If ever there was an adventuress on the Klondike trail it was that respectable, sturdy single woman journalist, Faith Fenton.

PART THREE

In the Palace Beautiful

XIII

Gold Fever

I do not care for anything that has no life. If you can put life into it; if you can make your ore pregnant with human history; or if you can imbue it with passion of suffering, or of love . . . then my interest would be unflagging.

Faith Fenton, "Woman's Empire," 1891.

GOLD. UNTIL THE CENTURY TURNED, that magic word dominated the news in Canada from the moment in 1896 when George Carmack, Skookum Jim and Tagish Charlie staked their claims on Rabbit Creek, a tributary of the Klondike soon to be known throughout the world as Bonanza.[1] Every advertisement section in the newspapers boasted a plethora of Yukon goods and chattels: clothing outfitters, drug outfitters, mining supplies, Klondike cameras, compressed Klondike horsefeed, Klondike stoves. And if your product was not directly useful for the Klondike, then you simply named it for the Klondike: Gold Dust laundry detergent, for example.

The saga of the Klondike gold rush gave a young nation heroes, heroines and villains as richly colourful as any created by Rider Haggard, and stories about the incredible riches in the valleys and hills of the Klondike read like pure fiction. People flocked in search of riches from all over North America and Europe.

But first you had to get there. Getting there, in fact, dominates the saga of the Klondike. There were various routes to the goldfields, and all of them required endurance and courage—most would have called it foolhardiness. All of them also involved crossing American territory, and since the two-hundred-strong Yukon Field Force had been specifically created to symbolize Canadian sovereignty in an area largely occupied by Americans, the so-called All-Canadian route was chosen—a slow, back-breaking slog of a route that killed half of those who undertook it. In reality it involved the use of American territorial waters, but they were waters on which navigation rights had been granted to Canada.

From Vancouver the route was a four-hundred-mile odyssey to Fort Selkirk, over a hundred miles south of Dawson City itself, where the Field Force would establish their headquarters. They would go by steamer from Vancouver to Wrangell in Alaska, then by river-boat up the Stikine River to the head of navigation in Glenora.[2]

At Glenora the true test would begin—a march of a hundred and fifty miles across a mountainous, mosquito-infested landscape of forest, bush and muskeg to the southern shore of Teslin Lake. There the Field Force would hope to coincide with the arrival of a steamer, or build the boats that would take them to the head of the lake, and then up the Hootalinqua River to the Yukon and to Fort Selkirk, established on the junction of the Pelly and the Yukon. It would be an epic journey to rival those of any of the story-book heroes of Alice's childhood, a pilgrim's progress of a journey in a northern landscape as alien and exotic in its own way as any in her beloved *Arabian Nights*. But there would be no magic carpet provided by the Sanford Manufacturing Company, no genie, no secret incantations to whisk Faith's hobnail boots over mountains and muskeg. She would have to manufacture her own.

When she arrived in Ottawa, Faith stayed in the Margaret Louisa Home, a women's hostel on Sparks Street, and had the unusual experience of facing interviews, rather than giving them. It is a rare opportunity to see Faith through someone else's eyes. She is described as practical, business-like, small, slight, alert and sympathetic. In one account she is characterized as "an enterprising and successful young woman who has helped to advance the popularity of journalism as a calling for women in Canada."

The use of the word "young" is interesting, because in the context of the nineteenth century, forty was far from young. The interviewer also adds that the years of struggle have left their mark on her, as if aware of a discrepancy between her appearance and her presumed age. Later on,

Faith would take a leaf from the Reverend Reikie's book on slowing the passage of time, but it was possibly at the start of her Klondike adventure that she first pared a few years from her age—perhaps to help obtain the certificate required to alleviate official concerns about her fitness.

It is also interesting to read the carefully selected biography Faith gives the unnamed interviewer. She said she was born in Toronto of English parents, that she came from military stock on her mother's side, that her mother was born in the Tower of London, that she had lost an uncle in the Crimean War and that her gift for writing probably came from her songwriter grandfather, Henry Fenton. She said that she was trained as a teacher, but began to write because "she could not help it." Apart from her place of birth, none of it was untrue, but the bourgeois side of her parentage and her father's trade are not mentioned—neither is her nineteen-year teaching career.

Faith also told the interviewer that she had been engaged by the Canadian Senate in 1894 to write a series of articles about the Upper House, and had lived in Ottawa during that time—suggesting that it was not *The Empire* that had sent her. When it came to selling what was now a public image, Faith was quite capable of giving the truth a more attractive twist, and no letters have survived to prove the matter one way or another.

"The Marchioness," a.k.a. Agnes Scott, had something to say about Faith's trip in her column, "The Social World," in *The Ottawa Free Press* on April 13, 1898:

> It was a surprise to hear that Faith Fenton, the enterprising journalist, was among those starting this spring for the Klondike. Miss Fenton of course intends "making copy" out of the trip, and is at present in New York making arrangements to that effect.
>
> It certainly requires courage in a woman to undertake this journey which calls for forced marches of eighteen or twenty miles a day over the most abominable country imaginable. But Faith Fenton has never shown lack of courage and we may look for articles from her pen that . . . will make us all long to go there. Her pen is always dipped in very rosy ink.

This is the only evidence there is that Faith went to New York to make "arrangements" before starting, and it is likely she tried to interest *The New York Sun* in running a series of articles on her journey across the country.[3]

The Ottawa interviews gave Faith a chance to reaffirm the essential truth she had lived all her working life: that no woman should be confined to "what is termed 'a woman's page' or sphere of work in journalism." She was on the threshold of giving her credo a breath-taking new validity.

There were six women in the party setting out in the company of the Field Force: Faith Fenton of *The Globe*; Filumina (Mina) Starnes, the French-Canadian wife of Inspector Cortlandt Starnes of the North-West Mounted Police, stationed in Dawson City; and the four members of the Victorian Order of Nurses—Georgia Powell, from New Brunswick; Margaret Payson, from Nova Scotia; Rachel Hanna, from Ontario; and Amy Scott, recently from Great Britain. The women left Ottawa ahead of the troops at the end of April. Among those at the station to see them off were members of two of Ottawa's leading families, the Ritchies and the Cambies, Sir Sandford Fleming, among whose many other achievements was the invention of Standard Time; and Lord and Lady Aberdeen, with their daughter, Lady Marjorie Gordon. Lord Aberdeen presented Faith and the nurses with bouquets of red roses, and Lady Aberdeen gave them each a lucky shamrock charm in a little case.

The Yukon Field Force was seen off on May 6 in spectacular fashion by Lord and Lady Aberdeen, Sir Wilfrid Laurier, and the Minister of Militia, the Honourable F.W. Borden. Both Lord Aberdeen and Sir Wilfrid addressed the troops, and the Governor-General's Foot Guards played a rousing march as the Field Force, in their scarlet tunics and white helmets, boarded the train. They had with them an arsenal of weapons that sound more impressive than they were: two Maxim machine guns and two obsolete field-guns, with cases of ammunition for them and for the Lee-Enfield rifles they were using. They also carried over two hundred tons of hard-tack biscuits, forty tons of tinned meats and nearly seventy tons of flour. An army not only marches on its stomach, but also only as fast as the supplies for that stomach, as Faith was to discover.

As they travelled across the country Faith had celebrated in her columns, and Alice Freeman in her classroom, she must often have looked out of the train window and thought of all those "dear far-off women" from Newfoundland to the "the great grain country" of the Prairies, for whom she had been confidante and companion for two decades. Perhaps she wondered about Wildflower and Prairie Lily somewhere out there where the horizon stretched for ever, soldiering on. Maybe on that journey she remembered the letter she had written to homesick L.F. of Manitoba, the Christmas of 1893:

> Now, little woman, let me give you some advice from a life fuller in experience than your own. Do not hold yourself aloof from the people around you, even though they may have less of culture. Try to assimilate somewhat with your surroundings. It is natural that the crops and the weather should be the chief topics of interest to people whose prosperity depends on these things. What if they do believe the Queen to be Tennyson's mother-in-law. Does it make them less kindly of heart or less noble in spirit? . . . Oh, I understand it all very well, for I have to fight against the same thing in myself. . . . Keep all of your dainty ways and manners, but do not scorn those who have forgotten them. . . . That's the right spirit for the North-West.

She who had cheered on pioneer women all those years was now about to discover how effectively she could cheer herself on in a world where the hierarchical structure she had lived with all her life was completely overturned. The solid burghers of what middle class there was toiled for low wages and with incorruptible respectability for the Canadian government. Commissioner William Ogilvie registered and regulated the claims of men who had become instant millionaires and never took a penny or staked a claim for himself. In this upside-down layer cake of a society he spent his time happily among men he would never have spoken to back east. Characters who could have walked out of a Dickens underworld or the crumbling mansions of Toronto's King Street carried pokes full of nuggets and pockets full of gold dust.

Women were at a premium—but would she have to take in laundry or hire herself out as a cook until her prince arrived? According to Ogilvie, these were the only occupations for a respectable woman. Faith knew the other kind of woman who would be there, and whether you called her an adventuress or a prostitute or a pitiful bit of straying humanity, she was to be found in any city of the civilized or uncivilized world. Faith would undoubtedly find her high visibility shocking. But for one who knew better than most women of her class the world of the Other Half, the presence of "the fallen woman" in that frontier society would come as no surprise.

Whatever doubts and fears she may have wrestled with on that long journey would have vanished when Faith arrived in Vancouver. As soon as she reached her hotel, she wrote John Willison, the managing editor of *The Globe*, such an enthusiastic letter of praise for the young city that he wired a request for an article along the same lines.

Even though they would have to wait a few days for the troops to arrive, time was at a premium, because many official engagements had been arranged for Faith and the four nurses. The hotel manager placed a top-floor room at Faith's disposal, "where she would be free from noise and molestation," and she completed the article in five hours and mailed it off to Toronto.

Under the heading "An Impressionist Sketch," in heavy type about half an inch high, followed by "Faith Fenton Pictures Vancouver and the West," the article took up about six columns of the May 23 edition of *The Globe*. As always, it was the contrasts that delighted Faith:

> We had gone to sleep in the heart of a great mountain world, white and still with the late April snow that clung in stretches to the bare, scarred heights, a world dark with vast looming shadows, sombre with solitude; we wakened in the freshness and beauty of soft air and sunshine, flowers, green lawns and blossom-laden fruit trees. . . . the sea air whiffs in our nostrils as we walk the city pavements. Vancouver has no long outreaching piers to build. China, Japan, Australia drop alongside in a delightfully familiar way—the whole of Asia and the Orient look in in almost daily greeting.

For many of the readers back east, it was probably their first introduction to Canada's Pacific gateway, and over the next few years portions of Faith's article extolling the virtues of living on the west coast were used in Vancouver guidebooks. Years later, in Dawson City, an old newspaperman from Vancouver, "Wings" Wilkinson, would tell Faith how important her article had been for Vancouverites and, standing in front of her, dramatically recited by heart the last prescient paragraph of her letter:[4]

Those mountain peaks shall some day look down upon a great city, whose streets shall be filled with commerce, whose warehouses shall be stored with wealth, whose harbor shall be thronged with vessels discharging the products of nations. All the gold of the northlands, the scented treasures of the Orient, the spices of the tropics, shall pass through your open lion-guarded gateway, and the time of the fulfillment of the vision is not far removed.

The Vancouver article was the public's first introduction to Faith Fenton as the Klondike correspondent of *The Globe*. In her memoirs, Laura Berton recalls that her only real picture of the Klondike and the Yukon came from the reports of Faith Fenton, and it is no exaggeration to say that thousands of women all over Canada waited eagerly for the latest despatch from their old heart friend.[5] Faith continued to show them that there need be no boundaries to what a woman could achieve. Intellectually, she had already made that clear. Now she was undertaking a physical venture that challenged the strongest of men. Certainly she was going well supplied and with an army of two hundred men, but it would be forty-one-year-old Faith Fenton who had to trek through a hundred and fifty miles of untouched, untravelled wilderness, and no one would be waiting for her to catch her breath and take an unscheduled rest.

Meanwhile, there were visits to Victoria, receptions as the guest of Lieutenant-Governor Thomas McInnes and his wife, lunches with bishops. *The Victoria Daily Colonist* reported: "There is little doubt that

[Faith Fenton's] company will be appreciated by both the nurses and the soldiers, as she possesses a faculty of being of assistance and adding life to any party."

Mina Starnes, in fact, found this outgoing woman journalist rather disconcerting. She described her later to members of her family as a young woman (that word "young" again) somewhat full of her own importance, but also full of life and enthusiasm, whose repartee and observations provoked gales of laughter on more than one occasion.[6] To a well-bred woman of the time, Faith's outspokenness and failure to remain quietly in the background would have seemed rather bewildering.

At the government reception, it had been arranged that each of the nurses "would say a few words, but they backed down when they saw the size of the audience, and to Miss Fenton was left the duty of delivering an address. She was fully equal to the occasion."

Fully equal to the occasion though she may have been, Faith's "interesting little talk on the Victorian Order of Nurses" led to controversy. Two days later *The Victorian Daily Colonist* carried two letters—one from "Quo Vadis," possibly a nurse working in the Royal Jubilee Hospital in Victoria, and the other from Amy Sweet, a nurse working in the same hospital, protesting against the implication in Faith's speech that other members of their profession would not have done what the VON were doing.

The nurses were particularly offended by Faith apparently claiming that "the Victorian Order do their work out of love for God and man whilst we work only for the sake of our fees." Faith was finding out that life as a public figure was full of pitfalls, especially if you were opinionated.

The Carlyle affair followed Faith all the way to Vancouver. A worried Herbert Johnson cabled her on May 9 for permission to contradict the Reverend Franklin's claims about her unauthorized copying of Carlyle's letters, and Faith cabled her authorization the same day. It must have been with relief as well as excitement that Faith finally embarked on May 15, amid cheering crowds, on route to Wrangell and away from controversy.

Right at the beginning of the journey, there were problems. Various gold-seekers, from a French count and his wife to a Chinese cook, had to be turned out of their cabins to accommodate the women and the officers, and this caused "a battle royal upon the wharf" and yet another delay, of three days. Faith's despatch describing the journey on the

Canadian Pacific steamer the *Islander*, written on May 16 at Wrangell, Alaska, was published in *The Globe* on June 4. It is typical Faith Fenton reporting, in that the scenery serves as a spectacular backdrop for the human beings who are in the foreground: "Mining engineers, who know the world as a very little place, surveyors, moneyed speculators, traders, working miners, with just enough to carry them through; and men of shady dress and shadier faces, weave a medly passenger list on any vessel bound for the Klondike."

As she loved to do, Faith moves from the general to the specific, turning the spotlight on two dining-room waiters who, during the course of the trip, produce an amazing range of musical instruments—guitars, mouth organs, jew's harps—that they then proceed to play with professional expertise: "They are, in fact . . . expert stage variety men, working their way to the Klondike."

As the steamer moved between the towering, snow-capped mountains and she listened to the guitar-playing waiters, Faith thought back to those early days of "Woman's Empire" in 1889, when she sat on the deck of the lighthouse supply boat, the *Canada*, and listened to the sound of a guitar played by "the merriest little lady of our party." Steamers also brought back memories of a lonely little girl on a far outreaching pier. Vancouver had no such piers, she said—only Faith and, possibly, some of her long-time readers would know the significance of that statement to her.

Two days later, the *Islander* arrived in Wrangell, a boom town with a dubious reputation and a history that went back to the Cassiar gold rush earlier in the century. Here, the troops would transfer their supplies to two smaller stern-wheelers or paddle-boats, the *Strathcona* and the *Stikine Chief*, to take them up the final leg of the Stikine River to Glenora—a treacherous stretch of shallows, sandbars and driving downstream currents.

Wrangell was Faith's first glimpse of a gold-rush boom town and she described it in her despatch as reminding her of "Quebec's lower town alleys reproduced in wood and canvas." Viewed from the steamer at low tide, as they came into dock, the town seemed, through the pouring rain, to be chiefly wooden wharves "propped on a thousand legs." The main hotel was only two months old and, she found, surprisingly good. But the majority of stores were only weeks old, and nearly everyone "squatted at will" in tents or shacks that were erected everywhere and anywhere. She gave her readers a thumbnail sketch of a population she described as "a pepper-pot sprinkle":

> The lady doctor from Los Angeles, with professional bag in hand, steps blithely out of her tent quarters to visit a patient in a six-bunked, single-roomed shanty across the way. Two young lawyers are having a game of poker on a soap-box outside the doorway of their "office." Correspondents and artists representing some of the world's biggest journals stroll about in roughing suits. . . Klondikers in the regulation yellow knee boots and sombrero are everywhere and the smell of pine boards and the sound of hammer and plane is over it all.

Lieutenant-Colonel Evans made every effort to prevent his troops getting into trouble on what was U.S. territory, in that sprawling, brawling, lawless town that was run by the cohorts of Soapy Smith, the uncrowned criminal king of Skagway. However, Evans was forced to authorize an unscheduled visit by Faith, accompanied by Mrs. Starnes, and probably an officer escort.

The incident was passed on by Mina Starnes to her family, but Faith herself never told her readers, and does not seem to have told her own family. It seems that Faith first appeared in her travelling outfit when they arrived at Wrangell and caused Lieutenant-Colonel Evans, an unmarried man, a nasty moment or two. The advocate of Rational Dress had had her gored skirt shortened until it came only just below her knees, and was wearing it without the regulation bloomers supplied by the Sanford Manufacturing Company. A studio portrait of Faith, taken in Ottawa, shows a skirt that looks quite end-of-the-twentieth-century, worn with what looks like some rather dashing spats cut close to her shapely calves, and a pair of tiny-heeled shoes in place of the hobnailed boots she would wear on the trail. Reeling in shock, Evans asked Mina Starnes to accompany Faith ashore and see what solution they could come up with.

Wild-west Wrangell's answer to the lieutenant-colonel's problem smacks more of dancehall-girl than maiden lady: a border of black satinette. However put out Faith may have been—and she was to be proved right many times over on the Teslin trail—she got a good look at Wrangell for her readers, "with its odor of unsanctity, material and spiritual." "We remember it as a blot," wrote patriotic Faith. "We realise with pride that such a town would be impossible in Canada. The United States has yet to learn how to govern annexed territory."

While they were tied up at Wrangell, the pastor of the Presbyterian Mission, Dr. Swing, came for dinner aboard the *Islander*, and was persuaded by Faith to tell the assembled company lurid tales of the crime and violence always present in that wild gold-rush town.[7]

Besides the four VONs, Mina Starnes and the Yukon Field Force, Faith had another companion on the trail: a kitten rescued from the streets of Wrangell—"a leetle yellow cat," according to Mina Starnes. Again, the kitten is only vaguely mentioned in her columns, but her family know the story, and two photographs survive—one of a young cat walking through the campsite, the other of Faith holding it on her lap. Presumably, Faith carried it over the trail in her pack and let it forage for itself when they camped, and one assumes it never took off into the wilderness.

With the supplies finally on board—the horses and some provisions had to be left until a third boat was available—and Faith's skirt decently lengthened, the two boats started to make their way against the heavy spring current and constantly shifting sandbars of the Stikine River, which, as Faith told her readers, "a little more than a month ago . . . was covered with ice, and dog-sleds were toiling over its surface."

Already at this stage of the trip Faith was realizing the difficulty faced by anyone trying to get accurate reports back east—that conditions changed at a rate more rapid than that of nineteenth-century methods of communication: "If it were possible to overtake copy on its journey eastward, much of it would be 'killed' by the correspondent who, at the time of writing, was expressing the exact truth."

She had been on many of the lakes and rivers of eastern Canada and had run the rapids at the Sault, but never had Faith seen a river like the Stikine, never before had she experienced the drastic change of climate of that stretch of the journey: "At the mouth it shares in the coast weather—a dank, warm atmosphere, a perpetual rain dropping from low mountain mists. . . . Half-way up the river we are still in the rain-belt, but high snow-covered mountains encompass us, glaciers gleam here and there, the rainfalls are chill with winter iciness. Another twenty miles and we are beyond the coast mountains . . . a glad, sunshiny, arid interior of summer heat. . . ." It was a foretaste of things to come.

Faith gave her *Globe* readers pictures of both the breath-taking scenery they passed through and the struggle of the boats against the heavy current. With her, they were up at three o'clock in the morning, teeth chattering in the cold, to view the passing of the Grand Glacier, "a vast, arrested river of ice. It is about two miles in width and stretches down the sombre mountains some 3,500 feet high. . . . Our boat creeps around the bank of it—a terrible bank of crushed stone that has been forced down in this awful avalanche of centuries ago, and now fringes the great ice-field. We look up the gleaming pathway, on and on to where it touches the horizon line fifty miles away. Nothing intervenes between the giant, jagged bed of blue ice and bluer sky."

From the awesome expanse of the mountains, Faith descends to a detailed and claustrophobic description of the appearance—and smell— of the river valley, seen at close quarters when the boats tied up each night, held by heavy hawsers against the current: "The low bank is like a slimy sponge; the Devil's Club and other thorny astringent plants spring thick from the soaking ground, permeating the air with a faint, offensive odor. Coarse mosses of varied texture and shade climb the tree trunks and throttle the slender branches. The snow-streaked, mist-curled moun- tains lock us chillingly about, and the rain falls. . . ."

Entire parties were often drowned on this stage of the journey. Faith told of a terrifying eight-day trip made in a boat similar to their own in which the passengers "had, at various times, leaped into the water, jumped to the nearest rocks, sat with life-preservers fastened waiting for the boat to go to pieces, and spent dreadful hours when the boiler—an old one—panting under the undue pressure of the steam, threatened an explosion."

Here, in this northern landscape, the scenery dominates the human beings who struggle through it, but there they unmistakably are, dotted along the trail and in Faith's columns: the men struggling along the river- bank, "with hands and faces briar-torn, with clothing soaked and in tat- ters," portaging their belongings; the party of three men in a seventeen- foot boat "in which a horse was standing, his four feet planted out firmly. He never moved; had he done so in this sweeping rock-walled canyon through which we were passing, the entire party would have drowned."

Faith would encounter those travellers every step of the way along the trail, "hungry, weary, sick or buoyant . . . full of eagerness, hope or despondency," and use the skills she had developed over two decades to sketch them for her readers, "with their faces turned upstream and Klondike-ward."

Five days after leaving Wrangell, they reached Glenora, and there they celebrated Queen Victoria's birthday on May 24 in "this little far north village of tents" with the firing of a *feu-de-joie* that startled the pack-mules and oxen, a march-past of the troops in dress uniforms, sports in the afternoon, and bonfires in the evening. Hundreds of Klondikers, many of them Americans, in "sombreros, knee-high moccasins, sweaters . . . unshaved and collarless," cheered with the troops and celebrated by opening a barrel of whisky. Here they would stay about a week while Lieutenant-Colonel Evans made preparations for the next stage of the operation: the journey along the Telegraph Trail to Teslin Lake.

The Telegraph Trail was a trail in name only. It was a track that had originally been blazed and named after a proposed overland telegraph line to link the west coast of America with Europe by crossing the Bering Strait, to hook up with another proposed Russian telegraph line across Siberia. Rising through the foothills of the Chechidla Mountains, it led travellers through a treacherous terrain of narrow rocky ledges and precipitous slopes, and often men, women and pack-animals climbed and descended to find themselves in creek beds of moss and algae in which they sank up to their knees.

The nights were chilly, the days hot and humid. Beneath the swamp water the ice remained, and the mud and moisture drenched the women's skirts, turning them to sodden dead weights around their waists—as Mina Starnes said more than once on that terrible journey, "Faith avait raison!" ("Faith was right!"), for their long skirts were cumbersome and treacherous. Even climbing from the valley brought no relief from the marshy swampland, for the very hills were composed of the same bog-like substance—and even if the humans made it through the muskeg, they often had to rescue the mules, who sank belly-high into the muck with their heavy burdens.

Sometimes the track passed through thick forest, where branches and brambles tore at mosquito veils and eyes, and gnarled roots and branches tripped and caught already weary legs. Parts of the countryside still smouldered from recent forest fires; here, the hot ashes rose up in clouds of dust to choke them, and the flames licked around them on the trail, bringing trees down with a sound like thunder. It was a landscape out of Dante's inferno, made more terrible by the clouds of mosquitoes that found their way beneath clothing and veils, clogged mouths and ears, bit every exposed area of skin, adding blood-poisoning and ulcerated sores to the torment of bodies aching with exhaustion.

Under these conditions the Field Force managed to cover about twelve miles a day—so, of course, did the nurses, Mina Starnes and Faith Fenton. And, under these conditions, Faith did what she had done all her life to survive: she looked on the bright side. "There is no royal road to Teslin Lake," she told her readers, and proceeded to find one. On the Telegraph Trail, that meant underplaying the Herculean struggle to survive, and her despatches lose some of the dramatic quality they might have had if she had allowed some of her personal pain to come through. There is a photograph of one of the officers, Major Young, checking Faith's copy, but it is much more likely that she censored herself.

What was clearly a deliberate choice must have posed an interesting dilemma to the journalist who rarely shrank from reporting a tough reality, even if she didn't seek it out. She even underplayed the mosquito menace— although calling them "those vampires among insects," she maintained that the mosquito veils and gloves enabled them to travel "in modest comfort" at the beginning of the journey, and when they were unbelievably bad she simply didn't mention them. Perhaps she saw herself as a propagandist for the VON and the Yukon Field Force, and therefore felt duty-bound to show fighting spirit without the struggle—but in making that choice—dipping her pen "in rosy ink"—she diminished not only her extraordinary achievement but that of the five women with her.

It is largely through the despatches of one of the nurses, Georgia Powell, who also wrote an account for *The Globe* and for the VON, and the diary of a soldier with the Field Force, Edward Lester, that one gets a true picture of that nightmare journey.[8] The human-interest stories in Faith's despatches from Glenora to Teslin Lake are about colourful characters along the trail, and are generally amusing rather than harrowing. The only real suffering she reports to her readers is that of the animals.

Here the woman who attacked the cruel treatment of streetcar horses in Toronto, and begged children to be kind to their pets and taught them to feed the birds in winter, pulls out all the stops:

> . . . it makes ones heart ache to see the condition of many animals that return from the trail—pitiful, weary creatures with great angry blotches like inflamed scalds upon their backs, the result of incompetent packing. Sometimes time is allowed for the wound to heal, but pack animals are valuable, and more often the saddles are readjusted, fresh loads put on over the chaffed and broken skin, and the animal walks on in dumb agony, with a festering fist-deep sore fresh goaded every moment by the load above it, until he drops on the trail and is mercifully shot.

Looking on the bright side may not only have been for propaganda's sake; it may have been because she knew it was what her public would expect of her, and that it was the only way she would get herself through the ordeal. Admitting to exhaustion and discouragement meant allowing that they existed, and Faith's method of getting through the Slough of Despond was to pretend it wasn't there. A record remains of only one of the books she took with her as inspirational reading on the trail. It is not "dear old" *Pilgrim's Progress*, not her favourite *Arabian Nights*, nor anything by Dickens—those she perhaps carried with her in her memory and her heart—but a book called *Prue and I*.

Faith had reviewed *Prue and I*, written by a British author, George Curtis, in one of her "Woman's Empire" columns, and adored it so much that her family had given her a specially bound volume for Christmas in 1894, covered in morocco leather, with her name stamped on the cover. It is a tiny book that would have fitted easily into pocket or knapsack, but it was for inspiration rather than convenience that Faith had chosen it. She returned to it more than once in her columns, and spoke of her "raptures" over it.

Prue and I is a cosily philosophical book about a happily married man whose wife, Prue, is the centre of his world, and who asks for nothing more of life than to return to her side at the end of the day. It is a book whose charm has not worn well; to a modern reader the emotion has become sentimentality, and the humour, whimsy. Nevertheless, it is a book that explains a great deal about Faith's motivation and frame of mind on the journey to the gold-fields.

When they set out on June 1, Lieutenant-Colonel Evans divided his force into three groups. He and about fifty men led the way, blazing the trail to the south end of Teslin Lake and the rear party, led by Major Young, was charged with establishing a base camp and being responsible for all the supplies that had to be carried up the line. The transportation officer, Major Bliss, moved up and down the line among the three parties, coordinating the transfer of supplies. They would work a fourteen-hour day and camp every night.

Faith was in the base party and she probably chose to be there. It was "the point of communication with the outside world," and her main concern would have been how to get her copy out. However, it meant that they moved slowly because of all the supplies that had to be reloaded onto the pack mules every morning—a skilled packer was worth his weight in gold, particularly when dealing with "green" mules.

Even travelling with the base camp, it would be risky and time-consuming getting despatches back to civilization. Faith would have to hand them over to pack-trains going in the other direction and trust they got to the nearest mail depot. Her despatch "At the Base: Of Supplies," for instance—one of her longer articles, complete with photographs—was written on June 28 and published as the main feature in *The Globe* magazine section on July 30.

Mina Starnes, Georgia Powell and Amy Scott were ahead of the base party, and Rachel Hanna was in the rear with Faith. Georgia Powell's account gives details of how the day went:

> We used to get up at 2 in the morning, breakfast at three, tents down and everything packed at 4 and all ready on the trail before 5. Our lunch, or midday meal, consisted of two hard biscuits and a cup of water from the nearest spring, and I am glad to say good water was plentiful, the only good thing on the trail. Then we had dinner just when the [mule] train came in, sometimes at 8 or 9, sometimes as late as 11 p.m.[9]

Already the VON were showing their value under the worst conditions imaginable. Word spread like wildfire along the trail that there were nurses with the Field Force, and men came from miles around to be treated for every imaginable affliction, from malaria to broken bones. One of the nurses, Amy Scott, seems to have had the toughest time on the trail, and at one time or another most needed the use of the one, woefully inadequate horse placed at the disposal of the women. Georgia Powell was exasperated by the animal, which she described as "a stupid, lazy old pony, whose one ambition was to bang up against every tree."

Faith Fenton characteristically turns the same recalcitrant beast into a fairy-tale symbol, saying, "May we also find our white horse and sturdy cavalier to lighten the way." And when the horse is put at her disposal, here is how she describes the scene, ignoring the rigors of the journey:

> A white horse . . . with pack saddle, and blanketed for trappings, and a woman in short walking skirt, high top boots and mosquito veil for rider. She carried a small cat and occasionally a gun belonging to the scarlet-coated orderly who walked beside her. Following came Joe, the pack train cook, who had gallantly placed his white horse at the service of the woman, trudging cheerfully behind humming Orange tunes, and close behind paced the long train of swaying, burdened-backed mules.

The scene has the striking quality of a moving picture rather than a snapshot, and Faith's faithful readers would have known by now who "the woman" was on that horse. Interestingly enough, she mentions a short skirt. Perhaps the satinette did not stand up to the conditions, or perhaps Faith took it off again when sensitive Lieutenant-Colonel Evans left with the advance party. In all the photographs that have survived of Faith on the trail, she is wearing an ankle-length skirt, perhaps saved for just such public occasions.

Faith may well have been given the horse at that point because she

was sick or exhausted—they had just trudged through mountain tor-
rents, muskeg and peaty slime after a week of continous rain—but that is
not part of the moment she chose to remember. However, when they
encountered the forest fires, Faith gave her readers some idea of the horror of that part of the journey:

> Our own way lay for interminable miles through dull,
> smoking trees and over logs yet licked by little flame
> tongues. We traced the trail as best we could through the
> hot ashes. . . . there were nights during the last two weeks
> of our march when the exigencies of distance compelled us
> to camp in forest so recently fire-swept that men were
> detailed to bring water from a near supply and quench the
> little aftermaths of smoke and flame creeping up from the
> coarse, tufted grass around our tents. We ate our evening
> meal standing. . . . Our tents were pitched upon the sooty
> ground. . . . it appears as though our way over the latter
> half of the Teslin trail had been through a world of ashes
> and blackness and desolation.

Faith wrote that report, "In the Muskeg country," on August 29, but it
was not published in *The Globe* until October 8.

Faith's Victorian sense of propriety about personal matters would
never have allowed her to discuss, however remotely, the particular difficulties faced by the women on that long march. Both men and women
would have been wet and filthy most of the time, but for Faith and the
other women their sex would have given them extra burdens.

Menstruation must have been a nightmare. Kimberly-Clark brought
out the Kotex sanitary napkin in 1921, and before that women made do
with flannel diapers that chafed, or homemade pads of absorbent material that they washed and reused. Possibly the physical hardship brought a
blessed temporary release from that monthly problem for some of the
women. One can easily imagine the difficulties for women in long skirts
and bloomers trying to urinate in privacy among "those vampires" of the
Teslin Trail, the mosquitoes, and an army of soldiers. And illness was a

constant worry, even with the presence of the VONs. Shortly after her arrival, Amy Scott had to be invalided out of the Yukon for a major operation. The nature of the surgery is not specified in any of the records, which suggests it was of a personal nature—possibly a hysterectomy.

Just as she had counselled L.F. of Manitoba to keep her dainty ways and manners, so Faith in the middle of nowhere kept up certain standards. Edward Lester records in his diary: "The women have not come in yet which is a blessing, as in the other camp they were an infernal nuisance their tents being so close to ours that they could overhear all that went on, and they were continually making complaints, Tommy's language not being always of the choicest. . . . I think Faith Fenton is at the bottom of it all." He was probably right.

But the journey to the promised land was not all hardship, pain and deprivation. There were moments that did not require an effort of will to turn them into pure pleasure and unalloyed joy. Faith's verbal snapshots of the characters along the trail are filled with her delight. Sometimes they are long-shots: ". . . men bound under heavy packs, each with a staff in hand and broad brimmed hat, recalling vividly the picture of burdened 'Christian' toiling up to the wicket gate in that famed old 'Pilgrim's Progress.'" Sometimes they are close-ups:

One of the pluckiest travellers over the route this season is a little American woman of Scottish descent. She came up over the Stikine River ice in the late winter, in company with her husband. . . . She has made two trips over the Teslin trail in the past three months. . . . They make the trip in easy journeys of ten, twelve or fifteen miles per day. . . . We have passed and repassed her several times upon our journey, and have grown quite friendly, so that the little sun-bonneted figure is always greeted with pleasure, and either tent by the trail side sends forth a genuine woman's invitation to stop and have a cup of tea . . . although she can drive a reluctant pack mule as well as any man, she can also enjoy "The Arena" and "The Scribner." To see a current number of such magazines lying in a Teslin trail tent admits of inferences, even if the tent's mistress does wear a short frayed skirt and sun-bonnet.[10]

The same pleasure is recorded in photographs of Faith with the pack-mules and pet dogs of miners and fortune-seekers she met on the trail, or sitting informally on the ground outside a tent with the great photographer of the Yukon, H.J. Woodside, who later became editor of the Dawson newspaper, *The Sun*. There is also a photograph of Faith writing up her despatches shrouded in her mosquito veil. From the rather unrealistic background it looks as if it was posed in the Ottawa studio, but still it reflects the reality of the trail.

One photograph is of a small tent and is simply labelled "Where I sleep"—Faith had her Kodak camera with her. Originally she had been sharing a tent with some of the nurses, but she was given a small tent of her own by a Presbyterian minister working in the Yukon, the Reverend John Pringle, when he caught up with them on the trail one day and found Faith sick in an overcrowded, small tent—something she herself never mentions. It gave her the much-needed privacy, and the time to herself and her thoughts she had always needed: "As the bugle sounds 'lights out' we look from our tent door through the soft, hazy atmosphere, and above the mauve shadowy hills to where the solemn, snow-clad mountains push their peaks into the strange yellow half light of an arctic midnight." There are echoes here, of the joy and contentment she had found in the solitude of the Laurentians—"oh the lovely aloneness of it all—so far away from men and women and bricks and newspapers."

The journey along the Telegraph Trail to the head of Teslin Lake took close to three months—from the beginning of June until nearly the end of August—and during that time Faith sent nine despatches back to *The Globe*, with the time-lag varying from three to six weeks. Some, of course, may have got lost. By the time the base party got to the staging area named "Camp Victoria" by Colonel Evans, the advance party was already on their way to Fort Selkirk on the steamer *Anglian*. The main concern now was to move the rest of the troops and supplies the remaining four hundred miles to Fort Selkirk before freeze-up, and there was no guarantee the steamer would be back in time.

Major D.D. Young, Evans's second-in-command, supervised the construction of four forty-six-foot scows, each with a large tarpaulin sail, and five row-boats, waited a few days for the return of the *Anglian*, and then gave the orders to set sail on August 29. They called themselves "H.M.S. The Yukon Squadron."

The little armada set out on its four-hundred-mile journey, and Faith Fenton, writing her final despatch from Dawson City on September 21, quoted Kipling to convey the thrill and elation of that final leg of the great journey:

> "Now there isn't no room to say ye don't know —
> They have proved it plain and true —
> That whether it's Widow, or whether it's Ship,
> Victorier's work is to do:
> And they done it, the Jollies—Her Majesty's Jollies —
> Soldier and sailor, too."

> And they certainly did it—our Yukon Jollies—with a right good will, on our long four hundred mile scow journey down unknown lake and river, through shoals and eddies, currents and rapids, to the golden Canadian Northland.

After the months on the trail, those thirteen days down Teslin Lake into the Hootalinqua, then the Lewes River and, finally, the Yukon, must have seemed easy. Camping on the shore each night, with the soldiers singing and the cooks preparing freshly caught salmon, Faith began to feel elation at her achievement and lapsed into romantic prose:

> Tents were pitched, and the evening meal served, the men moving about in a glory of sunset color . . . from deepest velvety purple, through shades of violet and heliotrope, to delicate pearly grey. . . . nothing was hard or violent, for a gentle warmth was in the air, and a cobweb breeze toned to delicate softness. . . . Come up to the Yukon, O artists of our country! . . . let our people know the rare summer beauties of this much-maligned land . . . our beautiful northern Canada!

The shoals of Teslin Lake were only minor irritations after the sand-banks of the Stikine—and, as for the Five-Finger Rapids, they were pure exhilaration for the woman who had shot rapids in a small canoe. Fifty miles of easy sailing later, they were at Fort Selkirk; an hour later, Faith was on a steamer bound for Dawson City. One journey completed, one journey about to begin.[11]

"Tonight—September 21—I write in a small tent snugly placed within a corner of the Mounted Police barracks. It has a flooring, and my little stove burns brightly. . . ."

As usual, optimistic Faith creates a cosy scene for her readers of the corner of the barracks square where Colonel Sam Steele, the legendary Commandant of the North-West Mounted Police, known as "the lion of the Yukon," had given her permission to pitch her tent.[12] But the bitter reality was that winter could come swiftly, at any time, and if she was going to get out she had to move before the steamers left and the river froze. Perhaps that was why she had been seen down on the dock on September 12. She had not planned a winter in Dawson City unless . . . , but here she was, and it seemed she would have to resign herself to cooking or sewing or washing clothes, as Ogilvie had suggested. Had she spent all her adult life avoiding the traditional tasks of women, only to end up in the kitchen?

Ten days later, Faith was still there. The nurses were gone, working under appalling conditions to fight the typhoid epidemic that had hit the city and would nearly take Georgia Powell's life. In a letter to Lady Aberdeen in September, Colonel Evans had foreseen just such a possibility: "It seems to be nobody's business to look after the sanitary arrangements of this town, which has grown in a year from 500 to 30,000 people. . . . Typhoid prevails in the town, and a worse epidemic may break out, as the smells are awful."

It was the first day of October, and by early afternoon the temperature was zero. The shore ice was already forming on the Klondike and Yukon rivers, and soon they would be frozen over. Faith was sick, cold, worrying about money and where she was going to live for the winter. Her money from *The Globe* had probably been deposited in the Dawson bank to await her arrival, as had been done for the nurses, but it would not last long in a city where the simplest of services and the most basic of necessities cost a fortune.

Most terrible of all, her little yellow cat was dead, torn to pieces by the police huskies at the barracks before anyone could do anything to save him. It was not a safe place for small pet animals: Spud, Mina Starnes's little black and white terrier who had been made the Field Force's mascot, had disappeared, his fate unknown. Grief-stricken, racked with guilt and fever and exhaustion, Faith Fenton had survived the journey only to reach the lowest point of her life. This was not the way it was meant to be.

She was sitting on a camp stool, huddled against her sheet-iron Yukon stove that afternoon of October 1. If ever in her life she had been plain, it was now. The photographs on the trail show a woman who looks considerably different from the woman in the knee-length skirt who had posed in an Ottawa studio—her eyes are hollow, her cheekbones stand out against her sunken face. Who knows when she had last had a chance to wash her hair, and even though standards then were different—Faith in "Woman's Empire" quotes a hairdresser recommending a hair-wash once a month—she must have felt dirty, desperate, deserted.

Fate did not come knocking, for there was no door. Presumably a voice outside the tent asked to come in and was admitted. And there he was: tall, with dark eyes in a face of great gentleness. He was probably wearing a hat—not only against the cold, but also because he was losing his hair at an early age. Men and women wore hats more frequently then, but John Brown often had his head covered in photographs, as if self-conscious about his early baldness.

What John Brown saw was not a homely, sick, forty-one-year-old woman in travel-worn clothes—"the last person you would notice in any gathering" sitting on a camp stool. He saw the woman he had observed making her way resolutely through the squatters and the tents on the riverbank on September 12—he would always remember the precise date of that moment, just as he would always remember what the temperature was, and the date and time of day, when he had entered the tent in the barracks square. He was given a seat on a soap-box by the writer whose columns he had read with envy and admiration in the reading-room of the old college building on Gerrard and Sackville streets, when he was studying medicine.

No story-book ending to the woman's quest could have been more fitting than this one. When Dr. John Nelson Elliott Brown looked at her, he saw the person Alice had become in her journey through the looking-glass: he fell in love with Faith Fenton.

XIV

That One Greatest Love

Of all the strange things Alice saw in her journey
Through the Looking-Glass, this was the one she always
remembered most clearly. Years afterwards she could
bring the whole scene back again, as if it had been only
yesterday—the mild blue eyes and the kindly smile of the
Knight—the setting sun gleaming through his hair, and
shining on his armour in a blaze of light that quite dazzled her.

Lewis Carroll,

Through the Looking-Glass, and What
Alice Found There.

ROUNDING THE BEND OF THAT GREAT SWEEP of river and seeing Dawson
City on its small apron of land against the scarred backdrop of the
mountain face, the traveller would have felt excitement in the air, in the
very fingertips, in the pit of the stomach. In the silence of the Dawson
waterfront today, the euphoria of that extraordinary time and the elation
of the thousands who saw it after the agony of the journey still hang
over that beautiful sweep of river.

Not silence then. Uproar—shouting, singing, the sound of hammers,
saws. The smell and smoke of small fires along the gravelly beach.
Boats, canoes, scows, rafts of every kind jammed the waterfront; steamers came and went between thaw and freeze-up, their whistles echoing
over the river. Sheds, shacks and hundreds of tents of every shape and

size littered the shoreline. And beyond the foreshore, masses and masses of humanity—or, rather, masses of men. There was scarcely a woman or child in sight.

In 1898 there were more people in Dawson than in Vancouver or Victoria. Three-quarters of them were American citizens, and most of them seemed to be clustered into the city blocks around Front Street, in the saloons, dancehalls and gambling-houses, with their gaudy façades tacked on to wooden constructions, hastily erected and frequently just as swiftly burnt down, during the extraordinary summer of 1898, when all the world stampeded to Dawson City.

John Brown's trip to the gold-fields had begun at two o'clock on the afternoon of August 4, 1898, at Union Station in Toronto, and ended a month and a day later, in Dawson City. In what was probably an uncharacteristically spontaneous move, he made a spur-of-the-moment decision to accept the invitation of a friend, James Sutherland, Minister of Works in the Laurier government, to join William Ogilvie's party and go to the Klondike. Like his brother, Homer, who was a missionary in China, he had always had the travel bug, but had been too busy establishing his medical practice to indulge it—too busy even to get married.

William Ogilvie needed a secretary on the trip to write official letters back to Ottawa, and John Brown was a godsend—not only did he have a typewriter, but he knew shorthand. Ogilvie also needed a doctor—he was suffering from severe boils that afflicted him the whole of the journey—and Dr. Brown had brought along his medical bag. Thus, John Brown found himself following the two careers he would combine in the Klondike for the next five years. Upon their arrival Ogilvie would appoint him Territorial Secretary and, later on, the Yukon Territories' Medical Officer of Health.

At Victoria, Ogilvie chartered a tramp steamer that took them north to Skagway in four days, where they set out for the White Pass, a forty-five-mile trail that Ogilvie himself had surveyed the previous year. According to John Brown's account, they covered it on horseback in what seems an incredible two days, met Colonel Sam Steele of the North-West Mounted Police at Lake Bennett on the headwaters of the Yukon, and went on by steamer to Dawson.

Although Ogilvie's experience made the trip comparatively smooth, there must have been adventures along the way. Certainly there would have been some tense moments in Soapy Smith's Skagway, where never a day passed without violence, murder and the sound of gunshots, but only the outline of the journey remains among John Brown's papers.[1]

John Brown's reticence about the more colourful aspects of his life and his feelings about the wide range of human beings and experiences he encountered in the course of a far-from-average existence make him a difficult character to read—but not untypical of a Victorian male of his class and background. When he set out to find freedom and adventure, he took with him the stiff upper lip of his British forbears. He may have permitted himself adventures and experiences outside his society's approval, but he did not give himself licence to talk about them.

Medicine was, in fact, only one of John Brown's passions. He had wanted to be a writer when he was at school, but had followed the advice of his headmaster, Isaac Lerau, and pursued a career rather than an avocation. Besides, it would undoubtedly have been what his parents expected of him. He was born in East Nissouri Township, Ontario, to John and Isabel (or Isabella) Brown, of Empire Loyalist stock—his grandfather had been a Methodist pioneer preacher in the area. He had attended school in nearby St. Mary's and started out as a teacher in a country school, before being accepted to study medicine at the University of Toronto in 1888.

His was a particularly brilliant group, and when he graduated with the class of '92, he was awarded the Silver Medal for his year. After graduation he became a house surgeon at Toronto General Hospital, and was appointed chief obstetrician at St. Michael's Hospital. It looked as if John Brown's life was set on a distinguished, but predictable, course.

He still found time to do some writing—the bug had never quite left him—and for Christmas 1897 he and three colleagues produced what they called "a four-fold greeting in numbers" that was privately printed. It was a series of poems each had written, and it isn't clear whether they read them out loud, or simply sent copies to all their friends. What is interesting about the document, besides what it demonstrates of the four men's highly classical education—John Brown calls himself "the most renowned Maister Johan N.E. Brown, Chirurgeon"—is what John Brown's offering, called "The Fear of Pan," reveals about its author.

The poem suggests a man highly responsive to the natural world—birdsong, the sound of rain on the roof, "the ocean's mighty roar"—particularly when that world around him was "filled to overflow with wine of life." John Brown would never have expressed his emotional frustration directly, but the poem reads like an apologia for a man who wonders if he is losing something by the restrictions imposed by his society:

> Or being moved, the impulse in his breast
> For joining in that chorus is suppressed.
> Dreading the censure of the little soul
> O'er whom a proper prudence has control.

When a friend said, "Come to the Klondike," and he remembered what his old headmaster had told him all those years ago, John Brown was more than ready to find release from the sense of obligation that had suppressed all other desires. Dunnage bags and typewriter in hand, he set out to escape "the censure of the little soul" and to find something to write about. Sadly for posterity, he never quite freed himself enough from that dread of censure to put on paper much of what he experienced in those early Klondike days.

As William Ogilvie had told Faith, there were already some women in Dawson City. They had started to arrive the previous summer, after word first spread about Bonanza. One woman, a coal-miner's daughter from Ohio, had made herself a small fortune by understanding the law of supply and demand. Belinda Mulroney had run—among other enterprises—a lunch-counter and a roadhouse, and was now building the grandest hotel in Dawson, with every luxury and convenience hauled in over the White Pass. The Fairview Hotel on Front Street had steam-heated rooms, Turkish baths, and an orchestra playing in the lobby.

But mostly the ones who had stayed on were the dancehall girls and the prostitutes, for whom life was much the same whether they were treading the boards in Seattle or San Francisco or Dawson, or taking their customers up to a filthy mattress on Victoria Street in Toronto, or into their cabins on Paradise Alley, just behind Dawson's Front Street.

To the young doctor from Toronto, they seem to have been a source of fascination. In the few paragraphs of his memoirs that have survived —possibly all he managed to write—John Brown "tells something about the women who had arrived there [in Dawson] a few weeks before Miss Fenton." Only, "a proper prudence" comes over him and he does not use his own words. He can only bring himself to quote from the memoirs of a Californian, Jeremiah Lynch, who in *Three Years in the Klondike* describes the women of Dawson and his experiences with them:

> So I ate a good dinner at the only decent restaurant, and squandered the evening in the dancing-houses. . . . All classes of beauties from all nations, but beauties all. Some had a history and some not before they came, but all had a history after arrival. There was no honest occupation for women. . . . Those who have lived and have not lost make excellent exemplars of virtue.[2]

Dawson City was an eye-opener for John Brown. A "bad" girl could be a good girl and make a fine wife for a miner or a lonely man. The prudence of eastern society made no sense in boom-town Dawson.

Among his papers remain two photographs of those girls. In one, four stand outside their cabins. They are young, pretty, in their Sunday-best outfits of freshly laundered and starched frills, their hair curled— they have made a special effort for the photographer. One is knitting, one holds a cat, another a dog. The fourth kneels in front of them, holding what looks like a tree branch (possibly an antler). Through the open door of one cabin, one can see a painting on the wall.

In the other photograph, three women stand just outside the doors of their homes on the boardwalk, a sea of mud between the one-room cabins. Glued to the back of this photograph is a poem written by John Brown, who has again encoded his feelings in verse. The opening lines are missing, but the message is quite clear:

. . .

In every city of the earth,
To hungry, polygamous men,
Your place has been a House of Mirth
Of roystering and jollity;
Of Transitory pleasures, sweet
Where primal appetites are cloyed
And music gay and dancing feet
Make wayward men oblivious
Of weary burden, of sad lots,
Of wives and sweethearts left behind,
Pure love and honour, quite forgot.

And if the young doctor *did* cloy his primal appetites on Paradise Alley—although he almost certainly would never have admitted doing so—he later felt no need to destroy the pictures or the poem, or hide them from his "pure love." The poem concludes:

Yet, may some weeping magdalen,
Or Naboth's wife's seducer, sad,
Deeply repentant, call to Heaven,
Confessing all, shall be forgiven.

If John Brown danced with those lace-clad women in their House of Mirth—if he did indeed taste those transitory pleasures—they apparently brought only shame and repentance. The women of Paradise Alley were not the answer; he was looking for something else.

The city was full of voices humming and buzzing with hope, with rumour, with dreams. Fear would have been part of that heightened state of emotion: fear of disease, fear of starvation, fear of failure. The winter of 1897 had been horrendous, with inadequate food and supplies for the earliest of the gold-seekers. Colonel Sam Steele now had ruled that no man could cross the Canadian border without a year's supply of food, but fear of that perilous Yukon winter would have been something Faith shared with the other adventurers in Dawson City that October 1898. When the miracle happened, and John Brown appeared on the scene, she had nothing but the clothes given to her by the Sanford Manufacturing Company, and the Reverend Pringle's tent.

In January 1899, *The Globe* carried a short news item on the work of the VON during the typhoid epidemic that concluded with the following statement: "Faith Fenton intended leaving the Klondike this winter, but has been retained in the Commissioner's office as assistant private secretary to Mr. Ogilvie."

The commissioner's head secretary was, of course, John Brown. Faith also could type and do shorthand—such rare skills to find among the women in Dawson City, where the law of supply and demand operated as almost nowhere else on earth at that time. With the help of a man, she had managed to find "an honest occupation."

It was not a swift courtship. Perhaps that was because neither of them was skilled at the game: John Brown was a shy man and the dictates of Faith's upbringing would have meant that this was one waiting game she would have to play, whether she liked it or not. Perhaps both were also afraid of rejection.

Besides, once she had decent lodgings somewhere in town and knew she had an income to rely on, Faith found her feet. In a city where there was no such thing as an outsider because everybody there was one, life was good for the woman who had never really fitted into nineteenth-century social structures. Her columns to *The Globe* continued—on average, about two a month, with her name prominently featured—and reflect the extraordinary richness and challenges of her new life. In fact, "the woman" becomes "the correspondent," as if she were reporting from a war-zone.

In November she watched the freezing of the Yukon, the ice first floating like feathers on the grey-green waters, gradually turning into great ice-blocks that moved sluggishly around the northern bend of the river and out of sight as the solid mass of ice crept out from the banks. One moonlit night, Faith stood on the bank and watched frantic attempts to rescue a man on a scow drifting through the ice-floes: ". . . it was impossible to help admiring the splendid soft winteriness of the night, the environing white-drifted hills, the white-moving river mass, with its dark-outlined victims of clumsy scow and frightened voyageur. . . ." We are not told the end of the story.

Soon there was no movement at all as the narrow centre channel froze over, and within two or three weeks the dog-teams were racing over the surface. Faith watched the "laughable incidents" as the young animals learned how to handle themselves in harness: "To bolt suddenly after some enemy, imaginary or real, and whirl the driver, if he's on the sled, into space, or if he is running beside the team, rush him on at breathless pace, to fall a-fighting, describe a series of curves and enmesh their master until he is bound with straps and cords like any Sampson. . . ."

And the skirt length suited Faith down to the ground: ". . . the women in fur coats, ankle-short or shorter skirts, moccasins and fur-bordered hoods." Dawson photographs frequently show women in ankle-length skirts, far better suited to the city's mud-filled thoroughfares—a length they obviously continued to wear even after freeze-up.

By December 1898, Faith Fenton was securely anchored in what respectable society there was, while at the same time moving comfortably through the wild uproar of Dawson's "Other Half"—in 1898, of course, virtually the whole city. That picture of Faith confidently handling her new world comes from the memoirs of Edith Tyrrell, who was married to the great explorer and geologist J.B. Tyrrell, and it is another rare opportunity to see Faith through someone else's eyes.[3]

As the wife of the man who explored the Barren Lands and Lake Athabaska, Edith Tyrrell was quite used to a life in which her husband was missing and feared dead—he had once survived a nine-hundred-mile walk from Churchill to Winnipeg on snowshoes. On this occasion she had arranged to join him in Dawson, bringing along their three-year-old daughter, Mary.

All went well on the journey, which actually began in the company of part of the Yukon Field Force, with Faith Fenton, whom Edith says she had already met several times in Ottawa. However, they parted company before the Telegraph Trail, and Edith writes in her memoirs: "The story of the long walk of two months was well told in Faith Fenton's despatches, although I thought she minimized the hardships."

When Edith Tyrrell reached Dawson, she found no husband to greet her. He was "out on the creeks," and his letter telling her not to come had not reached her in time. To her horror, she found herself alone with little Mary in Belinda Mulroney's Fairview Hotel, in a rough room on the top floor with no lock on the door—a room she had managed to get only because a young man she had known in Ottawa gave it up to her.

Next door a drunken party was raging—champagne corks were popping, furniture was flying, language not fit for a lady's ears filled the air. Weeping and terrified, Edith went down to the desk clerk to see what he could do and was told there was no need to worry: "We treat ladies on the square in the Yukon," he assured her. Back upstairs Edith put the only seat in the room, a three-legged stool, against the door, piled her luggage on top of it, and huddled in the one bed with her daughter.

In the middle of that sleepless, fear-filled night, there was a knock on the door and a friendly, familiar voice. Removing stool and luggage, she found Faith Fenton standing there and fell weeping into her arms. The desk clerk had gone out to look for one of the nurses, who were all out dealing with the typhoid epidemic, and had come back with Faith Fenton. Edith Tyrrell describes how Faith coped with the situation: "She soothed me and comforted me with the assurance that my husband was back on the creeks. She told me of the irregularity of the postal service and even made me laugh over some funny experiences of her own. She stayed with me for more than an hour and promised to come in the morning to see how I was."

When Faith returned the next morning, she brought with her the wife of the Collector of Customs, Mrs. Davis, who took Edith Tyrrell and her daughter into her home.[4]

The scene is typical of Faith in so many ways: not only the ability to look on the bright side and laugh at the tricks life played, but the capacity for finding some sort of practical solution to a difficult situation.

The city through which she passed that night with the chivalrous desk clerk, who did indeed treat ladies "on the square," would have been alive—in the dancehalls and gambling-rooms, the prostitutes' cabins, the Fairview and Regina hotels, business boomed through the long hours of darkness. But the small figure walking resolutely along by her unlikely escort's side through the freezing sub-arctic night and Dawson's midnight madness to rescue Edith and Mary Tyrrell was used to perilous journeys.

Behind those ornate, painted façades, the twenty-four-hour life of the gambler, the miner and the dancehall girl whirled and spun beneath the acetylene and oil lamps of the Opera House, the gas chandeliers and candelabra of the Monte Carlo dancehall, and the countless saloons and gaming-houses where the likes of Sweet Marie, Caprice and Diamond-Tooth Gertie plied their trade in a city that rarely slept. Only on Sunday was the ruckus stilled, by order of Sam Steele. Con-artist and government official, dancehall girl and lady correspondent, all were jumbled together in those few blocks around Front Street. Only the prostitutes were separated, eventually moved by Steele from Paradise Alley to an area behind the town that became known as "Hell's Half-Acre," and later across the river to Lousetown. But even they operated openly, their function cutting across every division of that boom-town society.

Faith had often walked through the dark midnight streets of Toronto with a male escort—or on her own. She had visited the shelters and the prison cells, gone undercover to share the life of Fighting Kate and Irish Mary at the House of Industry. She had heard a robin sing at first light at the corner of College and Spadina with only a paper-boy to share the moment with her. Like Sweet Marie, and Caprice, and Diamond-Tooth Gertie, she too had been a working woman with a professional pseudonym. As she passed the brightly lit windows of Front Street's palaces of pleasure and heard the music that spilled into the road—perhaps played by the showmen-waiters from the *Islander*—she was seeing life once again as a journalist, looking for a story.

Faith Fenton was not the first woman correspondent in the gold-fields—curiously enough, the few works that mention her are usually at pains to point out that fact—and in January 1899 she takes on one of the first, Flora Shaw of *The London Times*, who had crossed the White Pass in 1898.

Obviously the superior tone of Flora Shaw's article had offended quite as much as her criticisms of governmental corruption, and Faith delivers a swift verbal upper-cut against what she calls "Miss Shaw's Yukon animadversions:" ". . . There are difficulties of administration that even Miss Shaw, with all her ability, could not possibly comprehend within the limits of her two-week stay in the territory."

Faith may not have been the first woman, but she was the one who was staying on, and her euphoria is evident: "It is exhilarating to be in the Yukon at the present moment. One feels as if witnessing the birth of a nation. . . ."

It was certainly the presence of other correspondents, whether male or female, that brought about what could have been Faith's greatest professional fiasco, and the best-known story about her, although "best-known" is hardly the most appropriate expression to describe anything in Faith

Fenton's life. Maybe this was the story Faith shared with Edith Tyrrell to make her laugh at the Fairview Hotel, for she told it against herself in her *Globe* column in February 1899.

Not surprisingly, there were always problems getting mail out of Dawson. On November 1, 1898, there was a hanging scheduled for four men found guilty of murder, and Faith was determined to scoop the other correspondents who had stayed in Dawson City. It was over a month since the last steamer had left Dawson, but a man called Sandison, an experienced "ice-traveller," as Faith called him, was going out with his dog-team on the morning of November 1 and offered to carry any mail at a dollar a letter. The police mail was not due to leave until November 15, and Faith decided to use Sandison.

The only problem was that Sandison insisted on leaving at seven o'clock in the morning to catch all available light, and the hanging was scheduled for eight o'clock. Faith prepared and sealed two envelopes of copy for *The Globe* and drafted a telegram that needed only a few final words confirming the execution. Here is Faith's description of the events of that morning:

> Early on the morning of Nov. 1st the correspondent stepped out into the wintry twilight. Two hundred yards up the river bank the sentry was pacing back and forth before the barrack entrance. . . . Up the roadway newspaper men and one or two physicians [one of whom may well have been John Brown] were hastening. Turning in the other direction the correspondent passed quickly down the dim wintry street to a queer little saloon. Outside two patient dogs and a loaded sled were waiting; within the carrier was swallowing his last hot flap jack.
>
> Two of the long envelopes were handed over. From the third and unsealed one the telegraphic slip was taken out and hesitated over. There was a consultation of watches; each marked 7.10 a.m. The carrier strapped on his bag and tied his ear-flaps. . . . With one more glance barrackwards the telegraphic slip was unfolded, the few decisive words inserted. . . . and The Globe correspondent watched the carrier move up the river. . . .

And, of course, the unexpected happened—there was a last-minute stay of execution. In fact, there were two: one of twenty-four hours, and another for an indefinite period. In his memoirs Sam Steele describes Faith as an "enterprising young lady" who came to him in tears to ask him to send out a dog-team after Sandison. Faith does not mention the tears, but they had their effect: "Half an hour after the news . . . the writer was seated in the office of Col. Steele of the N.W.M.P., and twenty minutes later McBeth, the swiftest half-breed runner in the Yukon, was speeding up the river ice with orders to overtake the carrier and bring back the fateful telegram."

According to what Faith told her family, she paid a hefty fifty dollars for the services of McBeth, so it was not purely an act of gallantry on Steele's part, as has been suggested in other accounts. Faith concludes her story with humour: "The story of that hotly pursued telegram was carried up and down the river, and related with zest in many a miner's cabin, usually with the facetious comment that The Globe correspondent was the only one in Dawson who showed no hesitancy in carrying out the letter of the law."[5]

During that first winter—a fairly mild one by Yukon standards—Faith's feelings for the North began to take hold of her. As she had done for so many years in "Woman's Empire," she wrote a column on the turn of the year:

> Christmas has come and gone, and we close our letter in the last hours of 1898. A light wind has lifted the haze from the valley, and all the still white scene of ice-blocked river, twinkling cabins and mountaintops is lit by a clear, round moon. . . . this writer . . . confess[es] to an appreciation that is growing perilously akin to fondness for this unique and picturesque mining camp.

And at some point that winter, the mail brought her a card from the Aberdeens, who had left Canada in November 1898. They sent a similar card to most of their friends. Some say simply "Good-bye"; Faith's card was sent from the viceregal lodge in Dublin and says, "Au revoir."

No evidence exists that they met again, but it is possible they did. Ishbel would return again to Canada, once in 1909, and there is a letter from her to John Brown dated 1909, asking for his help for a group of visiting physicians. It does not read like a letter written after a silence of over ten years.[6]

During the last year of the century, Faith's letters to *The Globe* brought Dawson's story to Canadians back east. There were continuing problems with the mail, and accusations of inefficiency, but the two major events of that year were the enquiry by Commissioner Ogilvie into charges of massive official corruption, and the devastating fire in April that destroyed many of Dawson's principal buildings—from banks to saloons.

In between her coverage of these episodes, Faith gave her readers details of gold-mining methods, the miners' irritation at the royalty tax imposed on their findings, and the amount of gold taken out of the various creeks. She didn't tell her readers that she herself had registered a couple of claims, worth about two thousand dollars by the time the census was taken in 1901. She wrote about skiing—and the problem of women's skirts and skis—about the great ravens of Dawson, who, then as now, "cluster on the river ice in front of the town pecking at the piles of refuse and gabbling in husky tones." She talked of the longing for "the sight of a green thing growing . . . we missed them [flowers] most of all when the girl-wife [Faith does not identify her] died and all we could find to drape her coffin was her country's colors. She was a soldier's daughter, so we placed a tiny flag between her clasped hands and left her thus."

Spring finally arrived, and the green things grew again: "We walk some distance up one of the many gulches that lie like cradles between the hills. We sit upon a wayside log to rest and listen to the intensity of the stillness. . . . Across the river, which we have just traversed, the mouth of the Klondike opens wide, and our eyes travel up it to where Bonanza branches up to form a fork with the golden Eldorado. . . . A certain vividity of sense seems a peculiarity of dwellers in the Yukon . . . it may be the greater nearness to the primeval, but light and shadow, gradations of color, curve, form and sound . . . are intensified to a strange and special vividness in the Yukon."

That heightened awareness was attributable not only to the greater nearness to the primeval, but also to the fact that the one who walked the hills with her, and sat on a wayside log to rest and listen to that silence "filled to overflow with wine of life," was the Territorial Secretary of the Yukon, John Brown.

As the summer passed, Faith recorded the changes that were transforming Dawson from a mining camp to a little town "putting on the airs of a metropolis": new municipal offices were going up, heavy hydraulic and dredging machinery was being brought in to extract the gold, the shacks along the waterfront destroyed in the fire were being replaced by zinc-covered warehouses and Dawson's first brick building, and the first school in Dawson was about to open.

On September 28, it was *The Globe*'s correspondent who was given the privilege of sending out the first wire from Dawson City: "Greetings. Telegraph reached Dawson today. First press message goes to Globe. Hurrah! FAITH FENTON."

And, at some point that summer, Faith resumed one of the roles she had had back in Toronto—one of her younger sisters, Edith, joined her in Dawson City and became a stenographer in Ogilvie's office. Florence would join them later in 1901. Faith herself never mentions the fact that they came, or how they came, but they are mentioned in social notes in the local papers, and on lists of employees in Ogilvie's office.

Edith also appears in lists of helpers for what was to be one of the great social events of the year, the Ladies' Bazaar in aid of St. Mary's Hospital, which was organized from the home of Mina Starnes. Edith's sister would play a major role as editor of *The Paystreak*, a magazine of six issues brought out to publicize the bazaar.

St. Mary's Hospital had been opened in August 1897 by Father William Judge, known as "The Saint of Dawson" for his work of building almost singlehandedly, not only the hospital, but the Catholic church and homes for his staff. When he died in January 1898, the hospital was handed over to the Sisters of Ste. Anne, who also inherited an enormous debt. Faith would doubtless have got involved anyway, but one of the staff at St. Mary's was Georgia Powell of the VON, with whom she had become close friends.

Not only that, but John Brown was part of the men's entertainment committee, and the Bazaar Directorate lists the editor of *The Paystreak* as "Faith Fenton, assisted by Mr. Chas. Watts and Dr. J.N. Elliott Brown."

For the woman who had refused to reveal her church allegiance—"I have been a staunch Methodist this week. . . . I am born a Unitarian—perhaps"—and had enraged some of her readers by such remarks as, "For serene selfishness, commend me to . . . the average Toronto church member," the non-sectarian nature of Yukon church life must have appealed greatly. From the look of bazaar accounts, every middle-class woman and every one of the wives who had arrived in the Yukon that summer of 1898 got involved.

Even a casual glance at those accounts reveals the changing population of Dawson. "Respectable" women were arriving and reconstructing the society they had left back east. A year earlier it would have been impossible to find enough married women to organize the Fancy Work booth, the French booth and tombola, the Turkish booth, the Klondike booth, the refreshments and the fish pond. Hard as it was to find it in 1899, a year earlier it would have been impossible to find any paper at all on which to print *The Paystreak*.

In December temperatures of fifty below, the new middle-class of what had been a mining-camp a year before took over what was once the province of the dancehall girl and the stampeder, and partied for six days. Here is *The Paystreak*'s description of the opening at the Palace Grand, a huge dancehall on Front Street owned by Arizona Charlie Meadows, a sharp-shooting showman Faith might well have seen in Buffalo Bill's Wild West Show in Chicago—a combination of premise and cause that St. Mary's own magazine, *The Northern Light*, later aptly described as an "overlapping of the sacred and the profane":

> From eight o'clock onward guests arrived in a continuous stream. They crowded galleries and boxes, then overflowed down to the main floor. They laughed and chatted, drank cafe noir and fished in the water lily pond; they tried the wheel of fortune, visited the gypsy proprietress, purchased bon-bons, listened to the music, and when it grew irresistible, threw severity and formality to the winds, and danced—making the pretty picture more charming yet.

The scene at the Palace Grand could have come straight from "Woman's Empire," describing one of the subscription balls at the Horticultural Pavilion in Toronto. In fact, the style of *The Paystreak* is classic Faith Fenton, apart from some heavy-handed humorous contributions provided by assistant editor Chas. Watts: "The rainbow about Mrs. Clayton's booth reminds one of some policemen—never appear until the storm is over. . . . Quite a number of men in Dawson are attempting to pose as Apollo, but usually they are only an apolo-gy for one."

The King of the Klondike, Big Alex McDonald, was "one of the best patrons of the Bazaar"—beautiful Mrs. McDonald was helping to run the fish-pond;[7] the Dawson Electric Light Company donated hundreds of dollars' worth of lights; apologies had to be made to would-be advertisers to *The Paystreak* who were turned away: "the demand was so great that the advertising columns were filled within a few days"; a spirited contest took place over the most popular lady, with votes costing fifty cents each. John Brown was in charge of commercial contributions to *The Paystreak*, and Private Green of the Royal Canadian Dragoons contributed some skits and verse in the style of Rudyard Kipling. In a more serious vein there was a tribute in verse to Father Judge:

Mines of Monte Christo around him—wealth by millions
to be had;
Not one thought of earthly treasure—for the gold that
makes men mad.

There was a hockey match that ended in a tie. Outside, on the creeks, men huddled in their cabins against the deadly temperatures, dying of scurvy and frostbite, or of despair and by their own hand; inside the Palace Grand, a large blackboard on the stage fell on Mrs. Ward Smith's head and stunned her, but Dr. Brown came to her aid. On the stages of other dancehalls, beplumed and painted girls sang songs like "Such a Nice Girl Too," and, yes, even "Do You Remember Sweet Alice, Ben Bolt?" At the French stall in the Palace

Grand, the blue satin cushion was won by ticket No. 17, held by Mrs. J. Seely.

On Christmas Day, members of the NWMP and the Yukon Field Force presented Georgia Powell with "a gold medal-brooch of delicate design, bearing her monogram in the centre and letters of each force and date of presentation." She, like her VON colleagues, knew both sides of Dawson life as well if not better than any at the Palace Grand that December day.[8]

And what about the editor of *The Paystreak*—how was she faring in the midst of the parties and the dances of that week of celebrations? She was struggling to find paper and type, running a ruthless blue pencil through the superfluous "d——'s" in Commissioner Ogilvie's Western tale in spite of his protestations, appeasing Jeremiah Lynch when she had to cut his opening address to fit the limited space available—"and always [coping with] some aggrieved and overlooked worker to soothe with promise of notice in the next issue." Yet her mood was blissful in spite of the intense cold: "Fifty degrees below zero—and exhilarating to intoxication. We breathe ozone; we walk on air . . . we are electric spirits flashing about without consciousness of weight or weariness."

Faith's euphoria probably had little to do with the weather. She and John Brown had been thrown together, and he had seen Faith Fenton the writer at work. John Brown had also been sick in December when they were working together on *The Paystreak*—*The Dawson Daily News* reported that he was laid up with an attack of pneumonia—and perhaps Faith had been able to show her nurturing, "womanly" side by looking after him. Whatever the chain of events, at some point during that last week of the century John Brown had either proposed or finally persuaded Faith to marry him.

It is clear from the newspaper reports that the year-long romance had ended in a whirlwind marriage. *The Yukon Sun*, edited by Faith's old friend of the trail, H.J. Woodside, said that the marriage would come "as a pleasant surprise to the many admiring friends of the high contracting parties, as very few, it would seem, were taken into their confidence." *The Dawson Daily News* said that close friends had known for some time that the two planned to marry, "but the consummation, the wedding itself, came as a surprise to most."

So perhaps John Brown had proposed to her earlier; Faith herself said that, at the time of the bazaar, theirs was "a romance then in full bud." Perhaps, after waiting for so long, Faith had let John Brown court her before she gave her hand in marriage.

There is a photograph of Faith taken in 1899 with a Miss Edith Robinson, who also helped with *The Paystreak* and worked at the Dawson Post Office, that shows them standing in the snow. Faith, dressed in a slim-fitting coat with a white fur collar, is rather dreamily holding the bare branch of a tree. She looks quite different from the Faith of the Teslin Trail, different even from the Faith of the studio portraits taken in Toronto during her "Woman's Empire" days. Gone is that bold, direct stare—her eyes are turned demurely from the camera. Perhaps Dr. John Brown was there, out of the picture. Or perhaps it was just that she was in love.

They were married at eight o'clock in the evening on New Year's Day, 1900, in St. Paul's Episcopal Church in Dawson, also known as "the English Church," by the Reverend Dr. Naylor in the presence of a handful of friends, including Commissioner Ogilvie, the Collector of Customs and his wife, and Georgia Powell. Edith was her sister's bridesmaid, and John Brown's best man was his brother, Carman. Midwinter it may have been, but "the church was prettily dressed in flowers for the occasion."

Afterwards, Georgia Powell held the wedding supper at her home, and *The Dawson Daily News* reported that "business at the governor's office has been seriously interfered with by the congratulations that have been showered upon Dr. Brown, for no man in Dawson has more sincere friends." *The Yukon Sun* called John Brown "cultured and genial," and added: "the bride is widely known as one of Dawson's brightest and most estimable ladies and one of the cleverest woman writers and correspondents; her familiar nom-de-plume being 'Faith Fenton.'" Notices of the wedding later appeared in Toronto, Barrie and Bowmanville newspapers.

On the marriage certificate John Brown's age is stated as thirty-six; Faith gives her age as thirty-nine—where she paused until the 1901 census in October that shows her as still thirty-nine, and John Brown as thirty-seven. In fact, on January 14, 1900, she would be forty-three years old.

Afterwards, they would have walked the short distance to the corner of Mission and Seventh streets, where their new home was waiting for them, a log cabin as picturesque and "dainty" as anything Faith could have desired. It had unusually large windows by Dawson standards, but otherwise was typical of pioneer design, with one room divided by screens and curtains into bedroom, office and dining area. There was a small lean-to kitchen on the back, with a large store-room beyond. Centre stage was a large Klondike stove—their "star performer," Faith called it.[9]

Outside the cabin lay the still serenity of a Yukon winter night, barely disturbed by a breath of wind, sometimes misted with a dust of snow. Above, the shivering, shifting auroras of the Northern Lights streamed through the dark night sky over Moosehide Mountain and beyond the towering quartz cliffs above Bonanza Creek. Faith had first seen those dancing lights—*les marionettes*—on the Gaspé coast, but how magical they must have seemed when she walked through Dawson City with her husband on the first day of the new century.

Faith had found what she had once said was the best of gifts for a woman: the love of a good man. They were both romantics who had waited a long time to find each other, so it is perhaps not too presumptuous to suppose that, in those early, golden, Yukon years, theirs was a passionate love.

Faith Fenton-Brown's byline first appeared in *The Globe* on Saturday, March 31, 1900, and about this time she resigned from the commissioner's office. The column is about the beginning of springtime in Dawson, and the beginning of the exodus to Nome, where the first reports were coming out about the discovery of a new Eldorado. The ravens were out on the river, picking at the refuse heaps that were beginning to soften in the sun, and in the sunny Dawson streets the dog-teams were rushing joyously up and down—"Dawson owned many superb dog-teams in the early winter, but the best have been sold at high prices to Nome travellers." It is a column that foreshadows the fate of Dawson over the next few years.

The Globe's special correspondent in the Yukon was not unaware of the threat to the boom-town in which she had found happiness and a husband. The columns of 1900 are often Dawson propaganda: in April, Faith gives the population of Dawson as 5,400—"an increase of 1,000 since September last"—and predicts that "the coming wash-up will be big." At the end of April, in a column with the subheading, "A Future for Dawson," she quotes "the dismal prophecy . . . that in five years the coyotes would be roaming over a deserted Dawson," and uses the opinions of one of the pioneer adventurers of the Yukon, Captain John J. Healey, Manager of the American Transportation and Trading Company, to refute it.[10] In the same year she also wrote an article boosting Dawson for a glossy booklet complete with photographs that was brought out by *The Yukon Sun*.

On July 10, *The Globe* carried a column with an inch-high heading, "Quartz Mining in the Yukon," but just beneath it are two other subheadings: "Exodus to Nome" and "Hundreds Set Out for the New Centre." Farther on in the article, Faith firmly declares: "It is not to be inferred, however, that Dawson is dead. . . . the steamers are bringing hundreds of new arrivals. . . ."

By August, however, there was something new and exciting to write about: the visit of the new governor general, Lord Minto, and his wife, to Dawson City. Faith covers it in two columns for *The Globe*—one on the official reception, and one on the Mintos' visit to the creeks and the miners' presentation of a gold box filled with nuggets—without mentioning that she herself seems to have played an important role.

Among Faith's papers is a letter on crested notepaper from Mary Minto, written on the steamer *Sybil* after they left Dawson. In it, Lady Minto thanks Faith for the copies of *The Paystreak* and says what an experience it had been to see the mines. It ends: "with many thanks, yours sincerely, Mary Minto."

In fact, Faith Fenton-Brown seems to have created a network in Dawson much as she had done in her "Woman's Empire" days. In an article in the magazine *The Pacific Monthly*, titled "The Homes and Homemakers of Alaska," the author, Anna Shane Devin, extends her discussion to include Faith's Dawson City home. Her opening paragraph begins: "Quite literally speaking, the keys of Dawson were offered me by one of its most brilliant and distinguished women. . . . Mrs. Brown is better known to the outside world under her pen-name of 'Faith Fenton'. . . ."

According to the writer, Faith was at the centre of the new Dawson upper crust: "In Dawson, an introduction by Mrs. Brown is an effective 'open sesame' to all doors, and brought me equally into the sanctum of the governor, to the tea-table of madame 'the judge's lady,' or into the comfortable club-house where during the dark days of the long winter, Dawson society seeks diversion and surcease of ennui."

Dawson society was indeed finding more and different ways to divert itself. Alex Pantages, the well-known porter of the Opera House, had been promoted to manager—said *The Dawson Daily News*: "Alex has been thrifty in his habits and has saved quite a poke, which he is willing to chance in Dawson show business." It was, of course, the beginning of an extraordinary career that was to take Pantages and his poke far beyond the Yukon. In Dawson City, Greek immigrant Alex Pantages set the foundations for what was to become a multimillion-dollar theatre chain throughout North America.[11]

In 1900, however, the new manager was having to cope with his star, Blossom, being prostrated with heart failure during a performance of *Circus Girl*, by hastily substituting a farce called *Rooney's Lament*, after only one rehearsal. After all, he had to keep up with the competition: The curtain-raiser at the Monte Carlo, *A Hole in the Wall*, had them in the aisles, and the evening was rounded out with new "coon songs"— white performers in "black face" singing what purported to be the music of black America—and "ginger" acts—a wide range of novelty acts of all kinds, put in to "ginger" up the proceedings.

Leading ladies could be a problem: lovely Laura Lane, who dealt the game of Twenty-Nine at the Melbourne Hotel, had given up the precarious life of the stage for the easier riches that came her way from "the knight[s] of the green table." With a dashing fur cap atop her long, curling dark hair, "she now sits nightly before her table and deftly manipulates the cards with her jewelled fingers . . . bright black eyes restless with the fires of uncurbed caprices." (The bravura style of Dawson's newspapers perfectly capture that flamboyant era.) Why bother with the slog of playing Camille at the Palace Grand when she could merely "close the game and promenade to a champagne supper on the arm of an admiring miner"?

The old order had not yet given place to the new, but the writing was on the wall. The silence of the Dawson Sabbath was now broken by sold-out Sunday-evening concerts at the Palace Grand using very different material from that of the Monte Carlo or the Rivoli. *The Dawson Daily News* took this as proof that "a concert can be given suitable to a Sunday evening performance, void of coon and other shady songs and made up of classical and high-class modern music," and added that "Dawson contains a population today sufficiently large, intelligent and educated to fully appreciate it."

The Dawson Daily News was right. That educated population was setting about remaking boom-town Dawson in the image of Toronto, or Barrie, or Bowmanville—just as their forbears had created Toronto in the image of Bath or Bristol or London-town. By 1901 gaming-houses and brothels were officially prohibited within the town limits, and later a Women's Vigilance Committee was formed to keep an eye out for transgressors. Faith's family remember that she didn't approve of the dance-hall girls, and it is unlikely that she did. However, she is just as likely to have disapproved of a group of vigilantes.

Faith's attitude towards the Cad Wilsons and the Diamond Tooth Gerties was probably much like the feelings she had once expressed when some posters with dancing-girls were put up around Toronto to advertise a vaudeville show. At that time her chief concern was for other women walking past in the street who might encounter suggestive remarks and propositions—something she herself had experienced—rather than condemning the dancers.

Actresses certainly did not shock her; she loved and admired them. She had heard Julia Marlowe, one of the great Juliets of her age, speak in Chicago at the Women's Congress of the struggle that actors—and particularly women—had undergone for recognition. She quoted Canadian actress Julia Arthur, who told Faith in an interview that she had to go on stage because she had to earn a living. Faith unequivocally told her readers that one rarely met an actress who was intolerant or narrow-minded, and it is unlikely her marriage changed that view.

One of the stories she told her family suggests a lively appreciation of the eccentricities of her more footloose fellow Dawsonites: at one theatre performance she attended, an intoxicated member of the audience mounted the stage and made determined efforts to climb a staircase that was merely painted on the scenery, until forcibly removed by the theatre staff.

As for those pitiful pieces of straying humanity, "the scarlet women of the city," as *The Dawson Daily News* called them, now removed over the river to Klondike City—Lousetown—Faith is more likely to have been of the opinion of a local judge who "expressed the wish that the people who live off the earnings of such women were before him instead of the prisoners." She would probably have been well aware of the efforts of the NWMP to break up the gangs who brought young women into Dawson and Nome, "ostensibly to work in department stores that have no existence, but in reality to enter brothels and a life of shame in the two rich mining camps of the north."

The old order was passing with the departure of some of the men who had established it. Sam Steele left the Yukon in 1900 to take command of the Lord Strathcona Horse and to fight in the Boer War, and in 1901 Commissioner William Ogilvie retired from office. Faith and John Brown must have been sad to see old friends and colleagues go, but life was too good for them to look back. In fact, it was too good for Faith to be writing regularly any more for *The Globe* by the middle of 1901. The break occurred when Faith took her first trip "Outside," as Dawsonites called it, in July 1901.

From Dawson to Ottawa via Skagway and Vancouver, the trip took two weeks—how different from the journey that had brought her to Dawson City in 1898! While she was in Ottawa, Faith contacted *The Ottawa Journal*, whose interview with her was quoted in the Dawson *Nugget*. She apparently planned to visit Montreal and Toronto, returning in September to Dawson for which she told *The Ottawa Journal* she predicted "a large population."

One paragraph in particular must have given Faith pleasure: "Mrs. Brown is well known in the newspaper world, 'Faith Fenton' being a familiar name to most Canadians." She was gone, but not yet forgotten, on the "Outside." Perhaps *The Globe* dropped their special correspondent in the Yukon now that the rush was over, but it could also be just what Faith said to *The Pacific Monthly*: that she was much more interested in "being 'the wife of her husband' than in literary work [and] that she only consents to take up her pen under strong pressure of unusually interesting circumstances." Faith had waited too many years for the validation that marriage brought to a woman of her era not to relish every moment of her new incarnation as Faith Fenton-Brown.

Besides, being "the wife of her husband" in Dawson was a time-consuming occupation. There was no time off in the long arctic summer— parties and sporting activities could begin at midnight. And on Monday, January 8, 1900, a week after Faith's marriage, *The Dawson Daily News* carried the following announcement: "Mrs. J. Elliott Brown (Faith Fenton) will be at home to her friends on Wednesday and Thursday of this week and every succeeding Wednesday at her residence corner Mission Street and Seventh Avenue."

Even after Faith left Dawson, the elaborate structure of those "at-homes" was maintained. In her memoirs, Laura Berton says that it was not only possible, but necessary, to attend one every weekday afternoon, and that you were expected to return the call of every guest. The preparations beforehand were time-consuming—particularly since it was difficult to get servants—and the etiquette impeccable.

Mrs. J.N.E. Brown relished returning the courtesy, enjoyed putting in an appearance on the arm of her husband at such events as the first "at-home" of the season at Government House, held by Mrs. Congdon, the wife of the new commissioner. Faith and John Brown appear on the list of guests, as do Florence and Edith, Faith's sisters. With what genuine enthusiasm she would have served on the Entertainment Committee in 1900, put together to raise funds with a program of patriotic songs and tableaux for the widows and orphans of soldiers who had died in the Transvaal.

She and John Brown escorted Florence to the Tennis Club dance in 1902 and sat in the audience to hear Florence sing in the chorus of *The Bohemian Girl*, put on by the Dawson Amateur Operatic Society in the same year at the Auditorium, or play the piano at a concert to raise funds for the Dawson Free Library in April 1903. Things were definitely changing in Dawson—patrons of the library were expected to wash, be sober and avoid foul language.

There were children in Dawson now—lots of them. At the Agricultural Fair held in September 1903, more than a hundred children took part in what *The Dawson Record* called "a maze of counter-marches and drills." It was a far cry from the days when miners came from miles around to watch the baby son of Mrs. Fawcett, the wife of the Gold Commissioner, playing on the cabin floor, or lavished so much attention on little Mary Tyrrell that their women got jealous. In only three years that sub-arctic world had been transformed from the one in which the convent-educated teen-age wife of Swiftwater Bill Gates, "the Prince of the Klondike," gave birth to a baby girl in a cabin perched beneath the quartz cliffs of Bonanza.

Some things had not changed, although they were now the exception rather than the rule: "With a cigarette between his lips, Charles Arthur Wright, the vocalist, shot and killed himself last night (July 24, 1903) in the rear of the New Dominion . . . because Annie Graham, a dance hall girl, did not return his love."

And the Vigilance Committee had not managed to stamp out all traces of "the demi-monde," although they and the new law had succeeded in driving them underground. One of the juicier trials of 1903 was against one Dora Wells, who was accused of "keeping a disorderly house known as the San Francisco laundry on Second avenue." Much of the evidence revolved around whether the prosecution could actually prove the men were not bringing their laundry to Dora, whose lawyer strenuously objected when she was called "a fallen woman." According to the NWMP's Corporal Piper, he had witnessed ironing going on— "but never a sign of a washtub."

None of this would have troubled Faith. She had seen and heard as much or more from her Model School days in Toronto and her career as a journalist, when she had read about Jeannie Gilmour and written about Bertie Usher. The only difference here was that the contrasts were closer, around the corner and just up the street. You could see the bridge to Lousetown from the front step of St. Paul's Episcopal Church, where, on October 15, 1903, was held the élite church wedding of the year— what *The Dawson Record* called "one of the most elaborate weddings that ever took place in Dawson." It was the wedding of Faith's sister Florence to John Kerr Sparling, one of Dawson's leading lawyers.

John K. Sparling, solicitor, barrister, notary public, had come to the Yukon at the height of the gold rush, and now represented numerous British-based interests such as the Yukon Goldfields Ltd. (Eng.) and British Canadian Goldfields Ltd. He was also the sole agent in Dawson for various collection agencies and credit associations. He worked out of Victoria Chambers in the Monte Carlo building, and in September 1903 had represented the concession holders in a major dispute over concession rights.

At the age of thirty-one, Sparling was an influential man in Dawson, and the list of wedding presents alone gives some idea of his importance, as well as that of John Brown: Justice Craig and his wife gave a silver candelabrum, and Justice and Mrs. Macaulay a Wedgwood china tea-set. Faith and John's gift was a bird's eye maple writing-desk. In a white silk gown and a large picture hat of white velvet trimmed with ostrich plumes, Florence walked up the aisle on the arm of her brother-in-law, John Brown, to the bridal music from *Lohengrin*, and at the reception it was Commissioner "King" Congdon himself who proposed the toast to the bride.

It was a very different wedding from that of her sister, and probably represented a triumph to both of them. She may not have become a concert pianist, but through Faith's intervention, Florence had been spared the fate of her unmarried fifty-year-old sister, Mary, who still lived with their parents. Taking a leaf from her sister's book, Florence boldly dropped her age from thirty-two to twenty-six on her marriage certificate. Edith appears to have left the Yukon by this time, probably to continue with her journalistic career in the States, where she seems to have settled in Los Angeles, and eventually to have lost touch with the family.

In June 1904, Faith and Florence received what *The Dawson Daily News* called "the mournful intelligence" of the death of their sister Eva (by then Mrs. Frederick Stevenson) in Oshawa, Ontario, at the age of thirty-seven. Sad as it was, it is unlikely Eva's death had anything to do with Faith and John's decision to go Outside that summer for an extended trip—his first since he had arrived in 1898.

In fact, the primary purpose of the trip was for John Brown to study bacteriology at Toronto General Hospital and at Johns Hopkins University in Baltimore—"For Good of Yukon," as *The Dawson Record* put it in a giant headline. Brown also was to purchase an x-ray machine for Dawson. It was expected to be a long trip, lasting many months: "Dr. and Mrs. Brown are expected to return to Dawson over the ice. They will swing around through California and come north by way of the coast," declared the *Record*.

It was to be a journey of no return on the steamer *Dawson* for Faith and John Brown. While they were out of Dawson, the position of territorial secretary was abolished and, as *The Dawson Daily News* expressed it, "the question of the x-ray machine has since been shrouded in mystery."

The power-game against John Brown is also somewhat shrouded in mystery, but politics in the Yukon were byzantine. Liberal "King" Congdon, as he was called, played a game of favourites. With his lieutenant, William Temple, he had even managed to split the Liberal party into two groups, known as the Tabs and the Steambeers, by such tactics as rewarding personal support with favours—liquor licences, for example. An ambitious man, he built up a political machine that opponents declared as corrupt as Tammany Hall in New York at the turn of the century. In an attack on Congdon, *The Dawson Daily News* accused him of "spending the people's money like a Klondike millionaire among his little coterie of supporters," and claimed that five of the six departments of local government felt they could no longer support him, whereupon Congdon attempted to suspend members of those departments.

Congdon resigned his post in 1904 to run—unsuccessfully—in the federal election of that year, and presumably John Brown paid the price for his association with the commissioner he had served. It seems likely he would have worked as loyally for Congdon as he had for Ogilvie. Although the names of many government officials and employees appear in the various newspaper accounts and books written on "the Congdon Machine," perhaps it is significant that, in all the hurling of accusations, "genial" John Brown's name is not mentioned.

The Dawson Daily News in March 1905 reported with hope that "Dr. Brown intends to return to the Yukon and may bring the [x-ray] machine with him." However, it was not to be. The Dawson idyll was over for Faith and John Brown. They may have been thrown out of paradise, but those first years of their marriage in gold-rush Dawson would colour their lives for ever.

Faith Fenton-Brown grieved for her little log cabin on Mission and Seventh, left with all her goods and chattels and memories of her life with John. Deserted homes like Faith's are part of Dawson's history, abandoned with the contents intact as their owners drifted away to other gold rushes, other lives. Perhaps Florence packed up the most precious possessions and sent them Outside for her sister—she and her husband would eventually leave also, to live in Winnipeg.

The deserted homes eventually fell into disrepair, the more valuable contents put up for sale in the second-hand stores, the rest left to moulder and decay in summer heat and winter cold. Faith's home survives to this day, although it is hard to believe it is the same log cabin of the early pictures. Painted pink and with many additions, it still stands on the corner of Mission and Seventh Avenue, where she began her married life with John Brown.

Coyotes do not roam the deserted streets of Dawson, but the ghosts of those long-ago stampeders cling to the tumbledown shacks in the city and the cabins that still hang perilously on the hills above Bonanza. They hover about the remnants of that wild, wonderful era, not the re-creations of the Floradora or Diamond Tooth Gertie's saloon. But they cling closest to the graveyard on the hillside behind Dawson City, overlooking the river of their dreams.

From Japan, the United States, Scotland, Alsace, Finland, Germany, they came in their prime, to end up at the age of twenty-five, or thirty-five, in a decaying cemetery. Their gravestones are sometimes of stone, but mostly of wood and tin. Some graves have little picket fences around them, some have iron piping made into enclosures, with decorative finials. They look like babies' cribs, and one really is a crib, cut and thrust into the ground, holding baby Sheldon as it held him in life. Another holds two little boys who sleep together, their brief life-spans written on them: 1899–1904; 1904–1905.

Some of the trees have lifted the picket fences above their massive roots so they ride like ships on a stormy sea—ships of fools, their gold-mad passengers buried forever in the ground they hoped would make them rich beyond their dreams.

XV

Return from the Wilderness

The medical profession may be lucrative, but it must also
be full of grave responsibility . . . a doctor sees human
nature at the core; when all affectation and veneer are laid
aside and the real spirit of the man . . . betrays himself.

"Stella's Toronto Letter,"
The Northern Advance, 1887.

Our doctors are absorbed in petty rivalries and jeal-
ousies, in detecting breaches of etiquette, in taking legal
action against the unduly certified makers of bread pills.
What time have they for lesser things?

Faith Fenton, "Woman's Empire," 1891.

DAME RUMOUR HATH IT as the lady correspondent liked to say—that
Faith Fenton returned to Toronto and became a pillar of middle-class
society, pouring tea and entertaining her husband's colleagues and their
wives, while exaggerated and romantic stories proliferated about her
Klondike adventure. As with most rumours, some is true and much is
false. What is true is that she gave up her career as a full-time journalist.

It would be difficult to exaggerate her Klondike story, and Faith herself
always underplayed what she had achieved. In this part of her life she
became a very private person—"of a retiring nature," said one newspaper
commentary, "and shunning publicity"—who rarely spoke about her

colourful past, but possibly if she mentioned some of her early contacts with such political legends as John A. Macdonald, or stage legends like Emma Albani—if she told her visitors about shooting the rapids, or nearly hitting an iceberg off Newfoundland, or visiting the lone woman lighthouse keeper on Lake St. Louis, or braving in disguise the rats and misery of the House of Industry—the younger ones who had not read her columns would have found it all very hard to believe of the small, frail-looking and oh-so-correct middle-aged woman they saw across the tea-table.

As for becoming a pillar of society, there is no doubt she would have taken great pleasure in being mistress of a highly successful medical man's household, right in the heart of what had been enemy country for her friend and supporter, Ishbel Aberdeen. For when John Brown returned to Toronto, he was appointed house-surgeon and medical superintendent of Toronto General Hospital in July 1905, replacing the retiring Dr. Charles O'Reilly, the bitterly hostile doctor who had spear-headed the fight against Lady Aberdeen and the formation of the VON.

The old Toronto General Hospital was a palatial edifice set in park-land on Gerrard Street, east of Parliament Street, and Faith and her husband lived in a lodge in the grounds that was specially renovated for them. Faith must often have chuckled to herself over life's strange synchronicity and the whirligig of time as she poured the tea and bested the Toronto society ladies at a game she had played with the greatest of them.

Faith Fenton once said in a "Woman's Empire" column that she was glad she was not a genius—"nor yet the wife of one." John Brown may not have been a genius, but when he returned from the Klondike with Faith as his wife, his career blossomed. In the six years he was with Toronto General Hospital, he completely reorganized the institution, introducing a new cost-accounting system and extending the laboratory work—apparently partly at his own expense. He established weekly hospital clinics for post-graduate work, and travelled extensively in Europe, Great Britain and the United States to study hospital construction and administration. He spent some time in Germany and learned the language so well that he received requests from colleagues to translate letters and medical information.

The evidence is that Faith was generally with him when he travelled abroad. Finally, she was able to see the country of her mother and father, the London in which her grandmother had acted and sung, where her grandfather had written his poems and plays.

It was her husband who did most of the writing now. Over the years John Brown wrote on hospital planning, construction, organization and management; he wrote on folk medicine (with help, perhaps, from his wife's experiences with the Mennonites), tuberculosis, hospital kitchens, maternal mortality, hospitals in China (perhaps with input from his missionary brother). He wrote articles on subjects other than medicine—notably one on Oliver Wendell Holmes. His study "Evolution of Law and Government in Yukon Territory" is still consulted.[1] He was considered to have "an eloquent pen," and family lore has it that his secretary and editor—and in some cases the actual writer of the articles—was his journalist wife. Certainly, with the long hours he spent in surgery and hospital, it seems very likely to have been the case.

There was one place where being Faith Fenton still meant something, somewhere she could meet the women now in the profession she had pioneered. The Canadian Women's Press Club was formed in June 1904, when thirteen Canadian women journalists found themselves returning in the same Pullman car from covering the St. Louis World's Fair, and decided it was time they had their own organization. Kit Coleman was the first president, and Faith often dropped in to meet old friends, such as Jean Blewett of *The Globe*.

"Faith Fenton" also still meant something in publishing circles. When a young poet called Robert Service sent his first book of poems, *Songs of a Sourdough*, to William Briggs, the publishers sent a proof copy to Faith in 1907 for her opinion.[2] The Browns had left Dawson before Robert Service arrived there, but they became friends in later years, and entertained him to dinner in their lodge at the Toronto General Hospital.

Much as she had wanted it, adjustment to the traditional wifely role was not without its difficulties. Two stories have been handed down in Faith's family that suggest there were occasionally sparks in the Brown household. The first took place while Faith and John were in Dawson, and involved Faith's intervention when she saw a pack-mule being ill-treated by its owner and had him charged for using excessive violence against the animal.

The trouble was that the only witness for the defence was John Brown himself, who felt that the man was only doing what was necessary to get the job done. John Brown's testimony was believed, and the man was acquitted. Faith told her family there were a hard few days in the household until *she* came around to John Brown's point of view.

The second episode occurred when she was quite elderly. One of her nieces came to visit her on the day of a federal election, and found her aunt about to go out and vote. It was bitterly cold, and the niece suggested Faith should consider giving it a miss this time. "No, dear" was the response, "because your uncle won't promise not to go out and vote himself." John Brown was a Liberal, Faith a Conservative, and Faith obviously considered that each vote would cancel the other out. Clearly she never conformed to the then common wifely pattern of changing her allegiance to please her husband.[3]

There was little possibility, however, of Faith being bored in her role as "wife of her husband," because she was rarely in one place for any extended period of time. The Browns travelled extensively in Europe and the United States from 1904 to 1911, and then John Brown was appointed medical superintendent of Detroit General Hospital, which was also known as Henry Ford Hospital. From a freelance article Faith wrote for *The Mail and Empire* in November 1912, it seems John Brown first tried commuting to Detroit and returning to his Toronto home on weekends, and finally decided they would have to move to the United States.

The two-thousand-word article "Ordeals Encountered in Entering Detroit" is signed "F.F.B." and is vintage Faith Fenton. Reminiscent of the *opera buffo* style of her column on the *Globe* fire, it describes her problems with Customs and Immigration when she tried to cross the border with her Scottish maid, Maggie, and a sealskin coat in her luggage. When they had sorted out the immigration hassles—"there is so much riff-raff coming into the country that we have to be particular"—there remained the problem of the sealskin coat that Faith visited "behind the bars of the Customs locker of the G.T.R. depot at Detroit."

To the bewilderment of its owner, the Customs officials needed to know in what waters the seals were caught: "Fur coats are not needed in Detroit, except for a few weeks in the year. Why not store it in Windsor, and when you feel a desire to wear it, cross on the ferry and walk about Windsor for an hour or so?"

Besides demonstrating that the lady journalist had lost none of her skills, the article also shows that she had acquired the accoutrements of prosperity: a personal maid and, in fact, more than one fur coat. The doctor's wife was now able to indulge the longings a young Faith had felt in those lovely Quebec fur stores; she was also able to forget—as, of course, most of her contemporaries did—the "piteous, sad-eyed" seals she had once seen in Newfoundland.

The move to Detroit and the beginning of the First World War brought new opportunities for Faith to use her leadership skills and her drive. In both her obituaries and family records there appears the statement that she was "head of the Detroit Red Cross" during the First World War. However, files of the Detroit Red Cross in the National Archives in Washington show a Mrs. Russell A. Alger Jr. as General Chairman of the Department of Branches and Auxiliaries for the Detroit Chapter, when it was formed in 1917—when the United States entered the war—and it is possible that Faith headed a committee within that organization, perhaps liaising with the Canadian Red Cross.

With the unconditional patriotism of her generation, she would have had no crises of conscience over whether urging young men to go overseas to fight and die was morally desirable—if, indeed, that was part of what she did. A newspaper clipping of the poem "In Flanders Fields" is still among her papers.

In March 1914, the Browns were back in Toronto for the funeral of William Henry, who died at the age of eighty-five. The physician who signed the death certificate was his son-in-law, John Brown. His obituary lists his surviving children, who were now scattered across a continent—all except the oldest, now sixty-three, and the last on that list: "Miss Mary, at home."

By 1918 the Browns were back in Toronto, where John Brown took up private practice and broadened his medical horizons in other ways. He initiated the formation of the Canadian Hospital Association, was corresponding secretary of the British Hospital Association and on the editorial staff of numerous leading medical journals. The centre of his medical career was now closer to home than ever before in the twenty years of his marriage, because his surgery was in his home on Bloor Street when they first returned to Toronto, and his professional travelling much curtailed. They eventually bought a separate home on Blythwood Road, and then moved to 1178 Mount Pleasant Road.

Faith and John spent much time together during those last years of their married life. They now had a car, and in numerous fender-benders John Brown discovered to his chagrin that motor vehicles did not think as swiftly as he did. Meetings of the Toronto Medical History Club took place in their home, and as president of the Yukon Sourdoughs' Association,

John Brown must often have hosted meetings and celebrations on Bloor Street and Mount Pleasant Road. It is clear from the newspaper clippings kept by Faith and John, and the few recorded observations that remain, that those get-togethers with friends who had shared their Yukon experiences were precious. There would have been no need for lengthy descriptions or vain attempts to convey what it had been like in those glorious gold-rush days. They had all shared a unique experience that was beyond explanation.

In Toronto the Browns became guides, counsellors and loving friends to a generation of nieces and nephews. Faith's great-niece, the daughter of her beloved nephew Fred, suffered from mastoiditis as a child and required an operation. She recalls how her uncle John brought in the top specialist from the United States, who travelled to Toronto by car, his gloved hands resting on a pillow.[4]

The Browns also seem to have given financial support to young relatives furthering their education—Faith would never have wanted to see anyone deprived of his or her dreams. Books continued to be her solace and her joy, and she joined the Women's Reading Club, and kept up an extensive correspondence with friends all over the world. Only one of her letters is known to have survived. It is among the Laurier papers at the National Archives in Ottawa, and congratulates him on his election in 1896.

Faith went on writing freelance for magazines and newspapers in Canada and the United States. The last-known pieces are an article of hers in 1926 in an American magazine, *The Delineator*, and a piece about Laura Secord written for children, dated November 29, 1929, whose provenance has yet to be established.

As old age approached, Faith seems to have discovered the art of growing old, enjoying what she was still able to take from the moment. To the younger generation of her family, she was their legendary Aunt Faith who had been to the Yukon in the great gold-rush days. One of her nieces once asked her why. Faith paused a moment and then answered, "Well, dear, I think it was because of the binder twine." She had once sat up in the parliamentary gallery in Ottawa and listened to the country's leaders debate for hours over some sort of a problem involving binder twine, she recalled, and known she could never do what they were doing. It was too irrelevant.

When the actress Emma Abbott died suddenly in 1891, Faith wrote in "Woman's Empire," "It is well we do not know—that the hour is always hid from us." Maybe she had some premonition, some intimation of her own end, for in 1935 she began to put together her hundreds of articles and columns, to take a pencil to the work of forty years earlier and correct errors, cut paragraphs, alter phrases, as if she were thinking of putting them together for publication.

Faith had always kept her work, cutting out the columns and pasting them on to stronger paper, and it is from the backing of some of those columns that one can judge when it was done. Some are pasted onto letters to John Brown from drug companies and from colleagues and are dated 1935. One is from a garage, telling him when he can have his Buick back. In November 1935 she made her will, and the names from the beginning and the end of her life came together for almost the last time: "This is the last will and testament of me, *Alice Freeman Brown* ('Faith Fenton')."

Faith celebrated the turn of the year 1935 into 1936 by sending her greetings to *The Globe*, who used the opportunity to reminisce about "The Reporter Who 'Covered' Yukon for The Globe in '98." The writer of the article had looked out the files of *The Globe* for 1898 and found "scattered among the brown, brittle leaves thrilling accounts of Mrs. Brown's perilous journey. . . ." With her card Faith had enclosed a photograph of the Toronto Sourdoughs and a poem *The Globe* printed in full about those long-ago days "in that lone land of nightless June and dark December."

On New Year's Day, 1936, she and John celebrated their thirty-sixth wedding anniversary. A few days later, Faith was taken ill with pneumonia and died on January 10.

One of the notes John Brown kept after Faith's death was from the secretary of a home for the aged who recalled chatting with her "while she was waiting for you on a cold morning so recently." Some verses almost certainly written just before her death suggest that she was prepared to move on to "The Unseen Shore" that is the title of her poem:

> Sometime at even when the tide is low—
> I shall slip my moorings and sail away . . .

The poem concludes:

> But I shall have peacefully furled my sail
> In moorings sheltered from storm or gale
> And greeted the friends who have sailed before
> O'er the Unknown Sea to the Unknown Shore.

Without a shadow of a doubt, there would have been hundreds waiting for their heart friend as she completed that final adventure.

Faith's funeral took place on January 14—what would have been her seventy-ninth birthday. Almost three hundred mourners crowded into the funeral chapel to pay their last respects: among them were sourdoughs, former members of the Yukon Field Force, many writers whom Faith had encouraged in their early struggles. Among her pall-bearers were members of the Sourdoughs' Club, the president of the Toronto Academy of Medicine, and a member of the board of directors of the University of Toronto. She was buried in Mount Pleasant Cemetery, and her elegant headstone of unpolished soft pink granite reads: "In memory of Alice Freeman—Faith Fenton—1858–1936. Beloved wife of Dr. John N.E. Brown." Although the years had crept closer to the truth, to the very end Faith never admitted to her real age.

The death of "one of the glamorous figures of the gold rush of '98" made headlines in all the major newspapers. They called her "greatly beloved," "a pioneer woman journalist." They quoted her, they talked of "her rare ability and burning enthusiasm." They spoke of her "wide and sympathetic knowledge of general affairs," praised her originality and the "nice literary flavor" of her style. *The Mail and Empire* recalled how a whole generation "waited, wide-eyed, for these tales of great adventure. They were hardly more intrigued by what they actually read than by their imagination of the lone woman writer in the northern wilds. And their imagination did not exaggerate."

It is a fine epitaph, and one that would have pleased Faith: that the great adventure of that lone woman writer far outstripped in reality the wildest stretch of her readers' imaginations.

Postscript: Olive

Stories in this world tell themselves by halves. There is always a silent side, and none may know the life of another.

Faith Fenton, "Woman's Empire," 1889.

QUITE SOON AFTER HER SUDDEN DEATH, John Brown went to Faith's desk and tried to continue what she was doing. There are backing papers dated just after Faith died—old letters, bills, statements. The letters of sympathy flooded in from all over the continent and from Europe—from teachers, university professors, writers, government leaders—and he, or someone else, typed them all out together on sheets of paper, writing in the names, sometimes just the titles, of those who sent them.

John also attempted to write his memoirs—or, rather, her memoirs, "Memories of Faith Fenton." He set up two or three chapter headings, wrote a page or two, some opening paragraphs, and then apparently abandoned the attempt. Whether it was too painful, whether he still had problems putting his feelings on paper, or whether he was exhausted or unwell, can only be guessed at. But what is certain is that there was someone around who helped him through the year of 1936, and that in 1937 he married her. She was not only twenty-eight years younger than he was, she was Faith's niece, Olive Freeman, the daughter of Faith's "best friend" and brother Frederick.

The event caused a traumatic split in the Freeman family, with some of Faith's brothers and sisters accepting the marriage, some angrily rejecting Olive. One of those most distressed by the relationship was Olive's brother, Fred, the "Boy Blue" of Faith's "Woman's Empire" columns, who had been close to his aunt Faith.

Had she been observing such a marriage in her column, Faith might have noted the painful parallels between this story and the story of Thomas Reikie and Marion Thomson, but there are some important differences—the most significant of all being the role Olive had played in the lives of Faith and John.

One of the greatest sorrows Faith and John shared in their marriage was that they had no children. She loved teaching the little ones at school, she semi-adopted her nephew Fred and her sister Gracie—indeed, her readers sometimes thought they were her own children she wrote about. She sublimated her strong maternal instinct in her passion for animals. When Edith Tyrrell returned to the Klondike, she lived just down the road from the Browns, and she says in her memoirs that her daughter Mary spent a great deal of time with them.

In the December 1895 issue of the *Canadian Home Journal*, there is a full-page lullaby dedicated to Olive, called "Twilight." The theme of the poem is that there is nothing in this world that can compare with "Mother-love and Baby / In our old rocking chair," which is the refrain at the end of each verse. And when the Browns finally returned to Toronto, Faith resumed a close relationship that had started with Olive's birth in 1892.

Family lore has it that little Olive spent a great deal of time with her aunt and uncle, and that she even accompanied John Brown sometimes on his rounds as his "little helper." There are photographs of John, Faith and Olive in deck-chairs on a steamer or liner, so obviously she went with them at least once on their trips abroad. From the clothes and from Olive's appearance—she looks about twenty years old—the date would seem to be somewhere around 1912—certainly before the Great War.

To get some idea of Olive's character one has to rely on family memory, filtered through the anger and distress of those who were opposed to the marriage. She has been described as beautiful—and, indeed, she is very pretty in the few photographs that remain—but also "frigid." Apparently she had a reputation for turning men away, and never wanting to get married.

At this point a biographer starts asking questions. Was she "frigid" because she concealed a hopeless passion for her uncle John? Did John

Brown do anything to encourage or requite that passion? Did Faith know or suspect that there was anything to worry about—and was there, in fact, anything to worry about? It is much more likely that Olive was single because of her profession, her generation—even on this continent, the Great War had killed off so many young men—and a sense of duty towards her widowed mother, who may have relied heavily on her for emotional support.

One of the difficulties with unravelling John Brown's motivation is unravelling the character of John Brown. In the few contemporary references there are to him, he comes across as a kind, reticent, highly intelligent and popular—even much-loved—man. Even when he remarried, it was Olive who took the brunt of the criticism. He seems to have been a workaholic, completely committed to his medical career, only retiring shortly before his death. The accounts of his disagreement with Faith about the overworked mule, even perhaps his insistence on voting, suggest that he was exactly what one would expect of a Victorian husband: an authoritative, patriarchal figure, for all his kindness and geniality.

It is tempting to look at the only photograph of Faith, John and Olive together and see more than there is to see. Does pretty Olive look secretive? Does John look smug—almost rakish? Does Faith look grim, defiant? When it was enlarged, it revealed that Faith was wearing a veil over her face, perhaps in an attempt to flatter her features, particularly as her husband was seven years younger than she was, and now looked it.

The pattern of Olive's life interestingly followed quite closely that of her famous aunt: although she did not inherit the Freeman writing gift, she became a kindergarten teacher in the Toronto school system and taught in various schools up to the time of her marriage. She may have spent considerable periods of time as a child with the Brown family, but after the death of her father in 1917 from tuberculosis at the early age of fifty-six, Olive lived with her widowed mother, Elizabeth, until her marriage to John Brown in 1937. Olive and Elizabeth were reasonably secure financially, because Fred was a successful businessman, so Olive was not principally after her uncle John's money. What she would have been seeking most of all was that title that mattered so much: *Mrs.* Brown.

In the one photograph of John and Olive together, she looks all of her forty-five years—grey-haired, rather shy and, as far as one can see from what little remains of the picture, quite without the style of her aunt Faith, with much of her girlish prettiness gone.

Olive and Faith were almost exactly the same age when they married John Brown. Faith had been John's amanuensis, his travelling companion, his secretary, his kindred spirit, his everything. He could never have her back again from that unseen shore, but he found a woman who knew him almost as well as Faith—knew his ways, knew the way he had been with his wife, knew the way she had been with him. It is intriguing to think of Olive as Faith's new incarnation: Alice, who was Stella, who was Faith, who was Olive.

For some, however, Olive could never fill those tiny shoes. Among the letters that remain are two from the celebrated Canadians who were Faith and John's friends. One is from Robert Service to the second Mrs. Brown, politely turning down an invitation to visit with his wife, saying that they will not have time, not be down their way, etc. etc. The other is from J.B. Tyrrell, apologizing for not hearing the door-bell ringing when Olive visited with one of her sisters, and going into a long and elaborate explanation as to why that happened. Perhaps those refusals can be read as some sort of criticism of John Brown, who had been for many years a friend of both men. More accurately, they may reflect a rejection of Olive, since the Ontario-Yukon Pioneers, of whom John Brown was President, held a garden party to celebrate his remarriage in the summer home of the Tyrrells and presented him with a pig-skin travelling bag as a wedding present.

It is also worth noting that those two letters are all that remain of any correspondence there was between the Tyrrells and the Browns—there is one other letter from Robert Service—and that this is part of a pattern in the family archives. Apart from the photograph with Olive, the only known photograph of Faith and John together was found in the Yukon Archives at Whitehorse, and there is virtually nothing remaining among those private papers from the period of their marriage.

John Brown died in 1943. He is buried with Faith, beneath the pink granite stone in Mount Pleasant Cemetery. Olive is buried in the Freeman family plot. Faith Fenton no doubt would have approved of the discretion such an arrangement expressed.

On July 5, 1896, a few months after the great Historical Ball, Faith Fenton wrote a letter of congratulations to Wilfrid Laurier on becoming Prime Minister of Canada. Either he or his secretary thought enough of the letter to keep it, and it is among the Laurier papers in the National Archives in Ottawa. The printed heading on the notepaper reads: "The Editorial Department. *Canadian Home Journal*, Manning Arcade, Toronto." In it Faith says that she waited until the "shower of congratulations was past" to add her own, "from a Conservative." She adds that she is not sure that it is a matter of congratulation "to be chosen to the responsible office of premier—Sir John Thompson once told me it wasn't."

The letter continues by speaking of her disappointment that her party was not elected, "since as far as a woman can understand these things, I believe in its policy. Yet I know that our ministry has been making for its own defeat ever since Sir John Thompson died. Even women watching from the gallery see many things, you know."

She tells Laurier that she will always be proud of him, and that only one thing would have made her happier—"and that is to have seen you standing thus—only as head of the Conservative Party. You see I was born so, and just can't help it."

Faith concludes by apologizing for what is "hardly a conventional letter of congratulation," but assuring him of her sincerity, "and that in common with all Canada I shall be proud of our premier."

Certainly it is an unconventional letter, as was its writer, but the most striking thing about it is the comfortable familiarity with which the lady journalist addresses Canada's new prime minister. The tone of the letter suggests that she and Wilfrid Laurier had talked before, and that the conversation had been more than perfunctory. Faith is so absolutely sure of herself she feels free to put in a political observation—although she adds a self-deprecating comment that is not only tongue-in-cheek, but a touch flirtatious—but then, Wilfrid Laurier had that effect on women.

For the last thirty-six years of her life, her twentieth-century years, Faith surrendered the persona that had given her that kind of access to the leaders of Canadian society. She became what so many of her readers had been, a homemaker. Although she still did some writing, the author of the *Pacific Monthly* article was correct in saying that Faith Fenton-Brown rarely took up her pen, being content to be "the wife of her husband."

It seems hard to believe that the rebel would conform so easily, that the fires of reform would burn out so swiftly—Susan B. Anthony was still fighting in her seventies, after all. From remarks that Faith made in the later years of "Woman's Empire" it is clear she felt universal suffrage was just around the corner and that most of the struggle was over. By that she meant the fight to allow women into such professions as law and medicine to which they had been denied access. However, it was not because the mission was completed that Faith put down her pen; it was because she was the wife of John Brown. There is little doubt she believed the two roles to be mutually exclusive and, by the standards of her time, she was right. For John Brown to be as successful as he was in the medical profession, he needed a wife who could help him fulfil his social obligations and who would not alienate the medical Establishment—or any other Establishment, for that matter. He may have fallen in love with Faith Fenton, but it was Alice Freeman he needed by his side. One can only guess whether he loved the one as much as the other.

Faith Fenton the journalist lost something when she lost Alice. When she found her again, she probably enjoyed being Alice the conformist as much as she had Faith the rebel. The social imperative of that Victorian society in which Alice was raised was so powerful that the satisfactions of that "high and holy estate" more than compensated for the thrill of being familiar with a prime minister, or maintaining a secret correspondence with Canada's First Lady. Finally, Alice the castaway was accepted into the heart of the Establishment in her new role—as Faith Fenton-Brown.

One image stands out in the middle of the eulogies, the reminiscences, the tales told when that glamorous figure of the gold rush of '98 peacefully died. The writer of *The Mail and Empire*'s obituary quoted a young woman who remembered as a child being shown a photograph by her mother "of a human chain of persons going up an icy slope to a terrifying pass between mountains, the people looking like tiny black dots in the formidable scene; and she remembered her mother saying: '. . . one of those tiny black specks is Faith Fenton'. . . ."

The image of the gold-rush seekers on the Chilkoot Pass is one of the great images on the retina of twentieth-century imagination; in a century of photography, there are few more easily recognizable. That Faith Fenton did not take the Chilkoot Pass matters not. That she was female was important enough, but Faith was more than that to the women in Toronto and Winnipeg and Vancouver and Halifax. She was one of them who had dared to be different.

When that nineteenth-century mother identified one tiny black speck on the face of the mountain as Faith Fenton, she passed on to her twentieth-century daughter the lady journalist's great gift to her own generation: a new horizon of endless possibilities.

Chapter Notes

I: Undercover

1 Designed by Toronto's premier architect E.J. Lennox, the Toronto Athletic Club opened in 1894 and was bankrupt four years later. It was built in the Romanesque style of the medieval buildings of southern France, and contained the city's first indoor swimming-pool. Women were allowed to use the premises at certain hours and on Wednesday afternoons. It became a school, then a military headquarters, and was then used as police headquarters for over forty years. It has now been acquired for studio space by the Ontario College of Art.

2 John Graves Simcoe, who had served with the British army during the War of Independence, was appointed lieutenant-governor in 1791. Toronto was renamed "York" by Simcoe in 1793—which name it kept until 1834, when it reverted once more to "Toronto."

3 Goldwin Smith, former regius professor of Modern History at Oxford, had first visited Toronto in the 1860s, but did not settle permanently in the city until 1871, after a period of teaching at Cornell University, Ithaca, New York. In 1875 he married Harriet Boulton, widow of William Boulton, who had been both a member of Parliament and mayor of Toronto. Goldwin Smith was considered a leader of liberal thought, but had some unpleasantly unliberal views on racial minorities and on women. He was also an advocate of the commercial and political union of Canada with the United States.

4 The Family Compact, that "nest of dirty birds," as rebel-leader William Lyon Mackenzie called them, were a tight-knit group of families—the Boultons, the Baldwins, the Robinsons, among others—who controlled the land, the politics and the fortunes of early nineteeth-century Toronto under the leadership of John Strachan, the first Bishop of Toronto.

5 Jarvis Street, named after one of the most influential families of the Family Compact, was once the fashionable centre of Toronto and possessed some of its finest homes. See Austin Seton Thompson, *Jarvis Street; A Story of Triumph and Tragedy* (Toronto, 1980).

6 Timothy Eaton, founder of Eaton's Stores, opened his first emporium on Yonge Street in 1869.

II: A Certain Charm

1 After the creation of the Province of Upper Canada, Asa Danforth, an American,

contracted in 1798 to construct a roadway forty feet wide from Kingston, in the east, to Burlington, in the west, along the shoreline of Lake Ontario. Although it followed the contours of the shoreline, it was set inshore about a mile or so— both for military reasons and to avoid the marshland at the mouths of the many streams that emptied into Lake Ontario.

2 In 1852 a charter was issued to the Grand Trunk Railway Company of Canada to start construction on a main railway line between Toronto and Montreal, with much of the work being carried out by local contractors. All sections of the railway did not open at the same time, and the first through trains in both directions reached Bowmanville on October 27, 1856.

3 Thomas Hood (1799–1845) and Thomas Love Peacock (1785–1866) were celebrated enough in their day to be household names. Their poetry is very much of the "Gather ye rosebuds" genre—the best-known probably being Hood's poem on the Old Testament Ruth: "She stood breast-high amid the corn."

4 All the information on Mary Ann Lillie's background comes from hand-written notes recorded by her grandchildren, but there is a record of the marriage in Chelsea in 1851.

5 The Fenian Brotherhood came into being in Ireland in 1848, and eventually the movement reached the United States. By the early 1860s a faction of the organization believed that annexing Canada, calling it "New Ireland," and using it as a base of operations against England, would be more productive than trying to organize a long-distance rebellion in Ireland. By 1865 they had arms and supplies in depots along the Canadian border, and a hefty war-chest of funds. Nine companies of Canadian volunteers were set up to control the border and, in 1866, John A. Macdonald called up 10,000 men in the Canadian militia in anticipation of an attack on St. Patrick's Day. In fact, the attacks took place on June 1, when a body of Fenians from Buffalo invaded the Niagara Peninsula, landing in Fort Erie and retreating after two days in the face of advancing government troops. As in many communities along the shores of Lake Ontario, rumours of imminent invasion spread to Bowmanville, and an army of men, equipped with pitchforks and scythes and anything remotely resembling a weapon, turned out to defend their town at Barber's Creek, where they waited in vain for an advancing army.

6 There were an amazing number of private academies in Bowmanville for such a small community—obviously the immigrant population came from educated backgrounds and deemed such things important. In 1855 two local public schools and the Grammar School run in the old Town Hall combined to form the United Common and Grammar School—the Bowmanville Union School, which continued on Wellington Street until 1887, when the building burned down.

III: Liberty of Conduct

1 The Congregationalist, Methodist and Presbyterian churches came together in

1925 to become the United Church of Canada. The early Methodist circuit-riders, known as "saddle-bag preachers," travelled around the countryside taking their message to isolated communities, and had a profound effect on many early settlers—notably the great Egerton Ryerson.

2 The Royal Mail Line ran between Toronto, Kingston and Montreal—passengers changed steamers for the rapids on the St. Lawrence River. Steamers stopped at Bowmanville and Port Hope, and left Bowmanville every afternoon at 3:30 for Toronto. They left Toronto at 11:00 a.m. each day, and many more people at this time used steamers to travel between Toronto, Bowmanville and other towns along the shore than used the trains. Much of the cross-border trade went on by steamer, with coal coming into Bowmanville, and barley and apples going out, mostly to Oswego and Rochester. There was even a cross-lake exchange of baseball and other sports teams.

3 The octagonal parsonage still stands; it has now been divided into two apartments. See Margaret McBurney and Mary Byers, *Homesteads: Early Residences and Families from Toronto to Kingston* (Toronto, 1979).

4 For more information on George Brown, founder in 1844 of *The Globe* newspaper, Liberal leader and arch-rival of John A. Macdonald, see J.M.S. Careless, *Brown of* The Globe: *Statesman of Confederation* (Toronto, 1963).

5 The Ontario Bank, which operated between 1857 and 1906, was Bowmanville's very own bank. David Fisher was the general manager, and when the bank moved its headquarters to Toronto, he stayed on in Bowmanville as chief cashier.

6 Waverley Place is now the home of the Bowmanville Museum. It has been charmingly furnished in the style of its later occupants, the Jury family, who bought the house in 1901. However, much of the furniture dates from the 1880s and 1890s, and the setting creates a wonderful picture of how prosperous turn-of-the-century Ontarians lived.

7 In an era when teacher-training was either poor or non-existent, a series of authorized textbooks was essential and they were usually followed to the letter. There were little or no support materials. Bowmanville Union School had one or two maps and globes of the world, a magic lantern, and a library that was open to the public. Values such as the sacredness of private property and the virtues of industry and frugality were stressed. For the girls in the classroom, virtue lay in the glorification of motherhood and the shaping of life in the home.

8 The story of the Lady of Shalott will have been a familiar one to most of Faith Fenton's readers. In the poem of the same name, Alfred, Lord Tennyson, Queen Victoria's poet laureate, tells the story of a "fairy lady" doomed to live in one room of a great castle, seeing life only in reflection through a mirror: "A curse is on her if she stay/ To look down on Camelot." The younger generation of the twentieth century may have been introduced to the "fairy lady of Shalott" by singer Loreena McKennitt, who set the poem to music.

9 What Alice would not have known was that Dickens himself was "abandoned" by

his parents at the same age that she and David Copperfield were "abandoned." It took him years to tell the story of those childhood years to anyone and he never got over the pain of that rejection.

10 Marion Thomson is a story in herself. From information on the censuses it would appear that her mother died giving birth to her, and that her father remarried and started another family.

IV: Through the Looking-Glass

1 Robert Barr's semi-autobiographical novel, *The Measure of the Rule*, published in 1906, was set in the Toronto Normal School of the 1870s. Many of his characters were thinly disguised and easily recognizable as their real-life originals, and the chief interest of the book is the detailed picture it gives of life in the Normal School system. Born in 1850, Barr, like Faith Fenton, taught school while trying to get his writing career under way—which he did, successfully. He worked first for *The Detroit Free Press*, then moved to England to continue his journalistic career. He has some interesting observations on trying to be a writer in Canada: "Get over the border as soon as you can; come to London or go to New York; shake the dust of Canada from your feet . . . go back when all the rest of the world is acquainted with you, and you may find that Canada has, perhaps, some knowledge of your existence." And again: "What writer could wish for a more attractive hero than General Brock, or a more romantic hero than Tecumseh? Where, even in the history of Scotland, is there an act of more womanly devotion than the night excursion taken by Mrs. Secord . . . ? Literally, the woods are full of incidents like these."

2 Adolphus Egerton Ryerson (1803–1882) was brought up in a Loyalist household and raised by "a devout mother of Methodist sympathies," according to one of his biographical entries. Honoured as the founding father of the Ontario educational system, he first came to notice when he attacked the exclusive claims of the Church of England, headed by John Strachan, to the clergy reserves. However, he later disassociated himself from the extreme views held by William Lyon Mackenzie, who thought that only rebellion would bring about change. He was appointed first president of the University of Victoria College in 1841, when it was still based in Cobourg, and in 1844 he became Chief Superintendent of Education for Upper Canada, which position he held until his retirement in 1876.

3 John Howard (1803–1890), architect, surveyor, civil engineer, artist, was one of the great characters and creators of the city of Toronto. Originally called John Coltby, he changed his name to Howard when he came to Canada, and claimed to be the descendant of one of the dukes of Norfolk. He first taught drawing at Upper Canada College, where he made valuable connections for his later career as an architect and surveyor. His skills shaped the city in many ways—from the sewer system, to Gothic-style churches, to the Provincial Lunatic Asylum. And, like many Victorian gentlemen, he led a double life. His marriage was childless, but he had three children by another woman, a widow called Mary Williams.

4 See Frank H. Epp, *Mennonites in Canada, 1786–1920: The History of a Separate People* (Toronto, 1974).

5 William McMurray arrived in York at the age of eight, when his parents emigrated from Northern Ireland. He was taught by John Strachan at Upper Canada College and afterwards received his religious training from him. He was married to Charlotte Johnston, grand-daughter of an Ojibwa chief, whom he met in the Sault when he was the Indian agent there.

6 William Botsford Jarvis, High Sheriff of the Home District, whose Yonge Street pickets broke the back of the 1837 rebellion, had at least one escaped slave working for him on his 120-acre estate, Rosedale, in Toronto. See Sandra Gwyn, *The Private Capital* (Toronto, 1989), p. 26.

7 While still in his early teens, Sir Allan Napier MacNab fought in the war of 1812 alongside his father, who had been Lord Simcoe's aide-de-camp during the War of Independence. He was knighted for his services to the Crown during the Rebellion of 1837 after a circuitous route to prominence via carpentry, acting and the study of law. He became premier of Upper Canada in 1854. Dundurn Castle in Hamilton, which he named for the ancestral home he had never seen, was completed in 1835. Immaculately maintained, the castle stands at the head-of-the-lake, overlooking Burlington Bay.

8 In the War of 1812, the main thrust of the attack on Upper Canada was on the Niagara Peninsula and at Detroit. Apart from the civilian militia, Upper Canada was defended by a single regiment of 1,600 men, led by Major-General Isaac Brock. Scion of one of the great families of Guernsey, in the Channel Islands, Brock fought alongside the Shawnee leader, Tecumseh, and both were killed—Brock at the Battle of Queenston Heights, Tecumseh at the Battle of the Thames River. Early reports suggest that Brock could have survived if he had waited for the arrival of a thousand men from Fort George, but that he deliberately flaunted himself before the Americans and, having died with style, provided a much-needed hero for Canada. His monument at Queenston Heights—the second such edifice, because the first was blown up by a Mackenzie sympathizer—has a counterpart in Candy Gardens, St. Peter Port, the capital of Guernsey.

9 Robert Barr describes Dr. Davies as "bald-headed, red-whiskered, thick-pated, florid-faced [and] hot-tempered."

10 The Council of Public Instruction was a committee of teacher representatives and prominent members in public office set up to determine policy and conduct.

11 It is important to point out here that "Reform" in nineteenth-century politics has absolutely nothing to do with its twentieth-century incarnation. The Reform Party was another name for the Liberals, who were also known then, as now, as the Grits. The name sprang from the attempts of Liberals to break the power base of the Tory Family Compact, who controlled Crown and Clergy Reserves.

V: The Lady Vanishes

1 Alexander Mackenzie—no relation of the 1837 rebel leader William Lyon Mackenzie—led the Liberal Party from 1873 to 1878. He was about as different a Scot as can be imagined from John A. Macdonald—a dour, teetotal Baptist stonemason, born in a Highland croft. He was a great admirer of George Brown, and reluctantly agreed to lead the Reform Party when George Brown declined to return to elective politics after his defeat in 1867.

2 The Orange Organization was founded by Northern Irish Protestants and named for the Dutch Protestant king William of Orange, who defeated ex-king James II's Catholic supporters at the Battle of the Boyne in 1795 in County Armagh. Violently anti-Catholic, they had considerable influence and power in nineteenth-century Canada. Their parades on July 12 each year were a far more blatant and inflammatory display of bigotry than any jubilee church procession.

3 Jordan and Melinda streets lie in an area around and just to the north of King Street that was quite run down in the 1870s. Scott Street was not far away, in the same area. There were imposing buildings and prosperous businesses at one end, but the other was close to the wharves and docks of the lake, and consisted mostly of shacks and warehouses.

4 "Bees" in pioneer days were a cooperative method of building barns, churches and grist-mills, constructing roads, or clearing stumps from the land. It was not only an occasion for hard work, but also for heavy drinking. Perhaps this was when Jeannie Gilmour gave in to teacher Nattrass.

5 The story of Letitia Wright is taken from a series of historical studies based on documents from the archives of the Toronto Board of Education, researched and edited by Bruce Vance. This specific study is entitled *F.S. Spence and the Issue of Corporal Punishment, 1879.*

6 See Marian Fowler's *Redney: A Life of Sara Jeannette Duncan* (Toronto, 1985).

7 Before the era of movies, preachers were the stars of the church-going middle-class community. Actors, after all, were far too raffish and risqué to be worthy of respectable admiration—unless you had actor-ancestors, as the Freemans did.

8 James L. Hughes, a graduate of the Normal School in 1865, was Headmaster of the Boys' School from 1871 to 1874. He was appointed Chief Inspector of Public Schools in Toronto at the age of twenty-nine, a position he held for many years.

9 Mary Frances Scott-Siddons was the great-grand-daughter of the celebrated actress, Sarah Siddons. Her earliest appearances on the London stage were in 1867 as Juliet, and as Rosalind in *As You Like It*. She was described by contemporary writers as having a "neat figure, pretty face and pleasing arch delivery [that] qualified her for light comedy." The neat figure also made her an unqualified "saucy and attractive" success in Rosalind's male disguise of doublet and hose—even if she may have lacked "the grand air of the tragedienne" necessary for other Shakespearean roles. Her first American tour was in 1868 and, although she returned briefly to England, she seems to have enjoyed greater success in the United States.

10 For more on the life and career of William Howland, see Desmond Morton's *Mayor Howland: The Citizen's Candidate* (Toronto, 1973).

11 H. Rider Haggard (1856–1925) had his first major success with *King Solomon's Mines*, which was published in 1885. It caused a sensation, and its effect on the adventure story can still be seen in such twentieth-century movies as *Raiders of the Lost Ark*. *She* appeared in 1897, to equally great acclaim.

12 The Galt family played an important role in the development of Upper Canada, Ontario, and in nineteenth-century politics in general. Thomas Galt's father, John Galt, was a Scottish novelist and journalist who first became associated with Canada when he was appointed the London agent for those claiming compensation for losses sustained during the War of 1812. He first came to Canada in 1826, where he founded the town of Guelph in 1827. He was largely responsible for opening up the Huron Tract, and the town of Galt was named after him. One son, Sir Alexander Tilloch Galt, was the first Canadian high commissioner to London. Sir Thomas Galt was Chief Justice of the Court of Common Pleas from 1887 to 1894.

VI: *Canada's Dear, Far-off Women*

1 After many delays, and after refusing to use insanity as his defence, Louis Riel was finally hanged in Regina on November 16, 1885. To some a madman, to others a martyr, Louis Riel, in life and in death, altered the political balance of Canada in the nineteenth century so profoundly that the reverberations are still felt over a hundred years later.

2 A cartoon dating from 1883 shows E.E. Sheppard as a cowboy astride a bucking bronco labelled "Democracy." His holster holds a quill pen, and he is firing at a group of individuals whose banners identify them as "Globe Fogyism, anti-Canadaism, Retrogression"; "Telegram Nothingism"; "Irish Canadian Toryism"; "The Mail Toryism, Landlordism, Snobrule, Toadyism"; "World neither Fish nor Fowl." The title reads: "The Journalistic Cowboy." See Fraser Sutherland's *The Monthly Epic: A History of Canadian Magazines* (Toronto, 1989). The *Saturday Night* offices were also in the Grand Theatre complex, so presumably Faith knew many of the journalists there, although she never specifically mentions the magazine.

3 The fight for the right to build a westward extension of the railway system, and the ensuing débâcle, are a complex series of events, but it could be said to have begun in 1871, when Macdonald's government contracted to begin a Pacific railway which would take an all-Canadian route. There were two main rival syndicates or "rings," one of which was accused of giving huge sums of money to the government during the 1872 election. The "Pacific Scandal" broke the government and brought about the resignation of Sir John A. Macdonald.

4 Hector Charlesworth's volumes of memoirs give a fascinating picture of the world of journalism in turn-of-the-century Toronto. He chose the pen-name Touchstone after the Fool in *As You Like It* ("Call me not fool till Heaven hath

sent me fortune") when he became one of the first full-time theatre critics for a Toronto newspaper. He mentions Faith only once in passing, and it is possible that his journalistic nose was put out of joint by his colleague's popular theatre notes (Faith once apologized in one of her columns for encroaching on "Touchstone's domain") and prolific theatre contacts.

5 Emma Albani, one of the great divas of her era, was born in Chambly, near Montreal, in 1851. Her father, Joseph La Jeunesse, was a French Canadian, her mother a Scot. She took the stage-name "Albani" after the town of Albany in New York State, where she began her musical career. Her affluent international lifestyle was a constant source of material for society columns. A letter she wrote to Faith Fenton still survives, sending Christmas greetings to her readers, and Faith had the diva's signature reproduced for use in her columns. They met at least twice: once in Chicago and once in Ottawa.

6 Sir Charles Tupper, as premier of Nova Scotia, was one of the Fathers of Confederation, and a staunch supporter of Sir John A. Macdonald. At the age of seventy-five he became prime minister, succeeding Mackenzie Bowell in 1896, only to face defeat in the same year at the hands of Wilfrid Laurier. He detested Lord and Lady Aberdeen for their meddling in politics and their Liberal sympathies, and his antipathy may well have affected Faith's career in 1897. Certainly he allied himself with Toronto doctors in their fight against the VON.

7 J.H. Cranston's memoir, *Ink on My Fingers*, published by the Ryerson Press, Toronto, in 1953, gives some information on the sort of remuneration a journalist could expect. For instance, as late as 1901, Cranston was being paid $9 a week by the *Hamilton Morning Post*—"when there was money enough."

8 Emma Abbott's rags-to-riches story must have endeared her to Faith Fenton. Her father was a struggling music teacher, possibly struggling because the family were Jewish—Emma sang in the synagogue when she was a child. With her guitar, Emma played and sang her way to New York, where Clara Louise Kellogg heard her and financed further voice training for her. In Europe she was befriended by the Rothschild family. In spite of a romantic runaway marriage, she always maintained her maiden name and, in spite of critical abuse that was most probably as much anti-Semitic as anything else, she became one of the stars of her era. Faith Fenton was greatly distressed at Abbott's early death in 1891 at the age of forty-one.

9 The Mercer Reformatory was named for Andrew Mercer, whose estate was used to finance the construction of the Andrew Mercer Reformatory for Females, when he died intestate and without lawful heirs. The reformatory was on the south side of King Street West, between Fraser and Jefferson avenues.

10 There is no Doversville listed in the *Gazetteer of Canada* (Ontario), nor in Carter's *Place Names of Ontario*. Faith may have created it to avoid identifying the somnolent parliamentarian.

VII: The Spirit of Vagabondia

1 Mary Kingsley went to West Africa on the death of both her parents when she was thirty-one and died of typhoid fever when she was thirty-eight, having eaten hippopotamus and crocodile, paddled a canoe in the French Congo, made friends with cannibal tribes, written a best-seller on her adventures, and generally done more living in seven years than most of her female contemporaries managed in a lifetime. Isabella Bird travelled through Australia, America, Persia and Central Asia in the 1870s and 1880s. Gertrude Bell's love and knowledge of the Middle East was drawn upon by war-time military intelligence during the First World War. See H.V.F. Winstone's *Gertrude Bell* (London: Jonathan Cape, 1978). Margaret Fountaine, butterfly-net in hand, travelled all over the world in the 1890s and the early years of this century to Turkey, Africa, India, Siam and the United States. See W.F. Cater, *Love Among the Butterflies* (Harmondsworth: Penguin Books, 1982).

2 Martello towers were originally built in the early nineteenth century along the southern and eastern coasts of Britain, and in the Channel Islands, to provide protection and an early-warning system against possible Napoleonic invasion. This one would, of course, have been constructed to protect against invading Americans.

3 Just before Faith's visit, there had been prison riots in Kingston to protest against poor conditions, particularly overcrowding.

4 See Frances M. Heath, *Sault Ste. Marie; City by the Rapids* (Burlington, 1988).

5 For more on this original and gifted writer, see her *Winter Studies and Summer Rambles*, published in 1838. An abridged edition was published by McClelland and Stewart in 1965 for the New Canadian Library Series, with an introduction by Clara Thomas.

6 Until the 1880s the few women physicians practising in Canada—women such as Emily Howard Stowe and Jennie Kidd Trout—had trained outside the country. In 1883, two women's medical colleges opened: one affiliated with Queen's University, the other with Trinity College in the University of Toronto. But it was only after 1895 that students of the Ontario Medical College for Women could take the examinations that led to a degree.

7 Susan Brownell Anthony (1820–1906) came from a prosperous Quaker family with a tradition of strong-minded women not afraid to oppose the will of the majority— her mother adored music and dancing, for instance. Her father endeavoured to use cotton in his mill that had not been produced by slave labour, and encouraged his daughters to be self-supporting. After an early teaching career, she returned to the family home, which was now in Rochester, the centre of the women's movement. With such reformers as Amelia Bloomer, Lucretia Mott, Lucy Stone and Elizabeth Cady Stanton, she devoted her life to the cause of women's suffrage. The National Woman Suffrage Association was formed in 1869, with Elizabeth Cady Stanton as president, and Susan B. Anthony as chairwoman of the Executive Committee. Another association was formed the same year: The American Woman Suffrage Association, with Henry Ward Beecher as president. Susan Anthony and others felt

there was a problem with men in the association, because women fell back into their traditional role of follower as opposed to leader and trend-setter, reacting as opposed to acting. The two associations amalgamated in 1890. Susan B. Anthony was elected president in 1892, retiring in 1900 at the age of eighty.

8 The mayor in question was William Frederick Clarke, ex-editor of the official organ of the Orange Association, *The Sentinel*, and former deputy grand-master of the association in North America. He was mayor of Toronto from 1888 to 1891.

9 Emily Howard Stowe (1831–1903) had a Quaker background, as did many early women reformers. She had five sisters, and her only brother died in infancy, so the traditional division of labour did not happen in the Howard family. Her mother had been educated in Quaker seminaries in New York State and took over the schooling of her daughters herself. At fifteen, Emily became a teacher, and by 1856 she was a public-school principal in Brantford. Unable to train as a doctor in Canada, she took her degree in New York State and later practised in Toronto. She became the first president of the Dominion Women's Enfranchisement Association, when it was formed in 1889. Her daughter, Augusta Stowe Gullen, became the first woman to graduate with a medical degree from a Canadian university, and was closely associated with the early days of Women's College Hospital.

10 The slogan of *The Bystander* was "Not the party, but the people," a rather curious choice for a magazine whose favourite targets were socialism and the women's movement. Its subtitle was "A Monthly Review of Current Events, Canadian and General."

11 Before the Dominion Women's Enfranchisement Association was formed in 1889, there had been an earlier organization called the Canadian Women's Suffrage Association, formed in 1883. Although it accomplished much in the beginning— the foundation of two women's medical colleges and the passing of the Married Women's Property Act, for instance—it had become less active in the second half of the 1880s. It was largely due to the eloquence of Dr. Anna Howard Shaw, the American suffragist and preacher, that enough interest was revived to bring about the formation of the Dominion Women's Enfranchisement Association. During her visit, Anna Shaw stayed with Emily Stowe, and it is likely that Faith interviewed her there.

12 In the winter of 1885, a woman discharged from the Toronto General Hospital died in a doorway on Jarvis Street, because she had nowhere to go. The tragedy so moved an English visitor, Kate Evans, that she donated $10,000 to build a convalescent home for those without means. Hillcrest Convalescent Home was built on the corner of Bathurst Street and Davenport Road, then in the heart of the countryside, on a hill overlooking the city, and the home opened its doors in 1887. Under the heading "Children of Silence," Faith wrote a lengthy article on the Ontario Institution for the Deaf and Dumb, which was opened in 1870 on the Bay of Quinte, near Belleville, about one hundred miles east of Toronto. She was

obviously impressed with the work being done there and said she had written at such length because "even now . . . we find prejudice and superstition in regard to these inoffensive people yet existent, and because a man is deaf and dumb, he is counted also as demented."

13 In the Treaty of Utrecht that was signed in 1713 after the War of Spanish Succession, British ownership of the island of Newfoundland was recognized, with the French being given certain rights to the west coast of the island. The Treaty of Versailles in 1783 altered the limits of what became known as "the French Shore," but essentially matters remained the same until the invention of the canning process. Immediately, lobster became a valuable resource, and there were disputes over where lobster factories could be built. Finally, a *modus vivendi* was arrived at until another act was passed in 1891. The French finally gave up their rights to the French Shore in 1904. See Frederick W. Rowe, *A History of Newfoundland and Labrador* (Toronto, 1980).

VIII: *Shrieking Sisters*

1 St. James's was the Family Compact's church, from whose pulpit John Strachan had preached. The seating arrangement was a perfect reflection of the Victorian class system: benches for the poor around the edges, pews in the centre occupied in order by rank: members of Parliament, members of the bar, officers, gentlemen and their families. The pew of state for the lieutenant governor was topped by a canopy bearing the royal coat of arms.

2 See Marian Fowler, *In a Gilded Cage: From Heiress to Duchess* (Toronto: Random House, 1993), p. 112.

3 See Patricia Anderson, *When Passion Reigned: Sex and the Victorians*, (New York: 1995), Chapter Two.

4 The Association for the Advancement of Women began in 1873 when the Sorosis Club of New York issued a call for a congress of women that year. The object of the association was "to consider and present practical methods for securing to women higher intellectual, moral and physical conditions with a view to improvement of all domestic and social relations." For the greater part of their twenty-five-year existence, Julia Ward Howe was their president.

5 The Horticultural Pavilion was in the Horticultural Gardens, now called "Allan Gardens," between Carlton and Gerrard streets in the east end of Toronto.

6 Julia Ward Howe was more conservative in her views than suffragists like Susan B. Anthony, Anna Shaw and Emily Stowe. The focus of her organization's effort was not on women's suffrage, to which she was either ambivalent or opposed.

7 William Robinson Clark came to Canada from Scotland in 1882 to take up the chair of mental and moral philosophy at Trinity College in the University of Toronto. He and his wife were friends of Faith Fenton, and two of his letters to her survive.

8 Henrik Ibsen (1828–1906) created an uproar in England when his play *Ghosts*, written in 1881, was first performed in translation in 1889. The play was put on privately by the Independent Stage Company, because it had been banned by the censor. It was described as "a loathsome sore unbandaged . . . garbage and offal . . . as foul and filthy a concoction as has ever been allowed to disgrace the boards of an English theatre." Such a brouhaha about "the Scandinavian humbug" gives some idea of the courage and open-mindedness of Ellen Mitchell of Colorado. Interestingly enough, performance of the play was encouraged during the First World War to remind the war-time public of the dangers of promiscuity.

9 Tennyson's long narative poem "The Princess," became a focal point in the fight over women's rights. There were lectures pro and con Princess Ida (who wanted to found a university for women), letters to the press, even whole books written on the theme of the poem. A correspondent later told Faith that she regretted the princess's final decision to return and marry the prince after all, seeing it as capitulation, even if she had first "found herself."

10 Even though she never says so directly—and would certainly have known nothing about Sonya Tolstoy's married life—it is likely that Faith was reacting to the underlying misogyny of Tolstoy's work quite as much as to its pessimism.

11 William Valance Whiteway arrived in Newfoundland from England in 1843 and practised law before election to the House of Assembly in 1859. He was prime minister of Newfoundland from 1878 to 1885, and again, with a brief break, from 1889 to 1897.

12 George Monro Grant (1835–1902), born in Nova Scotia, was appointed principal of Queen's University, Kingston, in 1877. His son, William Lawson Grant, was headmaster of Upper Canada College. His grandson, George P. Grant, is the author of *Lament for a Nation: The Defeat of Canadian Nationalism*, published in 1965 by McClelland and Stewart, and one of this country's leading political philosophers.

13 The Canadian arm of the Imperial Federation League was formed in 1885 to preserve the unity of the Empire that many felt was threatened by attempts at reciprocity with the United States. The president was D'Alton McCarthy, and there were branches throughout Canada.

14 The National Club was formed in 1875 in connection with a movement called "Canada First." "Canada First" came into being after the Riel rebellion and its aims were to foster and advance a sense of nation within Canada, while at the same time remaining non-partisan and true to the British Empire. With Goldwin Smith elected president of the National Club, there were some divisions within the movement, many of whose members saw his belief in the ultimate independence of Canada as treason—not to mention his advocacy of economic union with the United States.

15 New York's Four Hundred were a coterie of extremely wealthy Americans such as the Astors, the Vanderbilts and the Belmonts, whose vast riches came mostly from railroads, tobacco and banking. The expression "Four Hundred" originally

came from the number of people Mrs. William Astor's ballroom could hold. They built what they called "cottages" in Newport where they spent their summers. Most of the so-called cottages rivalled Versailles in their elaborate splendour.

IX: Head of the Lady Journalists

1 Richard Cartwright had a long and distinguished career in Wilfrid Laurier's Cabinet as Finance minister, and Minister of Trade and Commerce. William Mulock became Laurier's postmaster general. George Foster had been Macdonald's Minister of Fisheries, and a letter from him to Faith, dated 1895, when he was with the Ministry of Finance, is still among her papers. Sir J.A. Chapleau had stood with Macdonald on the decision over the hanging of Riel, thus staving off an immediate government disaster in Quebec.

2 The pretty dark-haired wife was Zoë Laurier, who married Wilfrid Laurier in 1868. What Faith might possibly have heard—but would never have said—was that Wilfrid Laurier had had a clandestine relationship with another woman, Emilie Lavergne, for many years. See Sandra Gwyn, *The Private Capital* (Toronto, 1989).

3 Sir Peter Mitchell (1842–1899) led the fight for confederation during the election campaign which saw him elected premier of New Brunswick in 1866. He attended the London conference at which the British North America Act was drafted, and was appointed to the Senate in 1867.

4 Honoré Mercier's rise to prominence began with the hanging of Riel, when Mercier's fiery oratory united French-Canadian Liberals and Conservatives into a new party, the Parti National. The new party won a majority in the Quebec provincial elections in 1886, and Mercier became premier in January 1887. A year later, Mercier and his Cabinet were dismissed for corruption, which may explain the fact that his portrait was in the cellar.

5 The Ursuline Order was founded in Italy in 1535 and named after Saint Ursula, the patron saint of education. The Ursulines, headed by Mère Marie de l'Incarnation, arrived in New France in the seventeenth century and have had a profound effect on French-Canadian women's lives ever since. See Marta Danylewycz, *Taking the Veil: An Alternative to Marriage, Motherhood and Spinsterhood in Quebec, 1840–1920* (Toronto: McClelland and Stewart, 1987).

X: The White City

1 The Chicago Exhibition was called "The White City" because the pavilions and buildings were predominantly white and glistened in the sun. Faith's frequent use of the name has almost biblical reverberations.

2 Dwight Lyman Moody (1837–1899) and Ira D. Sankey (1840–1908) were the lead-

ing American evangelists of their day. Moody, who never sought ordination, was the preacher, and Sankey was the organist and singer. They started their revivalist crusades in England in 1873 and, by the time they came to Canada in the 1880s, they were one of the hottest tickets in town. On the occasion of their visit, Faith criticized the chic, upper-class Toronto audience, who were there only because it was the thing to do and the place to be seen: "What could even the Divine one do, with such magnificent audiences of well-to-do and self-complacent saints. . . . yes, I'm truly sorry for Mr. Moody. His work is harder than that of General Booth, since reviving such saints is infinitely more difficult than to convert sinners." Her mail-bag later reflected the indignation of those "saints." Faith was unrepentant: "I wrote as I was moved . . . and as I certainly believed, felt and still feel."

3   May Wright Sewall was on the executive committee of the International Council of Women and one of its founding members. She was particularly concerned that the organization should not restrict its interest to suffrage alone. A photograph of May Sewall is still among Faith's possessions.

4   For more on Mrs. Willoughby Cummings, Mary Macdonnell, and the history of the NCWC, see N.E.S. Griffiths, *The Splendid Vision: Centennial History of the National Council of Women of Canada, 1893–1993* (Ottawa, 1993).

5   The Palmer House Hotel was the place to stay in Chicago, whether you were a star of the stage or a member of the Four Hundred. It was named after one of the élite Chicago families, the Potter Palmers.

6   For more on the life of Ishbel Aberdeen, see Doris French, *Ishbel and the Empire* (Toronto, 1988).

7   Senator William Eli Sanford was born in New York, but brought up by an uncle in Hamilton after the death of his father. It was in Hamilton that he made his fortune, setting up the wholesale clothing firm of Sanford, McInnes and Company and becoming known as "the Wool King of Canada." He split from the Reform Party over protective tariffs, became a supporter of Macdonald's, and played a vital role in winning the Hamilton seat for the party in the 1878 election.

8   The Earl of Dufferin was Canada's governor general from 1872 to 1878. He took a great interest in the establishment of the educational system in Ontario.

9   From his early journalistic days as editor of *The Northern Echo* in Darlington in the north of England, through his editorship of *The Pall Mall Gazette*, to his subsequent prominence as editor of *Review of Reviews*, Stead played an important role in publicizing and defending the rights of women—sometimes spectacularly, as in his support of Josephine Butler's fight to raise the age of consent in Britain to sixteen in the Criminal Law Amendment Act of 1885.

10 See Sandra Gwyn, *The Private Capital*, p. 281.

11 William E. Gladstone first became prime minister of Great Britain in 1868, and shared both the spotlight and the post with Benjamin Disraeli over the next quarter of a century. He was not a favourite of Queen Victoria's, who much preferred Disraeli's elegant flattery.

12 John Philip Sousa (1854–1932) was "to the march what the Viennese, Johann Strauss, was to the waltz," as the *Dictionary of American Biography* puts it. He formed his own band in 1892, and one of its first major engagements was at the Chicago World's Fair, where Faith heard them play. He was a prolific composer of marches, and also wrote comic operas.

13 Isabella Beecher Hooker was ten years younger than her sister, Harriet Beecher Stowe, the author of *Uncle Tom's Cabin*. The book has fallen into disrepute in this century, and the expression "an Uncle Tom" has become a derogatory one. It is worth remembering, however, that the author and her husband hid escaping slaves in their homes as part of the Underground Railroad to the north, and risked losing their livelihood as teachers because of their outspoken opposition to slavery. Isabella Beecher Hooker devoted her life to the cause of women's suffrage, and was an expert on women's constitutional, legal and political rights in the United States.

XI: An Unheard-of Thing

1 Oliver Wendell Holmes's name is perhaps better remembered than any of his extensive output of essays, poems and articles. By birth he was one of what he himself called "the Brahmin caste of New England," and the last survivor of a group of celebrated New England writers: Hawthorne, Emerson, Longfellow, Whittier. He died only eight months after Faith visited him, at the age of eighty-five. His son, also named Oliver Wendell Holmes, achieved distinction as a Justice of the Supreme Court of the United States.

2 Faith may have been asked by the Chief of Police, Major Frank C. Draper, to help publicize his attempts to improve the efficiency of the police department. He was involved in a long-running battle with City Hall to get more money to build new police headquarters, and presented his report to them in 1885, complete with an appendix signed by one of Toronto's leading architects, E.J. Lennox, who designed and built Toronto's third City Hall in 1888. It apparently met with no success, and Draper resigned in 1886.

3 Hart and Riddell (Samuel Hart and Matthew Riddell) were wholesale booksellers, printers, stationers and engravers who operated a retail bookstore for a comparatively short space of time at 12 King Street West. By 1886, the Riddells Block included 31 to 33 King Street, where the bookstore was now called Hart and Company. It also housed the Beaver Publishing Company and produced *The Mechanical and Milling News*.

4 *Beautiful Joe* was based on the true story of a dog in Meaford, Ontario, where, in 1892, the author, Margaret Marshall Saunders, first heard his story. It was published in 1884 with a foreword by Ishbel Aberdeen, and was reprinted in a hundredth-anniversary edition by the Ginger Press, in Owen Sound.

5 The International Order of the King's Daughters and Sons was founded in 1886 in New York City and reached Canada in 1887. Its aims were largely philanthropic—

the maintaining of homes for the aged, for example—and its *raison d'être* was to encourage Christian beliefs and to foster the spread of the aims and ideals of Christianity.

6 The Château Frontenac bears the name of Louis de Buade, Comte de Frontenac et de Palluau, appointed governor of New France in 1672.

7 James MacPherson Le Moine (1825–1912) was a prolific writer, in both French and English. In one of her columns, Faith deplores the fact that English Canada had no chronicler of its history, legends and folk-tales like Le Moine.

8 *The Canadian Magazine* modelled itself along the lines of such upmarket American magazines as *Scribner's* and *Atlantic Monthly*. About the time Faith had her article published, the magazine merged with *Massey's Illustrated*, a magazine that had started life under the aegis of the Massey–Harris farm-machinery company.

9 Haddo House was the ancestral home of the Aberdeen family. See Doris French, *Ishbel and the Empire*.

10 See Donald Creighton, *Dominion of the North*.

11 The expression "the Boys," to denote the Ottawa Press Corps, is still in use.

12 In the late nineteenth century, the Muskokas were the Newport of Ontario's "Four Hundred." They are an area of lakes and rivers about a hundred miles to the north of Toronto, beyond Lake Simcoe.

13 For more on Toronto's nineteenth-century working women, see Caroline Strange, *Toronto's Girl Problem: The Perils and Pleasures of the City, 1880–1930* (Toronto, 1995).

14 In the catalogue of periodicals in the Canadian Institute for Historical Microreproductions' microfiche collection for 1994, only two issues are listed for the period when Faith was editor: January 1897, and November 1897. There were, in fact, nineteen issues (MacKay family archives).

15 Horatio Gilbert Parker (1862–1932) was one of the few Canadian writers of his day to have achieved a reputation beyond his own country—almost certainly because he left Canada in 1899 and continued his writing career in England. Not only was he a successful historical novelist, but he was a member of the British House of Commons, and was later knighted.

16 Catherine Parr Traill arrived in Canada in 1832, the same year as her younger sister, Susanna Moodie. Both were married to half-pay officers, and both came to find a new life in a new country. Catherine's book on immigrant life, *The Backwoods of Canada*, was published in 1836, and was an instant success in England and Europe. Her courage, resourcefulness and indefatigable optimism would have been very much to Faith's liking. Her *Canadian Wild Flowers*, published in 1868, and *Studies in Plant Life in Canada*, published in 1885, brought her fame as a naturalist. She settled in Lakefield, near Peterborough, after the death of her husband, and died there in 1899 at the age of ninety-seven.

XII: A Woman's Birthright

1 The resolution establishing the Victorian Order of Nurses was presented at the National Council meeting in Halifax in July 1897. Ishbel Aberdeen proposed the resolution and outlined five main aims for the order: see N.E.S. Griffiths, *The Splendid Vision*. For more on the early years of the VON, see John Murray Gibbon, *The Victorian Order of Nurses for Canada: Fiftieth Anniversary, 1897–1947* (Toronto: The Victorian Order of Nurses, 1947).

2 It would be impossible to find in nineteenth-century Ottawa a more distinguished group of families than these three: the Scotts, the Ritchies and the Desbarats. Faith was flying very high, indeed. For more on the role they played, and continue to play, in the social and political life of the country, see Sandra Gwyn, *The Private Capital*.

3 For an account of the detective work that uncovered this previously invisible journalist, see Sandra Gwyn's *The Private Capital*.

4 Emily Pauline Johnson—Tekahionwake, the Mohawk Princess—was a star performer in Canada and in England. She wrote all her own material, and her collections of poems sold successfully in her own country and abroad. See Betty Keller, *Pauline* (Vancouver: Douglas and McIntyre, 1981).

5 S.S. McClure was a giant in the world of journalism at a time when magazines and periodicals were enjoying great success. The Sunday supplement was his inspiration, and the list of writers he brought to the attention of an American audience reads like a Who's Who of the age's literary lions: writers such as Robert Louis Stevenson, Joseph Conrad, Rudyard Kipling and Conan Doyle. See Peter Lyon, *Success Story: The Life and Times of S.S. McClure* (New York: Charles Scribners Sons, 1961).

6 Faith kept all the correspondence between her, the lawyers, and the representatives of S.S. McClure, and her handwritten lists of the material made available to her at the Toronto General Trusts Company. They are in the MacKay family archives.

7 Lady Aberdeen's requests do not appear to have been successful. There is coverage of the gold rush, of course, but not by Faith.

8 Wilfrid Laurier's letter is in the MacKay family archives. There is no record of any column by Faith in the archives of *The Daily Mail*.

9 Knox College, a Presbyterian foundation, started life in 1844 in the private home of its professor of literature and science, the Reverend Henry Esson. It then moved in 1847 to Front Street West, where the Royal York Hotel now stands. In 1856 it moved again to Bay and Grosvenor streets, closer to the University of Toronto, into the home Lord Elgin had occupied when he was governor general. In 1875, when Faith was being escorted home by two of its students, it was on Spadina Avenue, north of College Street.

10 William Ogilvie tells his story in his autobiography, *Early Days on the Yukon and the Story of Its Gold Finds*, published in 1913, in an unromantic and unvarnished

fashion that speaks volumes about the character of this incorruptible and practical civil servant in a half-mad, gold-crazy world.

11 The information on John Brown's departure comes from his own typewritten account in the MacKay family archives.

XIII: Gold Fever

1 For more information on the gold rush, where better for a reader to turn than to Pierre Berton's epic *Klondike: The Life and Death of the Last Great Gold Rush*, (Toronto, 1958).

2 See Arthur L. Disher, "The Long March of the Yukon Field Force," *The Beaver* magazine, 1962.

3 The New York trip appears to have been unsuccessful.

4 The story about "Wings Willison," the circumstances in which Faith wrote the article, and its impact, are taken from John Brown's typewritten notes in the MacKay family archives.

5 See Laura Berton, *I Married the Klondike* (Toronto, 1954).

6 See Lucile Labelle, *Aux Avant-Postes du Canada. Sous le Signe du Bison* (Montreal, 1982).

7 See James M. Sinclair, *Mission: Klondike* (Vancouver, 1978).

8 For the romantic story of the discovery of Edward Lester's diary, its travels and its final return to Canada, see Brereton Greenhous, *Guarding the Goldfields: The Story of the Yukon Field Force* (Toronto, 1987). Greenhous also uses many of Faith's Klondike columns in the book, as well as some of Georgia Powell's despatches.

9 Both Georgia Powell and Rachel Hanna wrote accounts of their own. Georgia Powell also wrote for *The Globe*, and sent detailed letters to Ishbel Aberdeen and to VON headquarters in Ottawa; Rachel Hanna kept a diary that was preserved by her family, excerpts of which were published by Thora McIlroy Mills in *The Bracebridge Herald-Gazette* in 1971 and 1974.

10 *The Arena* and *The Scribner* were more like contemporary magazines such as *The Atlantic*, rather than, say, *People* magazine—so their presence did indeed "admit of inferences." The tough little American lady was well informed and highly literate.

11 In July 1899, half of the Yukon Field Force left the Yukon, and in October of that year the headquarters were moved from Selkirk to Dawson. Senior officers, such as Lieutenant-Colonel Evans, were now needed to lead the troops that were being sent to South Africa after the attacks by the Boers on Kimberley and Mafeking. By June 1900, it was decided that there was no need to keep troops in the Yukon, and the remaining members of the Yukon Field Force—now called "the Yukon Garrison"—were shipped out via Whitehorse and Skagway and thence to

Vancouver. See Brereton Greenhous, *Guarding the Goldfields*.

12 Samuel Benton Steele was one of those turn-of-the-century figures who led larger-than-life lives. Like William Ogilvie's memoirs—and the little John Brown wrote of his story—his autobiography, *Forty Years in Canada*, published in 1918, is a masterpiece of understatement.

XIV: That One Greatest Love

1 The account of John Brown's journey and arrival is taken from his typewritten notes.

2 Jeremiah Lynch had, at one time, been a senator in the California legislature. His memoirs are more colourful than those of Steele and Ogilvie.

3 Joseph Burr Tyrrell (1858–1957) was one of Canada's most distinguished geologists and explorers. He is particularly associated with the first explorations of the Barren Lands and the Northwest Territories. He and his wife, Edith, were lifelong friends of Faith and John Brown.

4 See Edith Tyrrell, *I Was There: A Book of Reminiscences* (Toronto, 1938).

5 In some of the family's accounts, it is recorded that *The Globe* paid her back the fifty dollars, because the story was such a good one.

6 In fact, the tone of the letter suggests that Ishbel Aberdeen had actually met John Brown. It is unlikely that she would have addressed a letter directly to him, and not approached him through Faith, if she had not done so.

7 By the time Faith met Big Alex McDonald, he was one of the wealthiest men in Dawson City, with interests in claims on the richest creeks in the Klondike: Eldorado, Bonanza, Dominion, Bear and countless others. He even owned part of Dawson itself. It is a measure of Faith's prominence in Dawson society that she seems to have known him and his wife very well—there are photographs in the MacKay family archives of Faith on a balcony with McDonald, and standing with John Brown in the front row of a crowd close to him on the floor of the Palace Grand.

8 Margaret Payson stayed in the Yukon and married a wealthy miner who courted her assiduously soon after she arrived. Georgia Powell served with the Field Hospital in South Africa, and married a sergeant with the NWMP. Amy Scott obviously made a full recovery from her operation, because she went on to nurse in South Africa. Rachel Hanna continued her nursing career in the Yukon, then went as Matron to St. Andrew's Hospital in Atlin, B.C., another gold-rush area, until 1914, when she accompanied the Canadian Contingent overseas. She returned in 1918 to private nursing in the Huntsville area, in Ontario.

9 The information on the Browns' cabin is from an article, "Homes and Home-Makers of Alaska," by Anna Shane Devin, in *The Pacific Monthly*, published in June 1906, after the Browns had left Dawson.

10 John Jerome Healey was a law unto himself and an epic story in himself. He ran away from home when he was twelve to join a band of renegades who hoped to

seize part of Mexico and establish a republic. Among other adventures, he had been a friend of Sitting Bull's, and run a whisky fort on the Montana–Alberta border. For more on this character for whom the word "colourful" seems particularly inadequate, see Pierre Berton's *Klondike*. In the context of Faith's story, it is another example of her access to the movers and shakers in any society, and of her ability to feel at ease with a dazzling array of personalities.

11 One of Pantages' original theatres, the Pantages on Yonge Street in Toronto, was recently restored to its former glory and opened for business.

XV: Return From the Wilderness

1 The information on John Brown's life and work comes from the obituaries on his death, and the wide range of contributions he made to many medical journals.

2 This proof copy is still in the MacKay family archives.

3 These anecdotes were written out and preserved by Faith's niece Ruth Freeman, and are in the MacKay family archives.

4 This story was told to the author by Phyllis MacKay, Faith's great-niece.

Selected Bibliography

Adams, Oscar F. *A Dictionary of American Biography*, 5th ed. Boston: Houghton Mifflin, 1904.

Anderson, Patricia. *When Passion Reigned: Sex and the Victorians*. New York: HarperCollins, 1995.

Baltzell, Winton J. *Baltzell's Dictionary of Musicians*. Boston: O. Ditson, 1918.

Barr, Robert. *The Measure of the Rule*. Toronto: University of Toronto Press, 1973.

Bears, J.H., & Co. *Commemorative Biographical Record of the County of York, Ontario*. Toronto: J.H. Bears & Co., 1907.

Berton, Laura Beatrice. *I Married the Klondike*. Toronto: McClelland and Stewart, 1954.

Berton, Pierre. *Klondike: The Life and Death of the Last Great Gold Rush*. Toronto: McClelland and Stewart, 1958.

Black, Martha. *My Ninety Years*. Anchorage: Alaska Northwest Publishing, 1976.

Bracchi, Carol Lee. *Liberation Deferred? The Ideas of the English-Canadian Suffragists*. Toronto: University of Toronto Press, 1983.

Briggs, L.L. *A History of Canadian Journalism*. Edited by a Committee of the Canadian Press Association. Toronto: Murray Printing Co., 1908.

Brown, J.N.E. "A Retrospect: The Class of '92." *Canada Lancet and Practitioner.* December 1933.

Burkholder, L.J. *A Brief History of the Mennonites in Ontario*. Kitchener: Mennonite History Society of Ontario, 1986.

Cannell, Kathleen. *Jam Yesterday*. New York: William Morrow, 1945.

Careless, J.M.S. *Brown of The Globe: Statesman of Confederation* Toronto: Macmillan of Canada, 1963.

Charlesworth, Hector. *Candid Chronicles*. Toronto: Macmillan, 1925.

———. *More Candid Chronicles*. Toronto: Macmillan, 1928.

———. *I'm Telling You. Being the Further Candid Chronicles*. Toronto: Macmillan, 1937.

Clark, Gilbert J. *Life Sketches of Eminent American, English and Canadian Lawyers*. Kansas City, Mo.: Lawyers International Publishing Co., 1895.

Coates, Ken S., and William R. Morrison. *Land of the Midnight Sun.* Edmonton: Hurtig, 1988.

Creighton, Donald. *Dominion of the North.* Toronto: Macmillan of Canada, 1957.

Cumming, Carman. *Secret Craft: The Journalism of Edward Farrer.* Toronto: University of Toronto Press, 1992.

Curtis, George William. *Prue and I.* Edinburgh: D. Douglas, 1894.

Dendy, William. *Lost Toronto.* Toronto: Oxford University Press, 1978.

Donaldson, Gordon. *The Prime Ministers of Canada.* Toronto: Doubleday Canada, 1994.

Duff, T. Clarence, with Sarah Yates. *Toronto Then and Now.* Markham, Ont.: Fitzhenry and Whiteside, 1984.

Epp, Frank H. *Mennonites in Canada, 1786–1920: The History of a Separate People.* Toronto: Macmillan of Canada, 1974.

Fowler, Marian. *Redney: A Life of Sara Jeannette Duncan.* Toronto: Penguin Books, 1985.

Francis, R. Douglas, and Donald. B. Smith. *Canadian History: Pre-Confederation and Post-Confederation.* Toronto: Holt, Rinehart and Winston, 1986.

Freeman, Barbara M. *Kit's Kingdom: The Journalism of Kathleen Blake Coleman.* Ottawa: Carleton University Press, 1989.

French, Doris. *Ishbel and the Empire.* Toronto: Dundurn Press, 1988.

Glazebrook, G.P. de T. *Life in Ontario: A Social History.* Toronto: University of Toronto Press, 1968.

———. *The Story of Toronto.* Toronto: University of Toronto Press, 1971.

Gough, Barry. *Gold Rush!* Toronto: Grolier, 1983.

Greenhous, Brereton. *Guarding the Goldfields: The Story of the Yukon Field Force.* Toronto: Dundurn Press, 1987.

Greenwood, Barbara. *Challenge of the Klondike: Rachel Hanna, Frontier Nurse.* Toronto: Grolier, 1990.

Griffiths, N.E.S. *The Splendid Vision: Centennial History of the National Council of Women of Canada, 1893–1993.* Ottawa: Carleton University Press, 1993.

Grove, Sir George. Edited by H.C. Colles. *Grove's Dictionary of Music and Musicians,* 3rd ed. Toronto: Macmillan of Canada, 1939.

Gwyn, Sandra. *The Private Capital.* Toronto: HarperCollins, 1989.

Hale, Katherine. *Toronto: The Romance of a Great City.* Toronto: Cassel & Co., 1956.

Hamlyn, Rupert G., Elsie Carruthers Lunney and David Morrison. *Bowmanville: A Retrospect.* Bowmanville Centennial Committee, 1958.

Hardy, W.G. *From Sea Unto Sea: The Road to Nationhood.* Volume 4 of the Canadian History Series, edited by Thomas B. Costain. Toronto: Doubleday Canada, 1970.

Hays, F. *Women of the Day.* London: Chatto & Windus, 1885.

Heath, Frances M. *Sault Ste. Marie: City by the Rapids.* Burlington: Windsor Publications, 1988.

Himmelfarb, Gertrude. *The De-moralization of Society: From Victorian Virtues to Modern Values.* New York: Alfred A. Knopf, 1995.

A History of Canadian Journalism in the Several Portions of the Dominion, with a Sketch of the Canadian Press Association: 1859–1908. Edited by a Committee of the Association. Toronto, 1908.

Houston, Susan E., and Alison Prentice. *Schooling and Scholars in Nineteenth-Century Ontario.* Toronto: University of Toronto Press, 1988.

Hulse, Elizabeth. *A Dictionary of Toronto Printers, Publishers, Booksellers & Allied Trades, 1798–1900.* Toronto: Anson-Cartwright, 1982.

Jones, F.O., ed. *A Handbook of American Music.* New York: Da Capo Press, 1971.

Kesterton, W.H. *A History of Journalism in Canada.* Toronto: Macmillan of Canada, 1978.

Kilbourn, William. *Toronto Remembered: A Celebration of the City.* Toronto: Stoddart, 1984.

Kluckner, Michael. *Toronto: The Way It Was.* Toronto: Whitecap Books, 1988.

Labelle, Lucile. *Aux Avant-Postes du Canada. Sous le Signe du Bison.* Montreal: Editions Beauchemin, 1982.

Laver, James. *Costume and Fashion: A Concise History.* London: Thames and Hudson, 1982.

Lownsborough, John. *The Privileged Few: The Grange and Its Peoples in Nineteenth-Century Toronto.* Toronto: Art Gallery of Ontario, 1980.

Lynch, Jeremiah. *Three Years in the Klondike.* London: Edward Arnold, 1904.

Martyn, Lucy Booth. *The Face of Early Toronto: An Archival Record, 1797–1936.* Sutton West and Santa Barbara: The Paget Press, 1982.

Matthews, J.B., and Laurence Hutton, eds. *Actors and Actresses of Great*

Britain and the United States. New York: Cassell and Co., 1886.

McBurney, Margaret, and Mary Byers. *Homesteads: Early Residences and Families from Toronto to Kingston.* Toronto: University of Toronto Press, 1979.

McCourt, Edward. *The Yukon and Northwest Territories.* Toronto: Macmillan of Canada, 1972.

McMullen, Lorraine, ed. *Re(dis)covering Our Foremothers. Nineteenth Century Women Writers.* Ottawa: University of Ottawa Press, 1989.

Morrison, David R. *The Politics of the Yukon Territory, 1898–1909.* Toronto: University of Toronto Press, 1968.

Morton, Desmond. *Mayor Howland: The Citizen's Candidate.* Toronto: Hakkert, 1973.

Ogilvie, William. *Early Days on the Yukon and the Story of Its Gold Finds.* Ottawa: Thorburn and Abbott, 1913.

Pascoe, C.E. *The Dramatic List,* 2nd ed. London: D. Bogue, 1880.

Polk, R.L., & Co. *Toronto Directory: 1884–1896.*

Prentice, Alison. *Canadian Women: A History.* Toronto: Harcourt, Brace Jovanovich, 1988.

Roberts, Wayne. *Honest Womanhood: Feminism, Femininity and Class Consciousness among Toronto Working Women, 1896–1914.* Toronto: New Hogtown Press, 1977.

Rowe, Frederick William. *A History of Newfoundland and Labrador.* Toronto: McGraw-Hill Ryerson, 1980.

Rutherford, Paul. *A Victorian Authority: The Daily Press in Late Nineteenth Century Canada.* Toronto: University of Toronto Press, 1981.

Sinclair, James. M. *Mission: Klondike.* Vancouver: Mitchell Press, 1978.

Stamp, Robert M. *The Schools of Ontario: 1876–1976. A Project of the Board of Trustees of the Ontario Historical Studies Series for the Government of Ontario.* Toronto: University of Toronto Press, 1982.

Steele, Col. S.B. *Forty Years in Canada.* Toronto: McClelland, Goodchild and Stewart, 1918.

Strange, Carolyn. *Toronto's Girl Problem: The Perils and Pleasures of the City, 1880–1930.* Toronto: University of Toronto Press, 1995.

Sutherland, Fraser. *The Monthly Epic: A History of Canadian Magazines.* Markham, Ont.: Fitzhenry and Whiteside, 1989.

Tausky, T.E., ed. *Selected Journalism: Sara Jeannette Duncan.* Ottawa: Tecumseh Press, 1978.

Taylor, Leonard W. *The Sourdough and the Queen.* Toronto: Methuen, 1983.

Thompson, Austin Seton. *Jarvis Street: A Story of Triumph and Tragedy.* Toronto: John Wiley and Sons, 1980.

Tyrrell, Edith. *I Was There: A Book of Reminiscences.* Toronto: Ryerson Press, 1938.

Wallace, Elizabeth. *Goldwin Smith: Victorian Liberal.* Toronto: University of Toronto Press, 1979.

Wickett, S.W., ed. *Government in Canada.* Toronto: University of Toronto Press, 1907.

Willison, Sir John. *Reminiscences Political and Personal.* Toronto: McClelland and Stewart, 1919.

Wilson, J. Donald, Robert M. Stamp and Louis-Philippe Audet. *Canadian Education: A History.* Scarborough, Ont.: Prentice-Hall, Canada, 1970.

Wilson, James Grant, and John Fiske, eds. *Appleton's Cyclopedia of American Biography.* New York: D. Appleton and Co., 1887–1889.

Manuscripts and Documents

The Aberdeen Papers and Diaries: 1892–1898. The National Archives, Ottawa

Keys, Alice M. *The Model School.* The Baldwin Room Collection of the Toronto Reference Library

The Diaries of Edward Lester: 1898. The National Archives, Ottawa

Manuscripts in the historical collection of the Toronto Board of Education

1871 Model School, Toronto: Course of Study with Time Breakdown of Each Subject. The Ontario Archives

Model School Teachers' Meetings Record Book, 1866–1877. The Ontario Archives

Model School Training Register, Females, 1871–1877. The Ontario Archives

Model School Boys Training Register, 1871–1877. The Ontario Archives

Toronto Board of Education, Personnel Records, 1844–1882

Newspapers consulted

Toronto:
The Empire
The Evening News
The Globe; The Globe and Farmer
The Mail
The Mail and Empire
The Mail-Express
The News
The Telegram

Ottawa:
The Ottawa Citizen
The Ottawa Free Press
The Ottawa Journal

Dawson City:
The Dawson Daily News
The Dawson Record
The Klondike Nugget
The Yukon Sun

Regional Newspapers:
The Bracebridge Gazette
The British Whig, Kingston
The Canadian Statesman, Bowmanville
The Guelph Mercury
The Montreal Star
The New York Sun
The Niagara Daily News
The Northern Advance, Barrie
The Owen Sound Advertiser
The Stratford Beacon
The Victoria Daily Colonist

INDEX

(An "n" following a page number indicates an endnote.)